CYPRUS AND THE EU

To my wife Helen

Cyprus and the EU

The Road to Accession

Edited by

CONSTANTIN STEFANOU (BA, MA, MPhil, PhD)
Institute of Advanced Legal Studies, University of London, UK
ISC, Queen's University, Canada

Routledge
Taylor & Francis Group
LONDON AND NEW YORK

First published 2005 by Ashgate Publishing

Reissued 2018 by Routledge
2 Park Square, Milton Park, Abingdon, Oxon OX14 4RN
711 Third Avenue, New York, NY 10017, USA

Routledge is an imprint of the Taylor & Francis Group, an informa business

A Library of Congress record exists under LC control number: 2004020412

ISBN 13: 978-0-815-38843-2 (hbk)
ISBN 13: 978-1-351-16028-5 (ebk)

Contents

List of Tables

List of Contributors

Costakis Christophorou is the Secretary-General of the House of Representatives of Cyprus.

Vicky Christoforou (LLB, LLM) is a Law Officer at the European Union Section of the Law Office of the Republic of Cyprus.

Christina Hadjidemetriou (LLB, LLM) is a former Law Officer at the European Union Section of the Law Office of the Republic of Cyprus.

Nicoletta Ioannou (LLB, LLM) is a Law Officer at the European Union Section of the Law Office of the Republic of Cyprus.

Alexia Kalispera (LLB, LLM) is a Law Officer at the European Union Section of the Law Office of the Republic of Cyprus.

Michalis Kamperis (LLB, LLM) is an advocate, legal consultant in EU Law and a former Law Officer at the European Union Section of the Law Office of the Republic of Cyprus.

Eleni Kouzoupi (LLB, LLM) is a member of Cyprus's permanent EU representation and a former Law Officer at the European Union Section of the Law Office of the Republic of Cyprus.

Anna Marcoulli (LLB, LLM) is a Law Officer at the European Union Section of the Law Office of the Republic of Cyprus.

Nicos Michaelides (LLB, LLM) Barrister at Law, is a Law Officer at the European Union Section of the Law Office of the Republic of Cyprus.

Dr Roderick Pace (BA, MA, PhD) is Lecturer in International Relations and European Studies and Director of the European Documentation and Research Centre of the University of Malta.

Elena Papageorgiou (LLB, LLM) is a Law Officer at the European Union Section of the Law Office of the Republic of Cyprus.

Dr Constantin Stefanou (BA, MA, MPhil, PhD) is a Fellow at the Institute of Advanced Legal Studies (University of London).

George Vassiliou is a former President of the Republic of Cyprus and the former Chief Negotiator for the accession of Cyprus to the EU.

Dr Helen Xanthaki (LLB, MJur, PhD) is a Senior Lecturer and Academic Director of the Sir William Dale Centre at the Institute of Advanced Legal Studies (University of London).

Markus Zalewski (Ref. iur., MBA, MIL) formerly with Neocleous and Associates, Limassol, Cyprus.

Abbreviations

AOC	Air Operator's Certificate
ATLA	Air Transport Licensing Authority
CAP	Common Agricultural Policy
CBC	Central Bank of Cyprus
CCB	Co-operative Central Bank
CCSS	Cooperative Credit and Saving Societies
CDCSR	Central Depository and Central Securities Register
CEEC(s)	Central and Eastern European Countries
CMLR	Common Market Law Reports
CFI	Court of First Instance
CFSP	Common Foreign and Security Policy
CGC	Cyprus Grain Commission
CEATP	Common European Air Transport Policy
CPC	Commission for the Protection of Competition
CRS	Computer Reservation Systems
CSEC	Cyprus Securities and Exchange Commission
CSCE	Conference on Security and Cooperation in Europe
CYTA	Cyprus Telecommunications Authority
DCA	Department of Civil Aviation
EAGGF	European Agricultural Guarantee and Guidance Fund
EASA	European Aviation Safety Agency
EC	European Communities/Community
ECAC	European Civil Aviation Conference
ECJ	European Court of Justice
ECN	European Competition Network
ECR	European Court Reports
ECSB	Statute of the European System of Central Banks
ECSC	European Coal and Steel Community
EEC	European Economic Community
EMU	Economic and Monetary Union
EP	European Parliament
ESC	Economic and Social Committee
EU	European Union
FDI	Foreign Direct Investments

GDP	Gross Domestic Product
GMO	Genetically Modified Organisms
IACS	Integrated Administration and Control System
IATA	International Air Transport Association
ICAO	International Civil Aviation Organization
IGC	Intergovernmental Conference
ILO	International Labour Organisation
IPRs	Intellectual and industrial property rights
JAA	Joint Aviation Authorities
JHA	Justice and Home Affairs
MANRE	Ministry of Agriculture, Natural Resources, Environment (Cyprus)
MEP(s)	Member(s) of the European Parliament
NAM	Non-aligned Movement
NATO	North Atlantic Treaty Organisation
N+N	European Neutral and Non-aligned countries
NPAA	National Programme for the Adoption of the Acquis
OECD	Organisation for Economic Cooperation & Development
OJ	Official Journal
OSCE	Organisation for Security and Co-operation in Europe
PEA	Preliminary Environmental Assessment
PHARE	Pologne, Hongrie, Assistance à la Réstructuration Economique
QMV	Qualified Majority Voting
SEA	Single European Act
TEU	Treaty on European Union
TRIPS	Agreement on Trade Related Aspects of IPRs
TRNC	Turkish Republic of Northern Cyprus
UK	United Kingdom
UN	United Nations
US(A)	United States (of America)
WEU	Western European Union
WIPO	World Intellectual Property Organisation

Foreword by President Vassiliou

On 1 May 2004 Cyprus was accepted as a full member of the European Union. The dream of all Cypriots had become a reality; we could now feel safe and hope that the accession would be the last step before the reunification of our island.

Relations between Cyprus and the EU can be traced back to 1962, when we made our first application to enter into a trade agreement. After nearly quarter of a century on 1 January 1988 the Customs Union Agreement became a reality while two and a half years later, in July 1990, the application to join the Union was submitted. Accession negotiations with the first 6 countries including Cyprus started in March 1998 and lasted for nearly five years. On 13 December 2002 in Copenhagen, Cyprus was accepted to become member of the EU.

Although the negotiations started in March 1998 a number of countries were not yet convinced that Cyprus could accede to the EU without first solving the 'Cyprus problem'. Consequently, our strategy during the whole period of negotiations had two main objectives:

i. to follow a consistent line on the national issue and cooperate closely with the United Nations in order to achieve the reunification of the island;
ii. to negotiate successfully with the EU and ensure that the harmonisation with the acquis communautaire progressed without any hiccups whatsoever.

All the time we were fully aware that we could not afford, under any circumstances, to fall behind. We fought hard and succeeded in protecting and promoting the interests of the Republic. At the same time we convinced our negotiating partners that we were taking the accession process very seriously. We were negotiating impeccably and doing our utmost to promote harmonisation. To be, as they say, 'the best pupils in the class'.

For the negotiations to succeed we had to:

i. study in depth and in detail every negotiation chapter (as it is well known the EU had classified the acquis in 29 chapters);

ii. prepare detailed positions addressing every single issue raised in each chapter, to undertake realistic obligations concerning harmonisation and convince the European Commission that we were in a position to implement what we undertook to do;
iii. be very careful in submitting claims for transitional periods, making certain that they were fully justified and necessary to help the economy and society of Cyprus to adapt to the needs and reality of the EU;
iv. ensure that harmonisation, i.e. the preparation, adoption and implementation of well over 1,300 new laws and Directives, progressed according to the plan. We were of course fully aware that we could not afford the luxury of not fulfilling all commitments that we were undertaking.

The task of preparing Cyprus for EU accession, conducting the negotiations and ensuring the harmonisation with the acquis, was undertaken by me. In all other candidate countries negotiations and harmonisation were two distinct tasks. The negotiations were conducted by the foreign ministry, while the harmonisation process was usually the task of one or two deputy Prime Ministers under the guidance of the Prime Minister. In our case I considered that it would be more efficient if all these tasks were combined. Probably this is one of the reasons that we succeeded in ensuring that the whole process progressed smoothly and enabled us to stay ahead for the whole period.

To guide the whole process we created a small management team consisting of:

- Mrs Leda Koursoumba and Mr. Constantinos Lycourgos from the Legal Service of the Republic.
- Mr Panicos Pouros and Mrs. Marina Jensen from the Planning Bureau of the Republic.
- Mrs Popi Avraam and subsequently Mr. George Zodiatis from the foreign ministry.
- Mr Costas Paschalis and Mrs. Maria Dionysiou from my office.

Legal harmonisation, in other words the transposition of the acquis communautaire into the legal system of Cyprus was one of the largest and most difficult tasks. The EU was to a great extent judging the progress of the whole process by the degree to which legal harmonisation was taking place. In parallel with the preparation of the new laws we had to address and solve a number of important issues. These were:

- The issue of the competent authority. According to EU regulations for every activity there has to be only one authority in charge. In Cyprus, as in many other countries, over the years various ministries acquired parallel and sometimes conflicting responsibilities. Addressing this issue was not as simple as it sounded but after many meetings and a lot of goodwill we succeeded.
- The introduction of hundreds of new regulations had an obvious and serious effect on the conditions of work as well as practices that people and trade unions were used to. There was an urgent need to explain the new regulations to hundreds of persons and organisations in various walks of life.
- Also vitally important was to decide the degree of detail required for certain legislation. For example, there were cases where we could create a 'framework law' while for other cases legislation had to be quite detailed and specific. Finally, it was important to establish the degree of the discriminatory authority that the responsible bodies would have. Otherwise they would not be able to take meaningful decisions that could be implemented.

This book, prepared under the guidance of Dr Constantin Stefanou, provides an in-depth investigation into a number of fields where significant legal work had to be undertaken in order to implement the corresponding EU legislation. Obviously it would have been impossible to deal in detail with all the problems encountered in order to prepare so many new legal acts and directives within such a short period of time. They had to choose and they did so wisely. They thus deal with sectors like agriculture, air transport, competition, environment, services, social policy and employment, the Cyprus Intellectual Property Law, the introduction of the Schengen regulations etc. In all these chapters a detailed description is given of the challenges that the legislators had to face and how they addressed them. I do not want to repeat what is very clearly and elegantly presented in the book. What is not necessarily obvious, however, is that in order to succeed with the legal harmonisation we had to completely change the procedures that were followed for the introduction of the new legislation.

The usual practice was for every ministry or relevant directorate to prepare a bill or regulation, under the guidance of the Attorney General's office. The bill was then checked by the legal office of the Republic and when approved it returned to the ministry to enable the relevant minister to submit it together with the justifying report to the Council of Ministers of the Republic for approval. After approval all bills were submitted to the House which allocated them to the relevant parliamentary committees for in-depth study. The parliamentary committees invited all interested parties to express their views and after a long process that sometimes lasted several months or more, decided whether or not to accept the bill and also what modifications to propose. Subsequently, the committee's report was prepared and the bill was sent to the Home Plenary Assembly for approval. Of course, despite a favourable proposal by the parliamentary committee it was often the case that voting on the bill was postponed, sometimes for a long time. On other occasions the bill was rejected and sent back to the relevant ministry for additions, modifications and re-submission.

It was obvious that if we were to follow the same procedures for the drafting and adoption of the various harmonisation laws we would have needed not four but twenty-four years. Therefore, a completely new simplified procedure was agreed and implemented:

- In the Attorney General's office, a special division was created under the leadership of Mrs Lyda Koursoumba – member of the negotiating committee – which employed more than twenty specially selected lawyers trained in legislative drafting. Depending on the case additional lawyers from the Public Attorney's office were asked to offer their services. All of them cooperated closely with the various Ministry lawyers but the responsibility rested with the office of Mrs Koursoumba's and not with the relevant ministry. Over 90% of all laws were thus drafted inside the new special division in the Attorney General's office. For a number of specialised pieces of legislation, which required special technical expertise, outside help was requested. For example, the bills for transport, telecommunications and for the regulation of the electricity market were all commissioned to international experts.
- Once the relevant bill was ready, it was submitted to the Council of Ministers of the Republic for approval under new simplified procedures. While all other bills were always submitted and supported by the ministers who were responsible for them, all harmonisation bills were submitted by the foreign ministry. The logic was that the Council

of Ministers did not need to study in detail those bills since they were in conformity with EU legislation already in place in the existing member states.

- Subsequently the foreign ministry sent the bill to the House. Here again, instead of submitting the bills to the various committees it was agreed that all harmonising bills would be sent to the special European Affairs Committee. This Committee met once or twice a week and dealt only with harmonisation bills. Another major difference was that while in the other committees all interested parties were invited to present their case before the committee, for all harmonisation bills the House did not hear any third parties. It was a condition, however, that the ministry responsible for the implementation of the bill had to ensure that all interested parties were informed of the bill's contents and given a chance to express any reservations. For this purpose a letter had to be submitted to the House, by the relevant ministry, specifying that all interested parties were given the opportunity to express their views. The European Affairs Committee was thus able to deal with the various bills efficiently and quickly and subsequently all these bills were approved by the Parliament usually without any discussions taking place.

The hard work of the various officials and the cooperation of all political parties made it possible to complete the huge harmonisation task within the very limited time framework available.

The various articles included in the book provide an overview of the prevailing conditions and the existing legislation and explain in detail the problems encountered in order to transpose and implement the acquis – a difficult and demanding task, which all authors have carried out impeccably. This book will prove very useful both to all students of the EU harmonisation process as well as lawyers actually working on similar tasks in candidate countries.

George Vassiliou

Preface

It is indeed with great pleasure that I welcome the publication of a book documenting the monumental achievement of Cyprus's accession to the EU. It is widely accepted amongst the public at large, that Cyprus's accession to the EU constitutes the single most important event that took place since Cyprus gained its independence in 1960; the prevalent view has for years been that Cyprus's accession to the EU would herald a new era of stability on the island, as well as offer its inhabitants a unique opportunity to prosper as members of the greater European family.

The preparation for accession to the EU was an enormous task due to the immense preparatory, as well as actual work that had to be completed in order to successfully harmonise Cyprus laws with the acquis communautaire within the tight time constraints agreed with the EU.

My position as Secretary General of the House of Representatives, has furnished me with first hand knowledge of the difficulties faced in the harmonisation of the national legislation with the acquis communautaire, and I am happy to know that the knowledge gained by my colleagues can be shared with others through this book. The knowledge and experience gained by Cyprus through the hard work of harmonisation, I believe, is of utmost importance both as an example that prospective EU member states may find useful to follow, as well as for use by researchers for reference purposes. This book, I believe, constitutes a useful guide to the particularities of Cyprus as a new member of the EU and also a guide through the labyrinth of mechanisms and processes developed to coordinate the civil service in the framework of fulfilling the harmonisation tasks speedily and effectively.

The House of Representatives, being the legislative body of the Republic of Cyprus, has had an instrumental role in the harmonisation process, which it did carry out with utmost success when the time came to bear. In view of the immense workload that the harmonisation process involved and the tight deadlines that the EU imposed on Cyprus, it was clear that in order to allow the House of Representatives to discharge its duties speedily and effectively, certain adjustments would have to be made both in the method of examination of bills of law and regulations of a harmonising nature, as well as regards its administrative structure.

The changes introduced at the organisational level involved the creation of the Parliamentary Committee of European Affairs and the transfer of the competence of examining bills of law and regulations of a harmonising nature from the former Parliamentary Committee of Foreign and European Affairs to this fledgling Committee. The above changes complemented the adoption of the fast-track procedure of examination of bills of law and regulations of a harmonising nature, through which speed and effectiveness was achieved.

On the administrative level, a decision was taken to establish the European Affairs Service, which would be entrusted with the task of providing technocratic support to the former Parliamentary Committee of Foreign and European Affairs and subsequently the Parliamentary Committee of European Affairs.

In conclusion, it should be borne in mind that just as the House of Representatives has had to proceed to necessary adjustments in view of the harmonisation process, virtually the whole of the civil service has undergone transformation. New departments were created and new mechanisms and procedures were introduced, which led to the successful harmonisation with the acquis communautaire. Therefore, this book, I believe, serves not only as an indispensable guide to the harmonisation effort, but also as a tribute to those who have contributed to this monumental achievement.

Costakis Christophorou
Secretary-General of the House of Representatives
Republic of Cyprus

1 Introduction

CONSTANTIN STEFANOU

When all the joy of the official opening of EU accession negotiations has subsided, when the last official has drank the last glass of champagne and wished the applicant good luck with their efforts to accede, the real work begins. And most of the work concentrates in one area: transposition of the EU acquis into national law. Yet, despite the fact that transposition constitutes the backbone of an applicant country's effort to complete the accession process it tends to receive very little attention. There are, of course, very good reasons for the 'low profile' of transposition. Being largely a process carried out by legislative drafters and national ministry officials in consultation with EU bureaucrats it is neither glamorous nor the subject of political posturing. It receives no media coverage and in academic terms it is usually the subject of dry, short commentaries about amendments to existing legislation.

This book concentrates on Cyprus's efforts to transpose the EU acquis into the Cypriot legal system and the problems experienced by an often neglected group of experts: the drafters who carried out the process of transposition. With the kind permission of the European Union Section of the Law Office of the Republic of Cyprus, a specialised unit set up to speed-up the process of transposition, the experts who transposed the acquis and assisted in the negotiations with their technical expertise have been allowed to contribute to this book. Their views, along with the views of other contributors, offer important insights into the rarely examined process of transposition, which chronologically coincides with the negotiation procedure between the EU and Cyprus.

The formal relationship between Cyprus and the EU[1] (see Table 1.1) dates back to 1972 and the EC-Cyprus Association Agreement which was temporarily abandoned following the 1974 invasion of the island by Turkey. Strictly speaking, Cyprus' efforts to harmonise go back to 1987 and the re-activation of the EC-Cyprus Association Agreement with the signing of a Protocol. However, as Cyprus always had close trade links with Greece and the UK, approximation and streamlining of national legislation with that of the EU was always on-going so that Cyprus's products would not be barred from the European markets, e.g. the EU's packaging Directive. In fact, it was the 1987 Protocol that provided for the harmonisation of accompanying policies on competition, state aids and the approximation of laws

The negotiation procedure of the EU with Cyprus was, of course, similar to that of the other applicant countries. It consisted of two phases.

- *Acquis screening*: the detailed examination of the laws, institutions and procedures of the applicant country in order to determine whether they comply with the acquis.
- *Substantive negotiations*: discussions/negotiations concerning transitional arrangements or derogations.

As the acquis communautaire consists of about 80,000 pages both screening and substantive negotiations are tedious and elaborate processes which are normally completed amongst groups of experts away from the limelight. The screening of the acquis is particularly important as it determines the breadth of work that the applicant country will have complete in order to close the 29 chapters – roughly one for each policy area – which the Commission hands over to all applicants. In total, there are 31 chapters, but only the first 29 are 'negotiable' and must be completed in order to be eligible for accession. These chapters are:

1. Free Movement of Goods
2. Free Movement of Persons
3. Freedom to Provide Services
4. Free Movement of Capital
5. Company Law
6. Competition Policy
7. Agriculture
8. Fisheries
9. Transport
10. Taxation
11. Economic and Monetary Union
12. Statistics
13. Social Policy / Employment
14. Energy
15. Industrial Policy
16. Small and Medium-Sized Undertakings
17. Science and Research
18. Education, Vocational Training and Youth
19. Telecommunications and Information Technologies
20. Culture and Audio-Visual Policy
21. Regional Policy / Structural Instruments
22. Environment
23. Consumers and Health Protection
24. Justice and Home Affairs
25. Customs Union
26. External Relations
27. Common Foreign and Security Policy
28. Financial Control
29. Financial and Budgetary Provisions
30. Institutions
31. Other

Table 1.1 Cyprus and the EU: a chronology

1972 December	EC-Cyprus Association Agreement signed: a two stage agreement aiming to eliminate barriers to trade and create an EC-Cyprus Customs Union (the second stage of the agreement was due to commence in 1977).
1974 July	Turkey invades Cyprus and the island is partitioned.
1977	EC postpones 2nd stage of EC-Cyprus Association Agreement.
1983	Turkish Republic of Northern Cyprus is proclaimed. It is not recognised by any of the 12 EC member states.
1987 October	Second stage of EC-Cyprus Association Agreement is activated and a Protocol is signed (effective from 1 January 1988). According to the Protocol the Customs Union between Cyprus and the EC should be completed by 2002 or 2003 at the latest. Cyprus undertakes the obligation to adopt progressively the EC's Common Customs Tariff.
1990 May	The office of the Delegation of the European Commission opens in Nicosia.
1990 July	The Republic of Cyprus officially applies for membership.
1991	A Joint Parliamentary Committee, consisting of members of the European Parliament and the Chamber of Representatives of Cyprus is set up. The Joint Parliamentary Committee meets twice a year.
1993 June	In its opinion the European Commission concludes that the application was made in the name of the whole island.
1994 July	The ECJ issues a ruling one a preliminary reference made by the British High Court, concerning imports from the occupied part of Cyprus, in which it states that the Republic of Cyprus is 'the only Cypriot state the Community recognises'.
1995 March	The General Affairs Council confirms that Cyprus is suitable for membership and establishes that accession negotiations will start 6 months after the end of the Intergovernmental Conference. The government of Cyprus establishes 22 working groups to start work on the different chapters.

Table 1.1 … continued

1997 December	The European Council in Luxembourg confirms that accession negotiations will begin in spring 1998. Turkish Cypriots are invited to be included in the Cypriot delegation.
1998 March	Accession negotiations commence ('acquis screening').
1998 November	Substantial accession negotiations commence. Commission publishes the First Regular report.
1999 October	Publication of the Second Regular Report.
2000	Pre-accession aid (€57 millions) is available to Cyprus to be programmed over 5 years.
2000 November	Third Regular Report on Cyprus' progress towards accession.
2001 November	Accession Partnership. Second Regular Report on Cyprus' progress towards accession.
2002 October	Fourth Regular Report on Cyprus' progress towards accession.
2002 December	Copenhagen European Council concludes Substantial accession negotiations. The European Council also notes that 'welcomes the commitment of the Greek Cypriots and the Turkish Cypriots to continue to negotiate with the objective of concluding a comprehensive settlement of the Cyprus problem by 28 February 2003 on the basis of the UNSG4s proposals'.
2003 April	Signing of the Accession Treaty in Athens
2003 June	Commission proposes a *goodwill* package for Turkish Cypriots.
2003 November	Fifth Regular Report on Cyprus' progress towards accession.
2004 March	UN secretary general Annan unveils the fifth revised Cyprus plan. The plan is supported by the EU.
2004 April	Referenda on the UN Annan Plan are held in the Republic of Cyprus and the occupied territories in the north. The Annan Plan is accepted in the occupied territories but it is rejected in the Republic of Cyprus.

When one looks at Cyprus's application and compares it to the CEECs it is obvious that Cyprus was a very straight-forward candidate in terms of the Copenhagen criteria for accession. With a population of only 620,000 and the highest GDP per capita amongst the applicant countries[2] the Republic of Cyprus met almost all the Copenhagen criteria and (after 2000) was well on the way to meeting the Maastricht criteria for the Euro. Unlike the CEECs Cyprus did not have to undergo major structural changes or liberalise its economy and develop rapidly.[3] Even Cyprus's 'political problem' was strictly speaking outside the Copenhagen Criteria in that it did not concern democracy or human rights but the division of the island and the occupation its northern part by a third country.

However, even though Cyprus's application was straight forward, being a small state Cyprus did encounter some practical problems related to transposition. To start with, after the end of the 'screening' process it became obvious that more than 80% of existing relevant legislation needed to be amended or in some cases abolished and replaced with new provisions. Although Cyprus had a Customs Agreement with the EU national legislation was not being updated regularly to keep pace with the regular flow of new Directives, Regulations or Decisions. From a practical point of view this meant that the volume of drafting required was heavier than initially anticipated and at the time Cyprus simply did not have enough drafters and certainly not enough with expertise in EU law. The European Union Section of the Law Office of the Republic of Cyprus did address the problem by appointing and training a group of young and well qualified drafters but the volume of work was such that – just like the CEECs – some of the work could not be completed in-house and private law firms were used. Just to give an example of the technical expertise required, at the Office of the First Parliamentary Counsel in the UK newly appointed drafters are expected to undergo a training period of 6-8 years as 'juniors' before they are allowed to tackle important pieces of legislation on their own. In Cyprus, such was the volume of transposition required that young drafters were thrown 'in at the deep end' after a few months of training. Inevitably, there were omissions, mistakes and duplication of work which slowed down progress in some chapters.

In terms of drafting methodology, as will be seen later in the chapters on specific policy areas, Cypriot drafters used both main methods of EU law transposition: direct and indirect. The *direct* method is the simplest in that the EU legal text is incorporated into the national body of laws "as is". For example, an EU Directive would be brought to Parliament as an Annex to a very short Act which would merely note that the Annexed Directive is incorporated into the legal system. The *indirect* method requires more work and is more time consuming in that the relevant EU provisions are organically absorbed into the legal system either through the introduction of a new law or through a series of amendments. It is interesting to note that some drafters comment that on many occasions they found it useful to consult different language versions of an EU provision as even slight variations can make a difference in the way a piece of legislation will fit in the wider legislative scheme. On rare occasions, using a different language version of a provision even made a difference in the quick passage of a bill through parliament.

Things became a little complicated as the first phase of the accession negotiations coincided with the publication of the Commission's 'Better Lawmaking Report 1998'[4] where the correct transposition of EU Directives into national law was mentioned as one of eight main guidelines for action introduced by the Report.[5] Suddenly issues of 'quality' were thrown into the very busy schedule. Inevitably, as the date of accession came nearer and more chapters had to be completed, the *direct* method of transposition seemed to win the day.

As can be seen in Table 1.2, the schedule for negotiations was very tight. Substantive negotiations generally started about one year after the screening with the notable exception of CFSP, audiovisual and culture policy, and industrial policy where substantive negotiations started five or six months after screening. The Cypriot drafters cooperated closely with Commission officials and were often present in the negotiations in Brussels and the House of Representatives where legislation often had to be rushed through to meet the tight deadlines.

What becomes obvious from following Cyprus's efforts to transpose the EU acquis is that small states face many practical problems as a result of the small size of their national administration. As one drafter pointed out, it was when the official dossiers on the CAP arrived – which run to about 11,000 pages – that the enormity of the task became obvious to all. The 80,000 pages of the acquis have to be transposed irrespective of whether the applicant country is Poland with a population of 38 millions and a large civil service or Malta with a population of 400,000 and a civil service a fraction of the size of larger member states. It was, in fact, this realisation that led the Commission to release €57 millions to Cyprus as part of its 'implementation of the pre-accession strategy for Cyprus and Malta'.[6] In 2001 for example, a good part of the €11.5 millions Cyprus received as part of the pre-accession strategy went towards 'acquis harmonisation'.

Table 1.2 Timing of negotiations for individual chapters

	Bilateral screening	*Submission of position paper*	*Substantive negotiations*
Free Movement of Goods	22-30/7/1998	18/12/1998	21/6/1999 & 7/12/1999
Free Movement of Persons	22-23/4/1999	1/12/1999	26/5/2000
Freedom to Provide Services	9-10/2/1999	17/9/1999	12/11/1999 & 7/12/1999
Free Movement of Capital	10/12/1998	27/5/1999	30/9/1999 & 7/12/1999
Company Law	17-18/6/1998	18/12/1999	19/5/1999 & 7/12/1999
Competition Policy	15/10/1998	18/12/1998	19/5/1999 & 7/12/1999
Agriculture	5-6/10/1998 20-21/10/1998 19-21/10/1998 25-26/2/1999 6-7/5/1999 1-4/6/1999	22/12/1999	13/6/2000
Fisheries	8/7/1998	18/12/1998	19/4/1999
Transport	16-17 /11/1998 & 17-18/3/1999	23/7/1999	12/11/1999 & 7/12/1999
Taxation	30-31/3/1999	23/7/1999	12/11/1999 & 7/12/1999
Economic and Monetary Union	21/12/1998	27/5/1999	30/9/1999 & 7/12/1999
Statistics	16/7/1998	18/12/1998	21/6/1999
Social Policy/Employment	9-12/11/1998	27/5/1999	30/9/1999 & 7/12/1999
Energy	8-9/12/1998	27/5/1999	12/11/1999 & 7/12/1999
Industrial Policy	19/5/1998	7/9/1998	10/11/1998

Table 1.2 ... continued

Small and medium-sized undertakings	25/5/1998	7/9/1998	10/11/1998
Science and Research (RTD)	4/5/1998	7/9/1998	10/11/1998
Education, Vocational Training and Youth	14/5/1998	7/9/1998	10/11/1998 & 21/6/1999
Telecommunications and Information Technologies	5/5/1998	7/9/1998	10/11/1998 & 21/6/1999
Culture and Audio-Visual Policy	13/5/1998	7/9/1998	10/11/1998
Regional Policy / Structural Instruments	4-5/5/1999	22/12/1999	6/4/2000
Environment	11-12/1/1999 12-15/2/1999 23/2/1999	23/7/1999	7/12/1999
Consumers and Health Protection	29/6/1998	18/12/1998	21/6/1999
Cooperation in Justice and Home Affairs	10-12/3/1999	22/12/1999	26/5/2000
Customs Union	8-9/10/1998	18/12/1998	21/6/1999
External Relations	21-22/9/1998	18/12/1998	21/6/1999
Common Foreign and Security Policy (CFSP)	9/6/1998	7/9/1998	10/11/1998
Financial Control	17/5/1999	1/12/1999	6/4/2000
Financial and Budgetary Provisions	30/6/1999	1/12/1999	26/5/2000

Source: *European Union Section of the Law Office of the Republic of Cyprus*

The rest of the book consists of 12 chapters on different aspects of Cyprus's efforts to transpose the acquis. Helen Xanthaki examines the stages of pre-accession negotiations using Cyprus as case a study. Anna Marcoulli gives us her view on one of the most difficult chapters for Cyprus, that of Agriculture, while Nicos Michailidis looks at the tricky chapter – for an island dependent on tourism – of air transport. In both cases the authors stress the difficulty of transposing EU law in hitherto highly protected policy areas. Vicky Christoforou examines Cyprus's efforts to harmonise with the acquis on competition and state aid rules and Christina Hadjidemetriou explores the difficulties in harmonising with the myriad of environmental regulations on an island with many already protected species. Looking at harmonisation in the areas of EMU and Free Movement of Capital, Alexia Kalispera makes some interesting comments about the use of different language versions of the same Directive while Elena Papageorgiou and Eleni Kouzoupi look at freedom of establishment and free movement of services on an island that was a heaven for off-shore companies. Markus Zalewski casts a critical eye on the tricky cumbersome process of harmonising Cyprus's Intellectual Property Law and Nicoletta Ioannou gives her views on the EU minefield which is of social policy and employment legislation. In examining Cyprus's efforts to harmonise with the Third Pillar acquis Michalis Kamperis also questions whether Cyprus can cope with its future role both as a member of the EU and as the external border of a Union of freedom, security and justice. The last two chapters of the book tackle more political issues. Roderick Pace looks at Cyprus as a small Mediterranean member state analysing the pros and cons that EU membership has to offer. In the very last chapter I look at qualitative issues related to membership regarding the ability of Cyprus to implement the acquis.

A final word about the selection of the nine chapters on specific policy areas. The aim has been to include 'easy' as well as problematic chapters. For example, agriculture and transport were the two chapters for which the Commission had expressed a 'serious concern' in its last 'Comprehensive Monitoring Report' of November 2003; the Commission had also asked for 'enhanced efforts' in environmental policy, the free movement of goods and services, and social policy and employment. In contrast, Justice and Home Affairs, EMU and other policy areas were seen by the Commission as problem-free or chapters where Cyprus had achieved a 'high level of alignment with the acquis'. In this sense the chapters on specific policy areas should be seen as representative of the efforts of Cyprus, its successes and failures.

Notes

1. For a detailed account of the EC-Cyprus relationship see www.pio.gov.cy/ir/cyptus_eu/recent_developments.htm
2. On the eve of accession negotiations the Economist reported that Cyprus had a GDP per capita of almost $12,000 compared to Hungary's $6,612 and Poland's $6,410. See *The Economist*, 20 December 1997, p.29.
3. See N. Nugent, 'EU Enlargement and the Cyprus Problem' in *Journal of Common Market Studies*, Vol.38, No.1, March 2000, pp.132-133.
4. See European Commission 'Better Lawmaking Report 1998: A Shared Responsibility', COM(1998)715 final.
5. See C. Stefanou and H. Xanthaki, "National Means of Implementation of Third Pillar Instruments", *European Current Law Review*, January-February 2003, pp.xi-xvii. Also see H. Xanthaki, "The Problem of Quality in EU legislation: what on earth is really wrong?", *Common Market Law Review* Vol. 38, 2001, pp.651-676.
6. Council Regulation (EC) No.555/2000 of 13 March 2000 on the implementation of operations in the framework of the pre-accession strategy for the Republic of Cyprus and the Republic of Malta (OJ L 68, 16.3.2000, p. 3).

2 The Route to EU Accession

HELEN XANTHAKI

The route to EU accession for aspiring member states

Accession to the EU is no longer purely a political decision. The route to accession is long, painful and requires determination, resources and skills. This chapter will explore the new requirements for EU accession and the efforts of the Republic of Cyprus to reach the goalpost and succeed in becoming an EU member state.

The three main criteria for accession to the EU were introduced by the Copenhagen European Council in June 1993.[1] Membership to the EU was dependent upon fulfilment of a political, an economic and a legal criterion. Compliance with the political requirements signified the existence of stable institutions which guaranteed democracy, the rule of law, human rights and respect for minorities in the candidate country. Compliance with the economic requirements signified a functioning market economy in the candidate country. The legal criterion required, for the first time in the history of the EU, the full adoption of the acquis communautaire before accession, as a means of securing that the candidate country already shared the EU's political, economic and monetary goals detailed in the constituting treaties and secondary legislation. The means of ensuring that the Copenhagen criteria were not only met but also were enforced by the candidate countries was the demand of the December 1995 Madrid European Council for the introduction of the necessary administrative structures for the gentle integration of the candidate countries with the EU.[2]

The first step towards the start of negotiations for accession is the evaluation of the candidate country's national legislation as a means of identifying areas of discrepancy. On the basis of this evaluation, which is undertaken by the Commission with the aid of candidate countries, a work programme is agreed and negotiating positions are defined.

The second step towards the start of negotiations is the inclusion of the work programme, negotiating positions and priorities for each sector of legislation in the accession partnerships of each candidate country. The aim of accession partnerships is to set clear goals for the reception of the acquis. The 'acquis' is the body of common rights and obligations which bind all the member states together within the EU. It is a dynamic body of stipulations which engulfs the content, principles and political objectives of the constituting treaties; secondary legislation adopted in application of the treaties and the case law of the European Courts (the European Court of Justice and to a lesser degree the European Court of First Instance); the declarations and resolutions adopted by the EU; measures relating to the common foreign and security policy; measures relating to justice and home affairs; international agreements concluded by the Community and those concluded by the member states between themselves in the field of the EU's activities. In other words, the acquis covers not only law *strictu sensu* but also general principles of Community law and measures of the second and third pillars adopted by use of the special legislative procedures in these areas of EU law. When the European Constitution comes into force and the three pillars will be restructured to one body, the meaning of the acquis will be greatly simplified. This will assist candidate countries in their understanding of the task laid before them: applicant countries have to transpose all if the acquis before they can join the EU. This obligation is of course subject to specific and expressly agreed derogations or periods of grace clearly introduced in the accession treaty for the particular country. Implementation of the acquis by the new member states begins on the date of their formal accession to the EU.

The third step towards the start of negotiations is the conclusion of a detailed programme for the adoption of the acquis. The programme takes into account the Commission's evaluation of the legislation of the country and the identification of areas of discrepancy with the acquis as detailed in the accession partnership. The aim of the programme is to organise the implementation of the priorities identified in the accession partnership, the introduction of a realistic and adequate timetable for the transposition of the acquis into national law, and the identification of the human and financial resources needed to achieve compliance with the timetable and final compliance with the Copenhagen legal criterion as a requirement for EU accession. Programmes and indeed accession partnerships are re-evaluated and adjusted regularly upon agreement of the Commission and the candidate country.

The main framework for accession remains the same and is based on Article 49 (former Article O) of the EU Treaty. Negotiations with candidate countries can only begin if all three central EU institutions are in agreement. What is required is support from the European Commission, agreement of the European Parliament and finally unanimous agreement of the Council. In other words, all existing member states and all EU institutions must be in agreement before even the lengthy period of negotiations for accession can begin. Apart from this *conditio sine qua non*, each candidate country must comply with the specific requirements for its own accession as negotiated and agreed in each particular case. Thus, specific conditions for admission, transitional periods and adjustments to the constituting treaties must be determined before negotiations for accession can begin and at a time when the candidate country has little, if any, negotiating powers. The legal nature of the agreement between the candidate country and the member states seems to be that of an international treaty. It is widely accepted therefore that national ratification requirements for all signatory states involved in the process must be respected and fulfilled before the agreement can acquire legal force.

The procedure for the start of accession negotiations was followed to the letter during the last enlargement. The relationship of the candidate countries with the EU began with the Europe Agreements namely association agreements with Central and Eastern European countries. In 1993 the Commission called for a structured dialogue of approximation between the associated countries and EU institutions. This dialogue was organised in the form of a number of meetings between national authorities of the associated countries and representatives of EU institutions. The scope of these meetings was to explore similarities and differences in the policies, economies and laws of the associated countries and the EU, to identify ways of approximation, and to introduce proposals for the facilitation of gradual closer cooperation. The essence of the exercise was expressed in the pre-accession strategy detailed in the December 1994 Essen European Council.[3] The Council focused this strategy to a triad of political, economical and legal approximation. This referred (at least for the time being) to the deepening of relations between the associated countries, the member states and the institutions of the EU, the introduction of financial assistance through the Phare programme of funding, and to the full adoption, implementation and enforcement of the Europe Agreements.

However, the task of identifying the precise manner in which this triple approximation was to take place was left with the Commission. The December 1994 Essen European Council invited the Commission to draft a White Paper on the preparation of the associated countries for integration into the EU's internal market.[4] The Commission responded with enthusiasm and in May 1995 the White Paper on preparing the countries of Central and Eastern Europe for integration into the Union's single market was ready.[5] The White Paper included an initial, indicative and incomplete table of the acquis which applicant countries had to transpose before accession to the EU. Associated countries were called to establish their own priorities in the fulfilment of the transposition requirement. In order to facilitate this work mainly by providing information on the acquis, associated countries were offered assistance by TAIEX, the technical assistance office. The White Paper was presented at the June 1995 Cannes European Council.[6]

On the basis of this White Paper the pre-accession strategy of the EU was further analysed by the December 1997 Luxembourg European Council.[7] First, the Council welcomed the applications for the accession of ten countries. After the positive response to these applications by the European Commission and ascent of the European Parliament the Council agreed to allow negotiations to begin. Second, the Council determined the legal instruments which would form the basis for negotiations with each of the ten applicant countries. For seven of the applicant countries negotiations would be based on the Europe Agreements and the accession partnerships and national programmes for the adoption of the acquis. A special pre-accession strategy was reached for Cyprus.[8] The 1998 pre-accession strategy for Malta also involved special pre-accession aid. The 1998 pre-accession strategy for Turkey included both pre-accession aid and a reinforced political dialogue. All applicant countries were allowed to participate to some EU programmes, agencies and committees. Third, the Council determined the subjects for negotiations. Negotiating session were held at the level of ministers or their deputies. This would be permanent representatives for the member states, and Ambassadors or chief negotiators for the applicant countries. Finally, the Council detailed the evaluation of the progress of negotiations. Progress for each applicant country was independent from progress of the other applicants: therefore, negotiations with each applicant would proceed as quickly or as slowly as the applicant's efforts merited. The evaluation of the applicants' efforts would be based on the degree of preparation of the applicant country and the complexity of the issues to be resolved.

The accession partnerships concluded by the Council in 1998 with each of the applicant countries (with the exception of Cyprus, Malta and Turkey) bring together in one document the aid provided by the European Community to each applicant country and set priorities for each sector in transposing the acquis. The accession partnerships were used as the framework for other pre-accession instruments, including the joint assessment of medium term economic policy priorities, the pact on organised crime, the national development plans and other sectoral programmes necessary for participation in the Structural Funds after accession and for the implementation of the Instrument for Structural Policies for Pre-Accession and the Special Accession Programme for Agriculture and Rural Development. They have also been the starting point for the development of action plans to improve administrative and judicial capacities in the applicant countries.

The EU institutions divided the group of ten applicant countries to first and second wave. First wave countries, namely states which were considered to be in adequate compliance – at least in principle – with the Copenhagen criteria were allowed to begin negotiations straight away. For Cyprus, the Czech Republic, Estonia, Hungary, Poland, and Slovenia negotiations began on 30 March 1998. For the second wave of candidate countries negotiations began when the EU felt that adequately rapid progress towards compliance – in principle – with the Copenhagen criteria justified the start of negotiations. Bulgaria, Latvia, Lithuania, Romania, Slovakia and Malta (albeit for other reasons) began negotiations on 15 February 2000. Accession negotiations were undertaken via bilateral intergovernmental conferences between the EU and each one of the applicant countries.

The main aim of accession negotiations is to achieve the highest possibly compliance of the national law of the applicant country with the Community acquis. Complete transposition must not be limited to the incorporation of the acquis to the national law of the applicant country. Implementation and enforceability of the acquis upon accession is an equally important part of transposition and indeed one which is often neglected by the applicant countries. It is the most technical and intricate part of their preparation for accession, as it requires the strengthening of the administrations and the legal system of applicant countries, as well as their drastic adaptation as a means of complying with EU standards. This is often a rather painstaking exercise especially in the very technical areas of agriculture, transport, energy and the environment. As a means of facilitating the intricate and often unbearable task of the radical prompt reform of the administration and the legal system to accommodate these requirements, the EU provides to applicant countries pre-accession aid.

Negotiations identify areas of difficulty, the measures required for transposition of the acquis and the timetable to be followed for complete compliance before the accession date. Moreover, negotiations look at the human and financial resources noted in the accession partnership in order to determine the nature and extent of pre-accession aid that the EU will award to the applicant country to support the gentle and effective incorporation of the acquis to the existing body of national laws. Lack of complete and timely transposition will signify failure of the applicant country to fulfil the legal Copenhagen criterion and therefore failure to accede to the EU. As a result, partial compliance is only acceptable if so agreed by the EU institutions. This can only occur in the minimal cases of derogation from the acquis or for transitional measures.

The role of the national authorities of the applicant country in accession negotiations is to clarify existing national law, to explore to which extent this complies with the acquis and to accept fully or partially the recommendation of the Commission on new measures to be introduced for the achievement of complete and timely transposition. Within this framework of negotiations national authorities have the opportunity to argue for favourable terms for the adoption, implementation and enforcement of the acquis by their legislatures, executive and judiciary. They may also request limited transitional arrangements when more time is needed for the full reform of legislation in a particularly difficult area or where the nature and extent of discrepancy between the existing national law and the acquis in a particular area of very limited scope could allow a derogation from the acquis which would not disturb the full integration of the applicant country to the EU. Traditionally, arguments for derogations and periods of grace are received with much scepticism from the Commission. Nevertheless, in a small number of cases genuine difficulties of the applicant country are recognised. Each applicant country draws up its position on each of the 29 'negotiable' chapters of the EU acquis; these form the basis of negotiations.

The subjects of negotiations are the existing member states and the applicant country. The applicant country appoints a Chief Negotiator, with a supporting team of experts. On the EU's side the subject of negotiations is neither the EU nor EU institutions: subjects are the existing member states. As a result, negotiating positions are presented by the President of the European Council as the representative of national governments and not the European Commission which, however, is very much involved in the actual meetings. Meetings at the level of ministers or their deputies are also chaired by the Council. The Presidency rotates every six months and applicant countries have the opportunity to push their positions forward under the Presidency of a number of existing member states. The role of the European Commission in negotiations is to propose the draft negotiating positions on the basis of pre-accession documents and outcomes of negotiations in the 29 chapters of the acquis. The Commission acts both as a facilitator of the applicant countries in the accession process but also as a guarantor of compliance with the acquis by the applicant country. The Commission is therefore in close cooperation with national authorities in order to advise them on solutions to problems and difficulties but also to apply pressure for the finalisation of all necessary measures for the timely and full transposition, implementation and enforcement of the acquis. In view of the role of the European Commission within the EU, this is not a task unknown to them. Although all Directorate Generals of the Commission take active role in the accession process for applicant countries, it is the Directorate General for Enlargement that has overall responsibility for the coordination of the effort on the part of the Commission.

However, administrative/secretarial support for accession negotiations is provided for by the General Secretariat of the Council and by the applicant countries themselves. At the negotiating stage the role of the European Parliament is to watch the work undertaken by the Council and the Commission and to evaluate the progress of the applicant countries. The European Parliament, as indeed national Parliaments of the accession countries, acquire an active role in enlargement only at the final stage of assent to the resulting accession treaties in the case of the European Parliament and the stage of ratification of the resulting accession treaties in the case of national Parliaments. The citizens of the EU are represented by the Council and the Parliament in the accession process and are awarded a direct active role in enlargement only in countries where a referendum is a constitutional necessity for the final approval of the accession treaties.

Negotiations for EU accession are conducted on the basis of four main principles. The principle of specificity limits the scope of negotiations exclusively to the terms under which the applicant country can adopt, implement and enforce the acquis. The principle of leniency allows transitional arrangements but delimits them in scope and durations as a means of ensuring that integration of the applicant country will not be harmed by them. The principle of differentiation prohibits the dependence of progress in negotiations from processes of negotiation undertaken in parallel with a group of candidate countries. Finally, the principle of catching up allows candidate countries to proceed quicker than previous applicants should their progress merit quicker advancement.

In the last enlargement accession negotiations started in March 1998. The first stage of negotiations was the detailed analysis of each applicant country's national law in each of the 29 chapters of the acquis and the evaluation of its compliance with the acquis. This constituted the lengthy screening process which took place in parallel for all 29 chapters and was conducted with the participation of the Commission and the applicant countries. Through the screening process for all applicant countries the Commission succeeded in creating a clearly signposted road map for the EU legislative measures that must be adopted for the accession of future applicant countries. As a result of the clear determination of the components of the acquis for the purposes of accession, the work of future applicants in the area of transposition will be greatly facilitated. The second stage of negotiations was the bilateral negotiations between the European Union and each of the applicant countries on the progress of development of the screening. The December 2002 European Council[9] in Copenhagen marked the conclusion of negotiations with the 10 applicant countries: Cyprus, the Czech Republic, Estonia, Hungary, Latvia, Lithuania, Malta, Poland, Slovakia and Slovenia, thus enabling them to join the Union on 1 May 2004. Bulgaria and Romania are expected to conclude negotiations in time for their accession in 2007. Turkey's candidacy will be re-examined in December 2004. The results of the negotiations were incorporated in the draft accession treaty.[10] This was approved by the EU and ratified by the member states and the applicant countries before May 2004 thus marking a successful end to the painstaking efforts of the ten new member states to achieve full compliance with the Copenhagen criteria.

The route to EU accession for Cyprus

Cyprus signed an Association Agreement with the EU in December 1972 and applied for membership on 3 July 1990. In the 1993 Copenhagen European Council the EU referred to the applications of Malta, Cyprus and Turkey as independent from each other; moreover, each application was to be considered on its won merits.[11] The application of the principle of differentiation in this case signified the start of negotiations with Cyprus liberated from the hurdle of parallel and dependent negotiations with Turkey which had to overcome the extra milestone of compliance with the extra milestone of the Copenhagen political criterion.

With reference to Cyprus's effort for EU accession it is interesting to explore the starting point for negotiations, as it was eloquently expressed in the 'Commission Opinion on the Application by the Republic of Cyprus for Membership'.[12] The Commission expressed no doubt about the legitimacy of the application: Cyprus's geographical position, its contribution to European culture and civilisation, the intensity of the European culture in the values and lives of its citizens, and its deep links with the EU rendered Cyprus's European identity and character unquestionable. However, things were far from simple. Cyprus's 'political problem', in other words the division of the island, was the main area of concern for the Commission and, consequently, the main focus of its Opinion. The Commission, and indeed the European Council, which endorsed this Opinion, expressed its regret for the division of the island and declared once again its support for a political settlement. In fact the Commission applied pressure on the government of Cyprus to finalise a political settlement on the island for three reasons. Firstly, a political settlement would assist Cyprus in its compliance with the Copenhagen political criterion: full restoration of human rights and fundamental freedoms across the island would encourage a pluralist democracy. Secondly, a political settlement would assist Cyprus in its compliance with the Copenhagen legal criterion: re-establishment of fundamental liberties – which form part of the acquis – would signify complete and timely transposition of Community law. Thirdly, a political settlement would not damage Cyprus's compliance with the Copenhagen economic criterion, as the economy of the southern part of the island is strong enough to carry the burden of the economic consequences of reunification. Nevertheless, despite the contribution of such a settlement to Cyprus's integration with the EU, the Commission declared its readiness to begin negotiations with Cyprus straight away. However, the European Council did not take up the offer and, at least formally, negotiations with Cyprus did not start.

The first assessment of the application of Cyprus cannot really be viewed as a positive one. Cyprus faced the stumbling block of the division of the island as a detrimental hurdle to its hopes of compliance with the political and legal Copenhagen criteria and, consequently, to its hopes of accession. The glimmer of hope for Cyprus lay with the possibility of application of the principle of differentiation on an internal/national rather than international basis. In other words, Cyprus's only hope was that its application would be considered independent of the results of continuing negotiations with the Turkish-Cypriot community. The Commission and the Council allowed a glimmer of hope by declaring that if inter-community talks failed the EU would reassess the application of Cyprus and its request for the start for negotiations in January 1995.

After the failure of inter-community talks however the EU was rapid in its advancement of the application of Cyprus. Although the benefits of a political settlements never stopped being mentioned, the 1994 Corfu European Council welcomed the progress towards the start of negotiations made by Cyprus and Malta.[13] Cyprus had already established 23 groups of experts with the mandate to familiarise themselves with the acquis in areas where transposition work would have to be undertaken in view of future accession. Moreover, Cyprus had proposed to negotiate representing both communities on the island should the Turkish-Cypriot community continue to refuse participation to accession negotiations. The combination of political will amongst the existing member states with Cypriot flexibility and legislative progress led the way to the beginning of negotiations. The 1994 Essen European Council confirmed that the next wave of enlargement would include Cyprus without mentioning the resolution of the political problem as a prerequisite.[14] Similarly, the 1995 Cannes European Council refrained from any references to the division of the island and reaffirmed that accession negotiations for Cyprus would begin six months after the end of the 1996 Intergovernmental Conference.[15] In fact the preliminary dialogue on the transposition of EU law continued and formal negotiations began in 1998 as foreseen in the 1995 Madrid European Council,[16] the 1996 Florence European Council,[17] the 1996 Dublin European Council,[18] and the 1997 Luxembourg European Council Conclusions.[19] The European Council at Luxembourg accepted the request tabled by President Clerides, on 12 March 1998, to include representatives of the Turkish Cypriot community in the negotiations as a means of facilitating progress in the dialogue between the communities and supporting the talks for a bi-zonal, bi-communal federation conducted under the aegis of the United Nations.

In its first Regular Report from the Commission on Cyprus's progress towards Accession of November 1998 the Commission reported that already 16 of the 29 chapters of the acquis were screened since 27 April 1998 when the analytical examination of the acquis started with Cyprus. In fact, Cyprus had already presented its negotiating positions on 7 chapters.[20] This was the main area of focus in the Commission's evaluation of the Cypriot efforts towards accession. The Commission assessed the progress made by the applicant country in the adoption of the acquis as detailed in the 1973 Association Agreement and the 1987 Protocol and praised the country for its rapid advancement. The Commission identified areas of concern on the basis of the discrepancy between the acquis and existing national laws. The internal market field and in particular the off-shore and financial sectors, maritime transport, telecommunications and justice and home affairs were noted as fields of law where increased effort for transposition was needed. Moreover, the Commission assessed the implementation and enforceability of the acquis after transposition and observed that these were not considered areas of difficulty for Cyprus in view of its administrative and judicial capacity. With reference to the political criterion the Report noted with regret that the Turkish-Cypriot community has not taken up the offer of participation to negotiations and even to programmers of financing. The Commission decided therefore to proceed with negotiations even though the screening of the acquis could not cover Cyprus as a whole. The economic criterion was not considered to present a problem for Cyprus as its government was considered to be committed to a stable macroeconomic environment and a favourable business climate. In fact, the economy of Cyprus was viewed strong enough to support the possible integration of the northern part of the island. One area of concern, which coincided with an area of concern with reference to the legal criterion, was the rapid increase of the international business sector in Cyprus, in particular the offshore banking sector, and the restricted domestic financial sector.

The 1998 Report on Cyprus's progress is a rather positive document. The country pleasantly surprised the Commission with its enthusiastic hard work and accelerated progress in the area of transposition, thus creating a momentum for an equally enthusiastic response by the EU. It is interesting to note that the political problem which was considered a major hurdle to accession that far was sidelined in favour of the encouragement for even deeper transposition. The Commission was pleased with Cyprus's interpretation of transposition which included not only legislation but also its implementation and enforcement and was reassured that the quality of transposition achieved so far and scheduled in the future would be of equally high standard. If there is one lesson to be learned from this process for future applicant countries, it is that hard work in the area of transposition is crucial for accession. Transposition must be complete: mere legislation is not enough. A second useful point for future applicant countries refers to the depth of assessment that the Commission is prepared to undertake in order to ensure complete transposition: even the administrative and judicial infrastructure of the applicant country will not escape the scrutiny of the Commission. A third lesson concerns flexibility as a means of demonstrating the importance awarded to EU accession by the applicant country: for Cyprus, encouragement of the Turkish community to participate in the negotiations was an exceptionally tricky step as it could be considered a *de facto* recognition of the Turkish-Cypriot administration. However, this may be considered as the move which resolved the gridlock preventing the start of negotiations, and indeed the goodwill gesture which liberated negotiations from the unsurpassable hurdle of a demand for a political settlement before the Copenhagen criteria could be considered to have been met. In the 1999 Regular Report from the Commission on Cyprus's Progress Towards Accession the political issue was only referred to in the very beginning where it was reported that little progress for a settlement had been made. Even so, the report declared that Cyprus met the political criteria anyway. With reference to the economic criterion the report reaffirmed that the main requirement, that of a functioning market economy, was already met. However, the Commission identified detailed areas of concern and proceeded to set goals for their attainment. Rapid economic growth and control of inflation were noted with satisfaction but the macroeconomic and financial imbalances and the unsustainable growth of stock market needed to be addressed. For this purpose the Commission asked for increased efforts in the areas of privatisation, deregulation, structural reform, capital account liberalisation; removal of the 9% interest ceiling; and appropriate fiscal measures to ensure macroeconomic stability.

In this Report, as indeed in the first Report, emphasis was given on the transposition of the acquis. The Commission presented areas of dissatisfaction with progress since the previous Report and provided a detailed analysis of areas where measures needed to be taken for the advancement of negotiations. Areas of legislative inactivity were the internal market where only 15% of existing European standards were adopted since March 1998; the liberalisation of capital movement; maritime safety; transport; immigration and the asylum; and the environment. The Commission also recommended specific measures for complete compliance with the acquis in areas where basic alignment was already in place: the subjection of public undertakings with special or exclusive rights to competition rules; the systematic control of state aids via the adoption of a framework law; the complete alignment in the veterinary and phytosanitiary areas; the strengthening of veterinary controls at border posts; and the further computerisation and harmonisation in the area of visa control. Maintaining its emphasis on complete transposition, the Commission recommended that Cyprus allocates sufficient budgetary and administrative resources to the environmental sector; that it introduces institutions in telecommunications, free movement of goods and justice and home affairs; and that it strengthens existing institutions in the areas of maritime transport and environment sectors.

The second Report of the Commission was much more detailed than the first Report. The Commission set aside the political problem and concentrated in the economic and the legal criteria. In fact it would be fair to state that the issue of transposition was awarded not only paramount but also primary importance. The detail of scrutiny of the existing national law by the Commission is impressive, especially in view of the novelty of the exercise both for the Commission and the applicant countries. Equally impressive was the extent to the rapid rhythm of reaction expected by the applicant countries: the adoption of 15% of the acquis in the field of the internal market within a period of 18 months was considered to be inadequate even at this early stage. The nature of screening, as detailed in the Report, was clearly twofold. Firstly, to identify areas where existing national law is so different from EU standards that general reform is needed. Secondly, to determine the specific points in need of legislative action in fields where alignment is already present. In the case of need for general reform the Commission recommends a framework law but refrains from detailing the specific contents of the proposed legislative text. In the case of specific points where transposition is needed the Commission does identify the specific content of the transposition efforts as a means of assisting the applicant country in its task to transpose the acquis fully. However, even in this case there is no recommendation or advice as to the exact nature of the response expected by the applicant countries: it is the applicants that will determine what type of measures are needed in each particular case for the complete yet gentle integration of the new laws to the existing national legal system. Nevertheless, transposition is again considered to include not only legislation but also implementation and enforcement. Such is the emphasis awarded to this by the Commission, that the Report also includes specific recommendations on the introduction of new institutions or the strengthening of existing ones.

The reaffirmation of the decreased importance of Cyprus's 'political problem' with reference to the Copenhagen political criterion came in the 1999 Helsinki European Council.[21] The European Council welcomed the launch of yet another round of inter-community talks in New York under the aegis of the UN and repeated that a political settlement would facilitate the accession of Cyprus. However, for the first time in the history of the Cypriot application, the Council declared in no uncertain terms that accession of Cyprus will not be dependent upon a settlement: the Council's decision on accession would be made without settlement as a precondition. Moreover, the strategy towards Cyprus would remain the same, as detailed in 'Council Regulation (EC) No 555/2000 of 13 March 2000 on the implementation of operations in the framework of the pre-accession strategy for the Republic of Cyprus and the Republic of Malta'.[22]

The decreased role of a final political settlement before accession could be contemplated became evident in most subsequent EU texts. Thus, in the 2000 Regular Report from the Commission on Cyprus's Progress

Towards Accession of 8 November 2000 reaffirmed that even without a political settlement Cyprus already fulfilled the Copenhagen political criterion. However, setting the trend for future evaluations of the Cypriot application, the Commission continued to repeat that a political settlement would be in line with the Accession Partnership and would therefore be very desirable for the EU. It is interesting to note that the Cypriot government did not sit back and enjoy the waiver from its most difficult hurdle to accession. In a continued demonstration of enthusiasm for the prospect of EU accession and of increased efforts to comply with the EU's desire for a political settlement at all cost, Cyprus continued intra-community talks and made substantive efforts for an agreement in the fourth round of proximity talks held in September 2000.

With reference to the economic criterion, the Commission continued to declare that Cyprus is, in principle, compliant with the Copenhagen economic criterion and is already a functioning market economy able to cope with the competitive pressure and market forces within the EU. Having already stated this in the two previous reports, this and subsequent reports re-stated the fact and proceeded to identify areas where further work was necessary. The Report called for general reforms such as increased efficiency of the market; preparation of the private sector to operate in the EU; and agreement on a structural reform agenda limiting state involvement in economic activities and addressing environmental constraints. The Report also included detailed recommendations for action in specific areas of concern: fiscal policy; complete price liberalisation; regulation of the co-operative banking sector; capital liberalisation. The Report acknowledged progress made already in the fields of liberalisation and structural reforms and welcomed the legislation on the abolition of the interest ceiling. In other words, the Commission continued to utilize a triple method of analysis: identification of work already undertaken, recommendation for reforms in areas of general concern and designation of measures to be introduced in areas of specific transposition tasks. The means in which the reforms were to take place were again left to the Cypriot government.

This pattern was also followed in the analysis of Cyprus's compliance with the Copenhagen legal criterion which continued to receive significant attention in the evaluation of progress towards accession. First, the Commission acknowledged the work undertaken in the areas of the health sector; the internal market; the financial sector both in the field of legislation and in the field of administrative capacity; taxation and VAT; fisheries; and transport. Second, the Commission identified areas where general reform was still needed: the state aid sector; and the environment. Third, the Commission referred to specific measures deemed necessary for the achievement of compliance with the acquis. The depth of detail found in the Report demonstrates the Commission's surprising diligence in the screening process and an equally surprising depth of involvement of the Commission to the pre-accession strategy of applicant countries. Thus, in the area of free movement of goods the Commission requested transposition in the fields of standardisation, certification and the New Approach Directives. In the area of free movement of capital the Commission required timely, orderly and complete abolition of restrictions. In the field of agriculture the Commission demanded full transposition of the acquis in the veterinary and phytosanitary fields and in the area of veterinary controls at border posts. For justice and home affairs the Commission identified the need for the enforcement of border control and for the efficient implementation of money laundering laws.

From this brief analysis of the 2000 Commission Report it becomes obvious that as negotiations progressed the Commission entered into finer details as to the transposition of the acquis by applicant countries. The common concept of pre-accession adoption of the acquis as a general exercise dealing mainly with the core primary and secondary Community laws in each field was already being shattered by the level of detail reached in the screening exercises. The Commission was indeed an excellent watchdog for the adoption and implementation of EC law and it began to gain confidence in extending this role to the applicant countries. The method of the Commission's evaluation of applicant countries accentuates the role of Accession Partnerships as a determination of the obligations to be undertaken by the applicant countries before accession can become a reality. Applicant countries need to acknowledge the long term effect of their agreement in the Accession Partnership and every effort must be made to view negotiations for the Partnership as a core part of the screening for the acquis. The Commission referred to Cyprus's compliance with the goals set in the Accession Partnership in the areas of fisheries, transport, the internal market, energy, and justice and home affairs.[23]

The increasing confidence of the Commission in its role as the watchdog of the Treaties even in pre-accession negotiations and the development of pre-accession negotiations in combination with the increasing urgency of the need for complete transposition within the approaching deadlines led to a lengthy and detailed 2001 Regular Report on Cyprus's Progress Towards Accession.[24] The depth of analysis of the state of play is further accentuated by the Accession Partnership included in the 2001 Report and by the 2001 Strategy Paper of the Commission on the progress achieved by all applicant countries.[25] Even the 2001 Regular Report itself was the lengthiest, most detailed one of its kind (at least on Cyprus) until that date.

Following the structure of past Reports, the 2001 Regular Report reaffirmed Cyprus's compliance with the Copenhagen political criteria since the functioning of democracy and respect to human rights was within EU standards. Compliance with the economic criteria was also reaffirmed as Cyprus is a functioning market economy which could compete within the EU. The analysis of the route to complete adoption of the acquis and compliance with the legal criterion took the best part of the Report. First, the Commission noted the progress made by Cyprus in the transposition of EC law in the following fields: structural reforms in the financial sector, the environment, and healthcare; liberalisation of the financial sector and the capital account; social security; financial services; capital movements; environment; transport with particular reference to maritime safety; and justice and home affairs apart from asylum. Second, areas where general reform was necessary were now limited to intellectual and property rights; and asylum. Third, there was considerable increase of recommendations for specific points of concern in areas where general law reform as a means of compliance with the acquis has already been achieved. Thus, the preparation of the private sector to operate in the single market should now include opening key sectors to foreign competition. In the area of free movement of goods the Commission requested compliance with the new and global approach principles and the New Approach Directives, as well as increased coordination of authorities for market surveillance. In the area of state aids the Commission required the introduction of a suitable tax regime for off-shore companies. In the field of agriculture further work was needed as regards the Common Market Organisations and the veterinary and phytosanitary sectors. In fisheries an area of continuing concern was the structure of the fishing fleet under Cypriot flag. With regards to taxation the level of indirect taxation and the special direct taxation for off-shore companies were still in need of harmonisation. The area of telecommunications needed the introduction of secondary regulatory instruments to transpose key parts of the acquis as a matter of priority. On asylum an independent appeals authority was also needed. Customs legislation needed further harmonisation with regards to temporary importation, customs procedures with an economic impact, and cultural goods. Cyprus's financial control system needed to address the internal control of revenues and the proper management of pre-accession funding and structural funds.

Finally, the Report included a detailed analysis of administrative structures needed in specific areas of legislation. This can be seen as a reflection of the continued emphasis awarded by the EU to the implementation and enforceability of transposition legislation.

The last Regular Report on Cyprus's Progress towards EU Accession[26] followed the same pattern emphasising the efforts of Cyprus to transpose the acquis fully and it time for EU accession. The Commission reported accelerated pace of alignment in an increased number of fields: social insurance, veterinary and phytosanitary inspections, pharmaceutical services, money laundering, ship inspection, inland revenue, planning, environmental services, consumer and health protection, and customs. Alignment was again interpreted broadly to include not only legislative reform but also administrative capacity for the implementation and enforcement of the new transposition laws. The Report observed that Cyprus had already achieved a good degree of alignment with the acquis in most areas.[27] Full alignment was reported in the fields of the free movement of goods, free movement of persons, freedom to provide services, free movement of capital, company law, competition, state aid, taxation, economic and monetary union, justice and home affairs, and regional policy.

However, further work was needed in a small number of areas. There, in recognition of the threateningly short deadlines for completion of the transposition effort, the Commission made detailed recommendations for the adoption of specific measures. Nevertheless, the nature of the measures to be taken was again left to the Cypriot government. Thus, in the field of public procurement further measures were needed on the notification procedure, market surveillance and product safety. In the area of energy Cyprus was requested to proceed with the progressive building up of oil stocks. Similarly, areas of environmental law needed alignment with the acquis with reference to air and water quality, industrial pollution control, chemicals, genetically modified organisms and waste management. In a number of areas the Commission declared full alignment in the legislative sphere but requested bigger administrative capacity for the implementation and enforcement of the new laws. This was the case with agriculture, fisheries, social policy and employment, the environment, financial controls and telecommunications. Moreover, intellectual and industrial property rights needed stronger enforcement capacity for border controls, combating piracy and counterfeiting. In the area of energy the new authority supervising oil stocks needed to be in place. In a number of fields the Commission urged Cyprus to proceed with its planned legislation for complete transposition of the acquis. This was the case with transport and especially aviation. Similarly, in the area of customs the Commission urged for the final adoption of planned legislation on inward and outward processing, temporary importation, cultural goods and procedural aspects.

The last Regular Report was a detailed analysis of progress achieved by Cyprus in its efforts to accession. The cycle of Reports started with a critical assessment on the adoption of a mere 15% of the acquis in 1999 and closed with praise on the almost complete adoption of the acquis in 2002. Within a period of four years Cyprus had managed to transpose most of EC law and to introduce the required administrative structures for its implementation and enforcement upon accession. In view of Cyprus's compliance with the Copenhagen legal criterion, attention was now turned to the political criterion and to a political settlement between the two communities on the island.

The 2002 Seville European Council affirmed that the Helsinki conclusions would constitute the basis for the evaluation of the application of Cyprus for EU accession.[28] Thus, a political settlement would not be considered a prerequisite for accession. However, the Council reaffirmed the EU's preference to proceed with accession of a unified Cyprus. For this purpose the Council was prepared to agree to a substantial financial contribution supporting the alignment of the northern part of a reunited island. The 2002 Brussels European Council reiterated the EU's preference for a reunited Cyprus to join the EU and urged both communities to reach an agreement before accession.[29] However, in the absence of such a settlement the EU would make its final decision on the application of Cyprus in the 2002 Copenhagen European Council on the basis of the 1999 Helsinki European Council: in other words in the event of non agreement between the two communities the island would have to accede divided.

Although the preference of the EU for a unified island as a member of the EU was expressed as 'strong',[30] the 2002 Copenhagen European Council declared that Cyprus would be admitted even without a political settlement. In the latter case the application of the acquis to the northern part of the island would be suspended until a subsequent unanimous Council decision based on a Commission proposal. This was reaffirmed in the 2003 Brussels European Council and the specific protocol on Cyprus to be attached to the Accession Treaty.[31]

The turn of attention to the political problem did not mean that the Commission allowed idleness in the ever dynamic area of transposition with the acquis. In its 'Comprehensive monitoring report on Cyprus's preparations for membership' of 5 November 2003 the Commission introduced a list of specific measures which still needed to be taken as a matter of urgency. Although these refer to very detailed issues within each of the negotiations chapter they nevertheless require attention from the government of Cyprus. Although accession would not depend on them as the decision had already been taken, upon accession the Commission enjoyed a full arsenal of data for the initiation of infringement proceedings before the ECJ against the new member state. As these carry with them the possibility of the imposition of a fine, the incentive for the fine-tuning of Cypriot legislation on these points is still very much there.

Thus, the Commission identified the need for urgent alignments on the following points: old sectoral legislation on the free movement of goods; investment services, securities markets and information society services on the freedom to provide services; protection of intellectual and industrial property rights in company law; in agriculture the Farm Accountancy Data Network, the veterinary control system, public health in agri-food establishments, transmissible spongiform encephalopathy (TSE) and animal by-products, common measures, animal nutrition and some aspects of phytosanitary legislation; in fisheries the resource and fleet management, inspection and control; in transport policy road transport and air transport; in social policy the European Social Fund and anti-discrimination; in energy security of supply, competitiveness and the internal energy market; telecommunications and information technologies, including postal services; audio-visual policy in the area of culture and audio-visual policy; institutional structures in the field of regional policy and co-ordination of structural instruments; nature protection and genetically modified organisms in the area of environment policy; market surveillance and non-safety related measures in the area of consumer and health protection; visa policy and asylum policy in the area of justice and home affairs; external relations, as regards screening of bilateral agreements with third countries and public internal financial control in the area of financial control. Moreover, the Commission identified two areas where immediate action was needed, agriculture and transport, and called upon the Cypriot government to regulate its Paying Agency, to prepare for the application of external trade mechanisms in agriculture and to finally provide for maritime safety.

Despite this, the Commission delivered its opinion on the Accession Treaty on 19 February 2003 and submitted the Treaty to the European Parliament which gave its assent on 9 April 2003. The Treaty was signed in Athens on 16 April 2003. Cyprus ratified the Treaty in July 2003. Cyprus became a member state on 1 May 2004.

The route to EU accession for future applicants

Are there any lessons that can be drawn from Cyprus's long and eventful route to EU accession? Can Cyprus's experience provide future applicants with valuable experience in the handling of their own applications, despite the obvious intricacies and idiosyncrasies of each application for EU membership?

What is beyond doubt is that, at least until the Copenhagen conclusions are amended by subsequent European Council conclusions, accession to the EU will be undertaken on the basis of three criteria. These are applied uniformly to all applicant countries and compliance with them is a *conditio sine qua non* for EU accession. The political criterion refers to a functioning democracy with respect to human rights and the values of the EU; the economic criterion refers to a functioning market economy; and the legal criterion demands complete transposition of the acquis before the accession.

The three criteria are rather general. One would have been excused for hoping that political will for the accession of the applicant country would allow gentle manipulation of facts to ensure that one way or another the applicant country would be found compliant with the generalities of the Copenhagen criteria. Unfortunately, for applicant countries, this could not have been further from the truth. Experience from the application of the Copenhagen criteria from the Commission for the purposes of the screening exercises demonstrates that the assessment of compliance with them is detailed, elaborate and multi-focal. In fact, one could state that vagueness in the expression of the Copenhagen criteria has been utilised to allow a global in depth analysis of the politics, economy and laws of applicant countries as a means of ensuring that all necessary reforms take place before accession. It is surprising to reflect the length of Regular Reports and their reference to all aspects of the politics, economy and law of the applicant countries. In indeed the blatant involvement to the government, economy and legal system of applicant countries can only be justified on the basis of the voluntary submission of their situation for EU assessment and of course on the basis of the advisory nature of Commission recommendations in these sensitive areas.

Although all three criteria have equal standing, the legal criterion is of paramount importance. Transposition of the acquis is demanded by applicant countries before accession and the Commission will scrutinise all national primary and secondary legislation in order to evaluate compliance with EC law. The amplified significance awarded to the legal criterion may be attributed to the interpretation between the legal and the other two criteria. Legal integration inevitably signifies compliance with the political values of the EU and the economic standards introduced by EC law. It would be difficult to contemplate compliance with the political and economic criteria if national legislation did not reflect this in the national legal provisions. By scrutinising and ensuring the amendment of national laws in line with the acquis, the EU ensures that the principles of democracy and the rule of law, respect to human rights, and actual functioning of an open market economy are materialised in the applicant country via its own legislation.

It is for this purpose that the analysis of Cyprus's route to accession must be undertaken on the basis of its efforts to transpose the acquis. Experiences drawn from this effort can be of immense use to future applicant countries and the lessons to be learnt are neither few nor insignificant.

The task of transposition begins with the detailed analysis of the acquis. Although it would be tempting for a future member state to conduct this analysis internally experience has shown that the presentation of EC law by the Commission and its interpretation by the ECJ constitute the only reliable source of information in this area. National legal officers from third countries tend to lack the know-how necessary for the correct identification of the sources of EC law, the appreciation of the hierarchy of these sources, and the objective determination of discrepancies between national laws and the acquis. Often the starting point for this process is different and the priorities of the EU and the Commission only become evident after the screening process has begun. Future member states have additional guidance in their initial efforts to familiarise themselves with the acquis. Firstly, the Commission's guide to negotiations presents the main points of each chapter for future negotiations and presents an accurate picture of EC law as it stood in June 2004.[32] Nevertheless, this is a very two-dimensional picture of the acquis which is inadequate for future use, as EC law is a dynamic, ever changing set of rules under constant review and interpretation by the European Courts. Secondly, the route to transposition is signposted by the efforts, faults and successes of the 2004 enlargement: future member states have access to complete reports on the Commission's priorities per chapter and the criteria for their evaluations.

Thus, work towards EU accession begins much before negotiations are even contemplated. Aspiring member states must have a strategy for accession even at the time that the initial international agreements with the EU are signed. Approximation pacts are far from the common perception of mere international agreements aiming to draw the country's attention to points of concern for the EU in exchange of hefty financial assistance. They constitute the basis upon which the assessment of the country's suitability as a future member state will be undertaken. In fact, points of concern identified in these instruments are often at the forefront of negotiations for EU accession as they reflect the EU's points of priority in the event of future enlargement. The agreement of the aspiring country in these pacts is often interpreted as an initial consent as to the existence of a problem in the areas identified in the text.

Negotiations for accession are crucial. They are not cosmetic and they can not be taken lightly. Experts participating in the screening process should be very much aware that their views will be binding for their country. Their presentation on the existing national provisions will be scrutinised very closely and any discrepancies will be brought to light. The best service that negotiators could offer to their country is to be frank and present the full picture of the existing legal provisions. Although compliance will have to be achieved, the Commission is more likely to agree on realistically longer deadlines and on understandable delays in full transposition if the intricacies of the applicant country's national legal system are made know to the Commission delegation. As the Commission' role is to facilitate transposition their experience from negotiations with a number of applicant countries may well lead to an innovative solution to any problems.

Of course the precise measures to be taken for complete and timely compliance with the acquis are determined and taken by the applicant country. The Commission advises on the points that the applicant country must address and expects adequate measures to be taken within the agreed deadlines. In theory the applicant country may ignore all Commission recommendations. The Commission's power in negotiations is only indirect: power is there only if the applicant country wishes to proceed with its application for accession to the EU; and the Commission's power lies on its instrumental role in the assessment of the applicant country's transposition of the acquis.

Transposition must be interpreted in its broad sense. Legislating for accession, be it one of the heaviest tasks on the drafters and administrative capacity of the applicant country, is only the first step for compliance with the acquis. Transposition also requires the introduction of agencies and institutions necessary for the implementation and enforcement of the new or amended legislation. Adequate transposition engulfs all three stages: legislation, implementation and enforcement.

Thus, the role of the Commission in the whole effort of the applicant states is to identify discrepancies between the existing national provisions and the acquis, to recommend the amendment of existing provisions or the introduction of new legislative measures in compliance with EC law, to assess the applicability and enforceability of the new measures, and to make recommendations for full alignment with the acquis. In other words, the Commission extends its role as the watchdog of the EU to applicant countries even before their actual accession. The only difference with the Commission's role with reference to member states is that in the case of the latter the Commission has the right and duty to refer them to the ECJ in infringement proceedings.

It would be fair therefore to state that the process of negotiations with aspiring member states begins long before the application for EU membership is submitted. The pre-accession strategy of aspiring member states must engulf any initial international agreements and approximation pacts with the EU. The route to EU accession is long and painful. Very often the required radical changes can prove destructive for the legal system of applicant countries. However, if accession is desirable, the route to it offers an invaluable opportunity to the applicant countries to acquire a realistic and insightful taste of the internal mechanisms of the EU, its legal system, its institutions and its values. And, despite the frequent criticisms of older member states, these seem to be highly enviable, if the decision of 10 new member states to accede to the EU is anything to go by.

Notes

1. See SN 180/1/93, 22/6/1993.
2. See SN 400/95, 16/12/1995.
3. See SN 300/94, 9/12/1994.
4. See SN 300/94, 9/12/1994.
5. See COM(95) 163, May 1995.
6. See SN 211/95, 26/6/1995.
7. See SN 400/1997, 12/12/1997.
8. See Council Regulation (EC) No 622/98 of 16 March 1998 on assistance to the applicant States in the framework of the pre-accession strategy, and in particular on the establishment of Accession Partnerships, OJ L85, 20 March 1998, p. 1.
9. See SN 1591/02, 29/1/2003.
10. Treaty between the Kingdom of Belgium, the Kingdom of Denmark, the Federal Republic of Germany, the Hellenic Republic, the Kingdom of Spain,

the French Republic, Ireland, the Italian Republic, the Grand Duchy of Luxembourg, the Kingdom of the Netherlands, the Republic of Austria, the Portuguese Republic, the Republic of Finland, the Kingdom of Sweden, the United Kingdom of Great Britain and Northern Ireland (Member States of the European Union) and the Czech Republic, the Republic of Estonia, the Republic of Cyprus, the Republic of Latvia, the Republic of Lithuania, the Republic of Hungary, the Republic of Malta, the Republic of Poland, the Republic of Slovenia, the Slovak Republic, concerning the accession of the Czech Republic, the Republic of Estonia, the Republic of Cyprus, the Republic of Latvia, the Republic of Lithuania, the Republic of Hungary, the Republic of Malta, the Republic of Poland, the Republic of Slovenia and the Slovak Republic to the European Union, OJ L236, 23 September 2003, pp. 17-930.

11. See SN 180/1/93, 22/6/1993.
12. See doc/93/5, 30 June 1993.
13. See SN 150/94, 24/6/1994.
14 See SN 300/94, 9/12/1994.
15. See SN 211/95, 26/6/1995.
16. See 400/95, 16/12/1995.
17. See SN 300/96, 21/6/1996.
18. See SN 401/1/96, 16/12/1996 where the settlement of the Cypriot problem is being mentioned again, albeit only as a note of Turkey's obligation to exercise its influence for its resolution.
19. See SN 400/97, 12/12/1997.
20. These were: Industrial Policy (chapter 15); Small and Medium-Sized Enterprises (chapter 16); Science and Research (chapter 17); Education and Training (chapter 18); Telecommunication and Information Technologies (chapter 19); Culture and Audiovisual Policy (chapter 20); and Common Foreign and Security Policy (chapter 27).
21. See 300/1/99, 11/12/1999.
22. See Regulation (EC) No.555/2000, OJ L68, 16 March 2000, p.3; also see Council Regulation (EC) No.622/98 of 16 March 1998 on assistance to the applicant States in the framework of the pre-accession strategy, and in particular on the establishment of the Accession Partnerships, OJ L85, 20 March 1998, p.1.
23. See Council Decision 2000/258/EC (OJ L 78, 29 March 2000).
24. See SEC(2001) 1745, 13 November 2001.
25. See *Making a success of enlargement: Strategy Paper and Report of the European Commission on the progress towards accession by each of the candidate countries*, COM (2001) 700.
26. See COM(2002) 700 final; and SEC(2002) 1401, 9 October 2002.
27. Also see *Towards the Enlarged Union: Strategy Paper and Report of the European Commission on the progress towards accession by each of the candidate countries*, COM (2002) 700.

28. See SN 13463/02, 24/10/2002.
29. See SN 14702/02, 26/11/2002.
30. See SN 15917/02, 29/1/2003.
31. See Act concerning the conditions of accession of the Czech Republic, the Republic of Estonia, the Republic of Cyprus, the Republic of Latvia, the Republic of Lithuania, the Republic of Hungary, the Republic of Malta, the Republic of Poland, the Republic of Slovenia and the Slovak Republic and the adjustments to the Treaties on which the European Union is founded, Protocol No 10 on Çyprus, OJ L236, 23 September 2003, p.955; also see 2004/511/EC Council Decision of 10 June 2004 concerning the representation of the people of Cyprus in the European Parliament in case of a settlement of the Cyprus problem, OJ L211, 12 June 2004, pp.22-23.
32. See 'Enlargement to the EU: Guide to Negotiations Chapter by Chapter', June 2004, European Commission: DG Enlargement.

3 Harmonising Cyprus's Agricultural Sector with the Acquis Communautaire

ANNA MARCOULLI[1]

Introduction

The Common Agricultural Policy (CAP) is considered one of the most important policies of the European Union (EU). This is reflected both in the volume of EU provisions dealing with agricultural issues as well as in the percentage of the Union's budget allocated to support the CAP. The enlargement of the EU with ten new member states, has a large impact on the CAP in several ways but primarily in financial terms. This is illustrated by the fact that, the financial arrangements in the area of agriculture were the final issue to be settled, before the Copenhagen European Council of December 2002, which confirmed the decision to proceed with the latest enlargement.

The enlargement procedure, which successfully ended in Copenhagen in 2002 started back in 1997 with the acquis screening, where the European Commission made it clear that the candidate countries would have to adopt the acquis communautaire before accession date and that only a limited number of transitional periods or derogations for its implementation would be allowed. The candidate countries started work having a twofold objective:

- to adopt all the necessary national legislative measures required for full harmonization with the acquis communautaire, and
- to set up the necessary administrative and technical infrastructure for implementing the transposed national legislation as well as the acquis communautaire.

This chapter, attempts to examine Cyprus's efforts to achieve the above objectives in the area of agriculture, by focusing mainly at the legislative side of this task, which in most cases is closely linked to the decisions associated with the administrative and technical side of the task. A brief overview of the development of the CAP on an EU level was also deemed necessary in order to give a more complete picture of what this policy is about and its aims.

A brief history of the CAP

The objectives of the CAP are set in Article 33 of the Treaty and have guided the policy makers of the EU in the formation as well as the subsequent reforms of this vital community policy both in economic and social terms. The targets set out in the said Article of the Treaty are:

a. increasing productivity in agriculture;
b. ensuring a fair standard of living for the agricultural community;
c. stabilising the markets;
d. guaranteeing security of supply;
e. ensuring reasonable prices for the consumers.

When setting up the CAP in 1962, these targets were found to be better served by the creation of Common Market Organisations (COMs) as provided in Article 34 of the Treaty, which nowadays cover approximately 90% of the agricultural products produced in the EU.

The mechanisms used for implementing the CAP back in 1962, were successful for the achievement of the targets of the Treaty in the following years. However, the excessive subsidising of the income of the farmers through the CAP mechanisms and mainly the use of intervention prices, led to the creation of surpluses in agricultural products and to massive spending of Community funds. It was necessary to introduce measures to control the funds of the Budget of the then EEC allocated to the CAP. Parallel to this, the need to diversify the scope of the CAP and to embark on a new approach also emerged. The result was the 1992 Mac-Sharry Reform, the first Comprehensive Reform of the CAP. This reform was broadly successful in lowering institutional prices for key products and offsetting the impact of these cuts on producer incomes by the introduction of direct payments. The first rural development measures were also introduced through this Reform. The continuous developments in this sector as well as the need to enforce the rural development measures led once more to the need to further modernise the CAP and this was achieved by the Agenda 2000 Reform, which deepened, extended and consolidated the 1992 Reform.

In June 2003, the Council adopted a new fundamental Reform of the CAP, aiming at completely changing the traditional way the EU supports its farming sector. In the future, the vast majority of subsidies will be paid independently from the volume of production. Member states will be able to choose to maintain a limited and restricted link between subsidy and production, in order to avoid abandonment of production.

A short history of Cyprus's agricultural sector and the accession negotiations with the EU

It is important to set the state of Cyprus agriculture in a general framework, both economic and historical, in order to understand the impact on this sector by joining the EU. When Cyprus gained its independence in 1960, the agricultural sector accounted for 17% of its GDP and 33% of employment. These percentages fell dramatically in 1974 when Turkey invaded Cyprus and occupied 37% of the island, which, unfortunately, was the most fertile land. The government has since initiated active policies and given generous incentives to both existing farmers to expand their activities as well as to young people to enter the field, without however much success. Physical and other limitations such as the shortage of water and the extensive land fragmentation leading to prevalence of small holdings, not only discouraged people from entering this field of employment but also pushed those already in, to find other sources of income. The current statistical data show a dramatic fall of the contribution of agriculture to the country's GDP to a level of 4% and that of the gainful employment in this sector, to 8%.[2]

The negotiation procedure between the candidate countries and the EU for the Chapter of Agriculture, as with the rest of the 28 Chapters, consisted of two phases: the 'screening' of the acquis and 'substantive negotiations'. During 'screening' the European Commission and the candidate countries examined in great detail the degree to which the body of law, institutions and procedures of the candidates complied with those of the EU, i.e. with the acquis communautaire. In the second phase, the actual negotiation of transitional arrangements or derogations took place.

In order to substantiate the requests and demands of Cyprus during the substantive negotiations the Ministry of Agriculture, Natural Resources and Environment (MANRE) which is the competent Ministry for this sector, prepared a well documented Position Paper. In this Paper, Cyprus accepted the principles and rules of the CAP in all sectors and stated that it was in a position to implement the acquis. The paper contained the requests made by Cyprus for transitional periods or derogations in implementing the acquis.

During the Copenhagen European Council, Cyprus confirmed the official closure of the last three outstanding Chapters including that of Agriculture, thus completing successfully its accession negotiations with the EU. More specifically, the Overall Final Agreement and the Global Agreement on all Outstanding Issues[3] are the documents reflecting the results of the final compromise between the EU and the candidate countries. According to the final package, Cyprus is given the possibility to complement direct aid, paid to a farmer under any CAP scheme listed in the Annex to Regulation 1259/99/EC,[4] up to the total level of support the farmer would have been entitled to receive in Cyprus prior to accession (2001). During the years 2004-2006 Cyprus has the possibility to co-finance the complementary national aid from its national rural development allocation under the European Agricultural Guarantee and Guidance Fund (EAGGF)[5] – Guarantee Section, under specified terms set in the final package. From 2007, however, all national complementary direct payments or aids will be financed exclusively from the national budget of Cyprus. Regarding state aid, in sectors where it provides a higher level of aid than presently in the EU, Cyprus may be given the possibility to grant transitional and digressive national aids until the end of 2010, in addition to the complementary national direct payments – again under specified terms. Cyprus also managed to get a fair compromise regarding its requests for the milk quota, the suckler cow premium, the beef premium, the slaughter premium and vine-planting rights. Moreover, Cyprus was given a five years transitional period for providing extra state aids to deprived areas and for the digressive adjustment for withdrawals of fruits and vegetables.

Horizontal issues

Legislative harmonisation in the field of horizontal issues of Agriculture, has mainly been completed. The most vital piece of legislation enacted regarding horizontal issues was the one on the establishment and operation of the Paying Agency.

Paying agency[6]

The support, restructuring and development measures of Cyprus's agricultural policy have similar characteristics to the relevant EU measures. Currently, in Cyprus the schemes providing financial assistance have similarities in the assesment criteria, competent bodies for handling applications, procedures for approval and disbursement of funds to farmers to those of the EU. The competent bodies for handling these schemes applications are the District Offices of the Department of Agriculture of the MANRE and the procedure followed after an application has been submitted regarding the technical specifications is completed within the various departments of the MANRE. The inspections and controls necessary for approval are conducted by technical services but an additional assessment and the final approval is the task of a Specialist Committee under the Department of Agriculture.

There is also a Committee responsible for internal audits. The Accounting Office of the Department carries out the financial control according to the rules and procedures issued by the Accountant General before the vouchers are sent for payment. The Auditor General acts as an external auditor for all the payments made under the schemes, according to international auditing standards. The actual disbursement of the payments to the farmers is done either through the Accounting Office of the Republic or the Central Cooperative Bank and the village cooperatives. A number of guarantee schemes are handled by semi-governmental organisations such as the Cyprus Grain Commission, the Vine Products Commission, the Olive Products Marketing Board and the Cyprus Milk Industry Organisation using similar procedures as described above.

All of the above were seriously taken into consideration by the MANRE, which is charged with the preparation of a study on how the Paying Agency would be set up in Cyprus. The proposal of the MANRE, which was presented and approved by the Council of Ministers at the beginning of 2002, suggested that the Department of Agriculture and the semi-governmental organisations would be reorganised to undertake appropriate roles in the context of the Paying Agency. The tight time limits were one of the major factors affecting this decision. The preparations proceeded according to the above decision until the end of 2002.

At this point, it should be noted that the European Commission had originally expressed some reservations on the choice of the Cypriot authorities to incorporate the Paying Agency into a restructured Department of Agriculture mainly due to the double role that the

Department would assume, both as the main policy maker in the area of Agriculture as well as that of the body responsible for the exercising the functions of a Paying Agency i.e. the authorisation of payments, the making of payments and the accounting. However, until the end of 2002, it did not object to this decision of the Council of Ministers. After all, there are already some member states whose Paying Agencies operate within their Ministries, i.e. they are not independent bodies.

Despite all of the above, at the end of 2002 the European Commission informed Cypriot authorities that they would have to change their original decision for having the reorganised Department of Agriculture accreditated as Paying Agency. Instead, the Commission requested the establishment of a new independent body for this role. As a result a new line of action had to be undertaken within an extremely limited time period. The first step was the enactment of the necessary legal framework for the setting up of the Paying Agency.

The legislation providing for the establishment, operation and other relevant issues of the Paying Agency was enacted by the House of Representatives in early June 2003. A Commissioner appointed by the Council of Ministers, is the head of the Paying Agency and is responsible for its management and proper operation. In his duties he is assisted by an Assistant Commissioner. Both the Commissioner and the Assistant Commissioner have been appointed at the beginning of September 2003 and have started work.

When drafting this legislation, it was decided that it would be correct to follow the text of Regulation 1663/95/EC as closely as possible, especially its Annex which sets guidelines on the criteria for accreditation of a Paying Agency. In fact, the provisions of the Annex was essentially copied into the national legislation, with necessary amendments, in order to guide the accreditation authority (the Minister of Agriculture, Natural Resources and Environment) on the elements that must be taken into consideration, in order to issue the Act of Accreditation which according to Regulation 1257/99/EC has to be issued before the Paying Agency starts operating. The Act of Accreditation must confirm primarily that the way the Paying Agency operates and the way it is structured ensure that its three main functions are kept operationally separate from each other. Furthermore, it must confirm that any delegation of the function of authorization of payments to other bodies is done according to the provisions of the Law and that the employees of the Paying Agency execute their duties according to the prescribed procedures set in Law and the acquis.

According to the Law, the Integrated Administration and Control System (IACS) which is a vital component to the whole procedure of running the schemes regarding both plots of land and animal identification. This system is set up under the Department of Agriculture of the MANRE and is expected to be fully operational soon. The Commissioner of Agricultural Payments is expected to delegate, the functions of the IACS to the Department of Agriculture.

It is expected that, despite the delay observed in the setting up of the Paying Agency, it will start operating shortly before accession and will be able to allocate to farmers the funds of the EAGGF.

Organic farming

In the field of organic farming, The Organic Production Law of 2001 and its implementing regulations[7] were enacted at the end of 2001 for full harmonisation with the provisions of Regulation 2092/91/EEC on organic production. This was one of cases where even though the acquis communautaire is in the form of a Community Regulation, which after accession will be directly applicable, there was a need to introduce national legislation before accession. This is because Regulation 2092/91/EEC on organic farming, requires the member states to establish the necessary national administrative structures in order to implement it; an additional reason was that the European Commission requested that the necessary infrastructure for implementing it should be operational and be tested to ensure that it can operate properly before accession.

This law names the Department of Agriculture as the competent authority for the application of its provisions and provides for the procedure for the registration of inspection bodies, which are responsible for the certification of organic products. The undertaking of an operator who wants to market organic products has to be subject to inspection by a registered inspection body in order to ensure compliance with the rules of organic farming. Once again the method chosen for harmonisation was the copying of the provisions of Regulation 2092/91/EC into the national Law. The Law and regulations are currently at their early stages of application.

Quality control

As regards quality control of agricultural products, the Agricultural Products Law was enacted in September 2002.[8] This Law mainly provides for the setting up of an Inspection Authority which will be responsible for the maintenance of the quality standards of these products. It also provides for the issue of subsidiary legislation which sets the quality standards for agricultural products according to the relevant common market organisation. A number of implementing regulations for different agricultural products have so far been adopted under the above Law.

Designation of origin and geographical indications

Regulation 2081/92/EEC on the designation of origin and geographical indications of agricultural products and foodstuffs, provides for a system, which aims at the production of agricultural products of higher quality under which the EU registers and thus protects a 'geographical indication' or a 'designation of origin' of an agricultural product or foodstuff according to the procedure defined therein. The relevant Cyprus legislation on Designations of Origin and Geographical Indications[9] introduces a system which is similar to that of the EU. All interested parties may prepare applications for the registration of an agricultural product that fulfils the conditions set in the Law, and submit them for approval at a national level.

The Law provides for the setting up of a national competent authority, which will be responsible for the examination and approval of the applications submitted at a national level. The national competent authority can be assisted in its tasks by government departments where necessary. The criteria for approval and registration as 'protected geographical indication and designations of origin' for any product at a national level are in full compliance with those of the Regulation.

After accession the national system set up under this Law will continue to operate on a national level but in addition to this, interested parties will be able to apply to the European Commission for the protection granted on the EU level. The Office of Registrar of Companies and Official Receiver, which is is the competent authority for this legislation, will also have the task of forwarding the applications of Cypriots under the Community Regulation to the European Commission. The applicants whose products have already been approved by the National Competent Authority of Cyprus are not expected to face difficulties when applying for EU level protection of their products if the criteria of the national legislation are closely observed by the National Competent Authority when granting the national protection.

Common market organisations

This part of the Chapter deals with legal and administrative harmonisation for agricultural products governed by Common Markets Organisations of the EU. The focus will be on the legislative measures enacted or to be enacted aiming at harmonisation.

As mentioned above, six marketing Boards of Agricultural Products are operating in Cyprus. Although each one will be discussed separately according to the agricultural product it represents, as a result of harmonisation the following two changes apply to all of them:

a. Monopolistic Powers: All the Boards enjoy monopolistic powers mainly in the trading and marketing of their respective agricultural products. In order to comply with Articles 31 and 86(1) of the Treaty, the monopolistic powers of the Boards have to be abolished. More specifically, Article 31 of the Treaty provides for the adjustment of state monopolies of a commercial character in order to eliminate any discrimination between citizens of member states; Article 86(1) of the Treaty provides for the enactment or maintenance by member states of measures contrary, to the rules of competition, when granting exclusive rights to public undertakings. The progress made to this respect will be examined for each Board separately.
b. Change of Competent Ministry: The responsibility for the Boards is transferred from the Ministry of Commerce, Industry and Tourism to the MANRE, in an effort to bring all the Boards that are dealing with agricultural products under the same administrative authority. This is a practical and useful approach which is likely to bring better results regarding the cooperation and coordination between the various Agricultural Marketing Boards and the MANRE.

Cereals

Cereals are the main rain-fed crops of the island and the level of production depends on the level of annual rainfall. Cyprus relies heavily on imported cereals and the market is currently regulated by a state monopoly, the Cyprus Grain Commission (CGC), which controls the entire marketing of the main types of cereals used in the country, including the functions of importing, exporting, purchasing and selling.

Useful as the CGC has been over the years, its monopoly will have to be abolished by the time of formal accession and, consequently, its role in the market will change. To this end, the CGC commissioned a study on the potential alternative role it can assume after the abolition of its monopoly. The study has been evaluated by its Board of Directors and although there is no formal final decision yet, there is an initial decision that the CGC will proceed with its transformation into two separate private companies. One dealing with the trade of cereals in an open market situation and under free competition and a second one providing storage services that will be available to both the trading company and the private sector on an equal basis. This second company is also expected to undertake the intervention function, should the need arise since Cyprus is a net importer of cereals.

Although the above decision has not yet been given a legal form it is not expected to create any difficult legal problems. However, it is expected to create some practical problems concerning the future of the CGC staff and assets since the two new companies will not be able to employ all the current employees of the CGC and certainly not under the same conditions, if the companies are to be viable and competitive. These issues are currently under discussion in order to find a fair solution for the employees.

Fruit and vegetables

The fruit and vegetables sector is a very important one for Cyprus, since it accounts for over 30% of the total agricultural output. Potatoes, citrus, table grapes and some vegetables, are the main exported products. The current policies of the MANRE for fresh fruit and vegetables offer the producers, a very protective environment especially regarding assistance for access to the market either locally or for exports. The MANRE is now ready to offer the producers the necessary assistance and advise in order to set up Producers Organisations.

The Producers' Organisations Law of 2002[10] lays down the procedures for the approval and monitoring of Producers' Organisations. Under this framework law, a National Accreditation Authority (CNA) is set up and is responsible for the recognition of Producers' Organisations. In doing so it applies the terms, conditions and requirements provided in the relevant Community Regulations and the domestic subsidiary legislation. In its task the CNA is assisted by a separate National Advisory Committee, for each product, which is made of expert government officials. The products for which Producer's Organisations may be established are specified in an Annex to the Law. It is noted that the Annex[11] includes the agricultural products for which a Common Market Organisation exists and provides for the creation of a Producers Organisation. The only product included in the Annex for which a Common Market Organisation does not exist on an EU level is potatoes.

For this law to become operational, it is necessary to enact the relevant implementing Regulations which will set out the specific criteria required for accrediting a Producer's Organisation and are different for each member state. The framework law also provides that the Producers Organisations may take the form of a private company or a cooperative association. The later form of cooperation between producers is already very familiar to Cypriot producers of fruit and vegetables. As a result it is expected that the producers will not encounter great difficulties in setting up their Producers' Organisations according to the Law. After being accreditated by the CNA, the Producers' Organisations will be eligible for the financial assistance provided in the relevant EU Regulation for the respective Common Market Organisation.

Olives and olive oil

Cyprus has a long standing tradition in the cultivation of olive trees which in 1998 represented 5.6% of the cropped area with about 2.5 million productive trees. The Cyprus Olive Products Marketing Board (SEKEP) was another Marketing Board that had a monopoly with regards to the management of domestically produced olives and olive oil. New legislation was enacted in 2003, amending the law establishing the Cyprus Olive Products Marketing Board[12] by abolishing its monopolistic powers. The Board now operates as an olive oil intervention agency. The quality standards currently in place in Cyprus are in line with the relevant acquis. The registration of olive growers has been completed. The preparations for setting up Geographic Information System (GIS), using computerised aerial photographs which is necessary for the calculations and the verification of the aid granted for olive trees, is also at its final stages.

Wine and alcohol

The wine sector is a well established area of agriculture which has a substantial contribution to the economy as well as to the social life and the environment of Cyprus. Under the Vine Industry (Regulation and Control) Law[13] a number of implementing Regulations have been adopted in order to harmonise Cyprus's legislation with acquis regarding wines, spirit drinks, sparkling wines, liqueur wines and aromatised wines. The wine sector is an area where EU Regulations were transposed into the national legal order, although they will only be directly applicable after accession for two main reasons:

a. the insufficient regulation in the sector, which could result in the wine industry easily found in breach of the acquis, thus affecting their exports; and
b. the need to familiarise with and starting to implement the acquis so that all interested parties, become accustomed with its provisions.

The management of the market organisation for the wine sector currently lies with the Vine Products Commission (VPC), a semi-governmental organisation. The VPC and the Oenological Section of the Department of Agriculture of the MANRE have the necessary know how and human resources for implementing the acquis.

At the beginning of 2002, the Council of Ministers after examining a number of alternative proposals regarding the future role of the semi-governmental bodies, given that they would all have to abolish their monopolistic powers in their respective areas, decided that the VPC as well as the Cyprus Milk Industry Organisation (see below) would maintain their status as semi-governmental organisations. After losing their monopolistic powers their role was going to be substantially diminished. The decision, however, provided that they would be maintained and given their expertise in their respective areas, the Paying Agency would be able to delegate work to them, according to the relevant national provisions Community rules. One of the main considerations for maintaining these two Bodies was the Council of Ministers' wish not to create employment problems for employees of the said Bodies. A draft law, amending the law establishing the VPC, has been prepared providing for the necessary legal changes accoding to the acquis and for its new role after accession. The draft legislation provides, among others, for:

a. the abolition of the VPC monopolistic powers,
b. the redefining of the VPC's competences, making it the national competent authority for some of the functions provided by them in line with Regulation 1493/99/EC on the common organisation of the market in wine
c. the delegation by the Paying Agency of its function of authorisation of payments in the vine sector.

Bananas and tobacco

Both bananas and tobacco are crops which are grown in the western part of Cyprus and are produced in small quantities. On an EU level they are regulated by Common Market Organisations. The harmonised quality standards for bananas have been adopted by regulations and are gradually being implemented. The local production of bananas is currently being 'protected' by imposing prohibitive tariffs on imports of bananas. Upon adoption of the EU banana regime, which will be effected mainly by lowering the tariffs for imported bananas, there will be a fall of prices and pressure on domestic producers. As a result, the producers will have to act promptly in setting up their Producers Organisations, as soon as the relevant Regulations under The Producers Organisations Law are enacted, in order to be able to claim the financial assistance from Producers' Organisations. The same applies for tobacco producers.

Dairy and beef

The cattle in Cyprus are bred for the production of dairy products whereas beef is a by-product of dairy production. The total milk production is around 180,000 tons of which 75% comes from cows, 14% from goats and 11% from sheep. Fresh drinking milk, cheese and yogurt is produced using cow milk and some traditional types of cheeses (halloumi, feta etc), yogurt and other typical Cypriot products are made by sheep and goats milk.

The Cyprus Milk Industry Organisation (CMIO) is the semi-governmental body having monopolistic powers regarding the purchase and sale of raw milk. The Board of the CMIO is made up of representatives of government, producers, the processing companies and independent experts. Today, the CMIO is responsible among other things for managing the quota system, and operating a private storage aid scheme for the traditional halloumi and fetta cheese. It also provides subsidies to exports of milk and other dairy products. To this end, a draft law has already been prepared amending the law establishing the Cyprus Milk Industry Organisation.[14] This law which has to be enacted before the accession date, provides among others for the following:

- the abolition of the CMIO monopoly in order to free the market,
- a change in the composition of the Board of the CMIO, by removing the members which represented private interests and leaving only the governmental officials and the independent experts. In this way its

decisions cannot be affected by the interests of any party which will probably be a beneficiary of subsidies under the schemes managed by the Paying Agency,

- the redefinition of the CMIO functions according to the new responsibilities that will assume, including the delegation of the function of authorisation of payments by the Paying Agency and the commercial exploitation of its laboratory which is one of the best in this area.

Sheepmeat, goatmeat and pigmeat

The only piece of legislation aiming at harmonisation for these products was the framework legislation entitled 'The Carcass Classification of Borine, Pig and Ovine Animals and the Reporting of their Prices Law of 2002'.[15] Its implementing Regulations provide for the introduction of a system of compulsory carcass classification as well as some aspects of price collection and reporting. These are pieces of legislation transposing the provisions of EU Regulations. The European Commission, deemed that Cyprus had to enact this legislation and start making the necessary arrangements for implementation before the date of accession so that the competent authories would be ready to fully implement it after accession. This was one of the cases where Cyprus was asked to transpose the provisions of EU Regulations which after accession will become directly applicable. This legislation along with some others, which have the same aim, will have to be checked closely after accession and amended to the extent that they include provisions which go further than those which are necessary for their implementation. Maintaining any other provisions of the EU Regulations would be contrary to the principle of direct applicability of EU Regulations.

Eggs and poultry

Cyprus introduced the necessary legislative measures for regulating the production, grading labeling and marketing of eggs and poultry meat:

a. 'The Production and Use of Hatching Eggs and Chicks Law'[16] which is fully harmonised with Regulations 2782/75/EEC and 1868/77/EEC. The competent authority is the Department of Agriculture which provides for the collection and compilation of monthly statistical data on hatching egg production and hay-old chick hatchery.

b. 'The Production, Grading, Labelling and Marketing of Edible Eggs Law'[17] (Regulations 1907/90/EEC and 1274/91/EEC) which is expected to lead to an increase in the number of egg packing plants and to strengthen the tendency for consolidation of slaughterhouses into bigger units, capable of meeting the more demanding standards set by the transposed acquis communautaire.
c. 'The Production, Labelling and Marketing Standards for Poultry Meat Law'[18] (Regulations 1906/90/EEC and 1538/91/EEC) has already been enacted. However, its enforcement may be delayed pending the enactment of relevant veterinary legislation on poultry slaughter-houses. At any rate full compliance with the acquis will be achieved before accession.

Potatoes

Potatoes are the only commonly used product in the EU for which a Common Market Organisation does not exist. However, given the importance of this product for Cyprus's agriculture and economy (it is one of the main export products), the European Commission agreed to allow potato-producers to create Producers' Organisations under legislation mentioned earlier. This sector was managed by the Cyprus Potatoes Marketing Board, another marketing Board which is responsible for the trading and marketing of the product under a monopolistic regime. This Board will also have to abolish its monopolistic powers through the necessary amendment of the legislation establishing the Board. A study for the future of the Board suggested that the best way forward in this area is the setting-up of Producers' Organisations (which will be financed by State funding), which will eventually lead to the full abolition of the legislation of the Board since its role will be taken over by the Producer's Organisations.

The reform in this sector, through the amendments on the legislation[19] regulating the functions and competences of the Board was not uncontested. The producers remain very reluctant to accept the new state of affairs introduced with the gradual abolition of the role of the Board and the need to adjust and operate in a new environment. Their main concern is that the protective environment in which they operated until today will be replaced by an open competitive market in which they will have to act both as farmers as well as managers within the producers organisation.

Rural development

This is an area where no legislative action was necessary. Cyprus recognised the importance of rural development and its direct link to the protection of the environment and this is reflected in its 5-years strategic development plans. The agricultural components of the multi-annual plans amount to operational programmes for specific sectors and are materialised following a process of consultation between the Planning Burean, the Ministry of Agriculture and Natural Resources and Environment and other government Departments involved. Detailed annual programmes are then drawn up and incorporated into the Annual Budget of the Republic to become operational.

Cyprus's rural development policy objectives and instruments are largely in line with the acquis, while new projects are evaluated for conformity with the acquis before approval. Conformity of a project with the objectives of Council Regulation 1257/99/EC which sets the respective criteria for approving a project on an EU level must exist in order to be approved.

A New Rural Development Plan has been prepared and was presented in September 2003 by the MANRE where it sets a 10 years' plan for the development of Cyprus's rural areas. The Department of Agriculture has been designated as the managing authority for the Rural Development Plan. A formal draft Rural Development Plan for expenditure which are proposed to be financed by the EAGGF-Guarantee Section has been forwarded to the European Commission.

Concluding remarks

The process of harmonisation in the area of agriculture was a long procedure, which has not yet been fully completed. The necessary harmonising legislative measures are almost in place. The work for setting-up the infrastructure either technical or administrative is also at its final stages. Cyprus is expected to be able to implement properly the acquis communautaire in this area from the day of its accession to the EU. The setting up and operation of the Paying Agency is currently the biggest issue pending, regarding harmonisation, because if it is not operational before accession date there is a danger of losing the Community funds allocated to Cyprus's agriculture.

The Agricultural sector covers a vast area of Community legislation.

In this Chapter, I tried to include some of the features of Cyprus's harmonisation relating to legal and administrative measures as well as the results of Cyprus's negotiations for the closing of this Chapter during the accession negotiations. The competent authorities proceed in full speed their preparations in order to be ready to respond to the demanding environment which will be created after accession. Although the CAP is a common policy of the Union and the decisions are taken on that level, the member states have a very active role both as part of the decision-making process and as the responsible authorities for the proper implementation of these decisions. Given Cyprus size it is not expected that it will play a critical role in this sector. It can, however, use the considerable expertise of its human resources, in order to achieve positive results in areas of major importance for the country and its people.

Notes

1. The views expressed in this Chapter are the personal views of the author.
2. Information obtained from Cyprus's Position Paper on Chapter 7 – Agriculture.
3. The Overall Final Agreement, The Global Agreement on all Outstanding Issues, and the EU Common Position Paper include the European Unions' full final position on all the issues under the Chapter of Agriculture.
4. Regulation 1259/99/EC on establishing common rules for direct support schemes under the common agricultural policy.
5. Community spending on agriculture is made through the European Agricultural Guarantee and Guidance Fund, which as its name suggests, consists of two sections which finance different measures under the CAP according to Regulation 1258/99/EC on the financing of the common agricultural policy.
6. Regulation 1663/95/EC laying down detailed rules for the application of Regulation 729/70/EEC regarding the procedure of for the clearance of accounts of the EAGGF Guarantee Section, and Regulation 1258/99/EC on the financing of the common agricultural policy.
7. Law 160(I)/2001, and The Organic Production (Labelling, Production, Control and Marketing) Regulations of 2001 (SI 506/2001).
8. Law 129(I)/2002.
9. Law 7(I)/2002.
10. Law 164(I)/2002.
11. The Annex includes fruit and vegetables, processed fruit and vegetables, bananas, tobacco, olive oil, olives etc.
12. Law 23/1963 as amended.

13. Law 52/1965 as amended.
14. Law 4/1969 as amended.
15. Law 49(I)/2002.
16. Law 88(I)/1999.
17. Law 118(I)/2000 as amended.
18. Law 101(I)/2000 as amended.
19. The Potatoes Marketing Board Law 1964 (59/1964) as amended.

4 Harmonizing Air Transport

NICOS MICHAELIDES[1]

Introduction

Air transport is an important industry in the EU, generating approximately 1% of the Union's GDP. In Cyprus, air transport is one of the most important industries, since a large income comes from tourists. In 2000, for example, tourist inflow reached 2,686,205 as against 2,434,285 in 1999. In 2000 the average expenditure per tourist increased by 8.1% compared to 1999 and receipts from tourism reached CY£194 millions in 2000.

The implementing authority is the Department of Civil Aviation (DCA), which is under the Ministry of Communications and Works and is responsible for the smooth and efficient operation of the airports. It ensures that the international standards and recommended practices adopted by the International Civil Aviation Organization (ICAO) are applied and co-ordinates civil aviation matters with the various international organisations such as the International Civil Aviation Organization (ICAO), the European Civil Aviation Conference (ECAC), the Organization of the Safety of Air Navigation in Europe (EUROCONTROL) the International Air Transport Association (IATA) and the Joint Aviation Authorities (JAA). There are two International Airports in operation, one in Larnaka and one in Pafos (the Nicosia International Airport is not in operation because of the Turkish invasion in 1974). Both have undergone extensive improvement and development works to the tune of CY£7.7 millions. In Cyprus the basic legal instruments in the area of Civil Aviation are the Colonial Air Navigation Order of 1955,[2] the Aerodromes Law,[3] and the secondary legislation issued in accordance with the provisions of the above mentioned instruments.

For the EU the turning point which led to the adoption of a Common European Air Transport Policy, was the confirmation by the ECJ, in the *Nouvelles Frontieres case*,[4] that competition rules applied to air transport even in the absence of an implementing Community Regulation (a ruling which led to the three liberalisation packages). Furthermore, Community legislation was developed in the areas of package travel, computerized reservation systems, environment, denied boarding, personnel licensing, baggage controls and technical requirements and procedures.[5]

The purpose of this Chapter is to outline the relations between Cyprus and the EU, compare Cyprus's law with Community law,[6] discuss the efforts for harmonisation already made and evaluate the whole situation in the field of Air Transport.

The need to harmonize

The first stage of the accession negotiations with the EU was initiated on 3 April 1998 and involved the analytical examination of Community law, which was separated into 29 chapters. During that stage (acquis screening) the European Commission presented and explained the acquis in certain areas while Cyprus presented its own policy in the area and then the two were compared. During that process, Air Transport was part of chapter nine. Cyprus agreed that it will bring into force the measures which are necessary for harmonization by the date of accession to the EU. Cyprus did not ask for any derogations or transitional periods for Air Transport for two main reasons: firstly, because of the need to ask for transitional periods in other sensitive areas, such as the special tax regime that applies in the case of offshore companies; and secondly, because the conclusions of a study conducted by Cranfield University were taken into consideration.

The conclusions of the study were as follows:

- a new entrant low cost carrier is most likely to enter the Larnaka-Athens route because the route has high profitability, fares are medium to high, it has good potential for business and leisure traffic and this will have a downward pressure on fares and a boost in the number of passengers
- an increase in UK visitors to Cyprus is expected because of the downward pressure on fares and the expected boost of the Cyprus to London traffic as a result of the possibility of using seat-only charters
- traffic to member states other than UK and Greece, is not expected to increase significantly, even though traffic originating in Cyprus can use seat-only air fares to member states
- a small increase of the traffic from other member states to Cyprus is expected because of the downward pressure on fares

- Cyprus Airways will face intense competition both from scheduled but especially from charters and low cost carriers
- an increase in total movement to and from Cyprus is expected, having a positive impact on both employment and value-added tax and therefore an increase in the rate of growth of the economy

The Luxembourg European Council decided that, starting in the latter part of 1999, the Commission will submit regular reports to the Council. Cyprus's progress with harmonisation in the field of Air Transport was evident by 2002. As the Regular Report of 9 October 2002 noted:

> In the field of air transport, regulations on air traffic management equipment and systems for the adoption of EUROCONTROL standards entered into force in February 2002. A law was passed in March 2002 ratifying the Montreal Convention for the Unification of Certain Rules for International Carriage by Air. A study of the capacity of Larnaka and Paphos has been completed.[7]

This Regular Report is supplemented by a 'Comprehensive Monitoring Report on Cyprus's Preparations for Membership' which also noted:

> In the area of air transport, the relevant framework legislation has been transposed and is largely in line with the acquis, but some modifications are needed, notably with regard to slot allocation and noise restriction. Implementing legislation is still being adopted. Administrative capacity needs further strengthening. Full membership of the Joint Aviation Authorities (JAA) remains to be achieved and efforts will need to be made to become a full member before accession as required by the acquis and irrespective of the setting up of the European Aviation Safety Agency (EASA).[8]

On 16 December 1998, the government of Cyprus decided the full liberalization of the air transport sector by 1 January 2003,[9] thus contributing towards compliance with Council Regulations (EEC) No. 2407/92, 2408/92 and 2409/92 forming the Third Aviation Package of Liberalization and Council Directive 96/67/EC on access to the Ground Handling Market at Community Airports. More specifically, the government of Cyprus decided, inter alia, the following:

- 1 January 2003 to be the date for the full liberation of the air transport sector with the adoption of the Third Aviation Package (market access, licensing of air carriers fares and rates)

- 1 January 2003 to be the date for the full implementation of the provisions concerning access to the market of ground handling activities

A committee[10] was set up by the Council of Ministers of Cyprus[11] to take decisions regarding the gradual implementation of the Third Aviation Package and the liberalization of the ground handling services. The committee appointed a technical committee in order to submit proposals. However, the only decisions taken so far concern the liberalization of air transport services between Cyprus and Greece. It was decided to grant permission to a second air carrier to provide scheduled services between Cyprus and Greece and to permit charter flights from Greece (excluding Athens and Thessaloniki). No other decision was taken because Cyprus had already started negotiations to join the European Common Aviation Area – which were never concluded and there is no need to be concluded anymore because the Treaty of Accession has already been signed.

Cyprus requested to be included in the negotiations for a Multilateral Agreement on the establishment of a European Common Aviation Area between the EU, the CEECs,[12] Norway and Iceland.[13] The Agreement entered into force in early 2002, subject to specific transitional arrangements such as:

- the provisions on third-party handling contained in Council Directive 96/67, affected by the plans to privatize the operation and ownership of Larnaka and Pafos airports, which is expected to be completed by 2004
- the prohibition of Chapter 2 airplanes from third countries between the territory of Cyprus and those third countries in derogation of the provisions of Directive 92/14 on the limitation of operation of airplanes covered by Part II, Chapter 2, Volume of Annex 16 of the Convention of International Civil Aviation
- the obligation to be full members of the Joint Aviation Authorities, as provided in Article 5 of Regulation (EEC) 3922/91.

The Agreement incorporates Community legislation related, directly or indirectly, to air transport. A joint committee will be established, which will be responsible for the administration and implementation of the Agreement. This joint committee will consist of representatives of the Contracting States and act by unanimity, unless they decide to apply majority voting. The provisions of the Agreement will be interpreted in conformity with the relevant ECJ judgements and Commission decisions reached prior to the date of signature of the Agreement. The implications of judgements and decisions reached after the date of signature will be considered by the joint committee.

Comparison between Community law and Cyprus law and efforts already made for harmonization

Computerized reservation systems

The aim of Regulation (EEC) 2299/89, as amended by Council Regulation (EEC) 3089/93, is to inhibit anti-competitive practices. It covers only air transport products, either alone or in combination with an inclusive tour arrangement. The Regulation applies to all Computer Reservation Systems (CRS) operating in the EU. A computer reservation system operator must allow any airline the opportunity to participate on terms which are not discriminatory, unreasonable or exclusive, display information about its services clearly and without bias and allow the airline access to relevant information.[14]

With respect to subscribers, an airline owning an interest in a computer reservation system must not encourage the use of a specific computer reservation system, must make the computer reservation system distribution facilities available on terms which are not discriminatory, unreasonable or exclusive and must oblige the subscriber to present the data in an accurate and non-discriminatory manner.[15] Furthermore, a computer reservation system operator must ensure that its individual reservation system is separated from the computer reservation system,[16] that technical compliance is monitored by an independent auditor, and not to discriminate against a competing computer reservation system by refusing to provide information about its services to, or to accept reservations for its services made through, such other computer reservation system.

In Cyprus there is no legislation covering computerized reservation systems. The inclusion of the above provisions in the new legislation will be more than enough to achieve harmonization in this area, considering the fact that Cyprus Airways, as owners of the Sabre CRS, is applying in practice the provisions of the Regulation which will be directly applicable upon accession. Besides Sabre, Amadeus and Galileo are the two other CRSs operated in Cyprus. The provisions of this Regulation will be part of the twenty third chapter of the Civil Aviation legislation under preparation.

Denied boarding compensation system

Council Regulation (EEC) 295/91[17] established common rules for a denied boarding compensation system in air transport. It covers all scheduled flights departing from an airport in a member state. It does not cover non-scheduled flights, flights from third countries and cases where a passenger is travelling free of charge or on reduced fares not available to the public.[18] It obliges air carries to pay compensation and to provide additional services to passengers who are denied boarding. It also obliges the airlines to lay down the rules it will follow in the event of denying passengers to board an overbooked flight, and to make these rules available to the passengers.

The passenger has the choice of reimbursement or re-routing at the earliest opportunity or re-routing at a later date of the passenger's convenience.[19] Irrespective of the passenger's choice, he/she is always entitled to compensation of minimum €150 for flights up to 3,500 Km and €300 for flights of more than 3,500 Km. This compensation is paid in cash or, with the agreement of the passenger, in travel vouchers or other services. In addition to compensation, the carrier shall offer the passenger who is denied boarding the expenses for a telephone and fax message to the point of destination, meals and refreshment and hotel accommodation when an additional stay of one or more nights is necessary.[20] It is noted that the EU submitted a proposal for a Regulation which aims at establishing common rules on compensation and assistance to air passengers in the event of denied boarding and of cancellation or long delay of flights.[21] If this proposal is adopted, Regulation (EC) 295/91 will be replaced by a new regime which will cover scheduled and non-scheduled flights and impose compensation in case of cancellation or long delays of flights and higher compensation rates in case of denied boarding, compared to the compensation rates specified in the current regime.

In Cyprus there is no legislation, which adopts the above provisions. A passenger who is denied boarding may claim damages for breach of contract in accordance with the general provisions of the Contract Law.[22] The general provisions of the Law do not cover in detail and specific terms the issues of remedies for denied boarding specified in the Council Regulation. A party claiming damages for breach of contract will be entitled to receive such damages arising naturally under the usual course of events or as may reasonably be supposed to have been expected by the parties at the time the contract was made.[23] A case which concerned overbooking (delay in transferring goods by ship) was *Thunder Shipping Co. Ltd v. Lloyd Triestino*,[24] where the Supreme Court of Cyprus stated that the plaintiff will be able to claim damages only related to the expectations of the parties and only if the plaintiff was not able to recover any losses resulting from increase in the exchange rate.

Mutual acceptance of personnel licences

Community law[25] imposes an obligation on member states to accept licenses issued by other member states. With respect to pilots' licenses a member state shall accept any licence issued in accordance with the requirements of Annex 1 to the ICAO Convention, if the bearer satisfies the special validation requirements prescribed in the Annex to the Council Directive 91/670/EEC.[26] Annex 1 to the ICAO Convention is part of Cyprus's legal order through section 4 of the International Convention of Civil Aviation (ICAO) 1944 and its Thirteen Protocols 1947-1984 (Ratifying) Law, No.213/88. However, the remaining provisions are incompatible with the Air Navigation Order 1955, which provides that the Council of Ministers of Cyprus may issue a validation for a licence, which was granted outside Cyprus. The Council of Ministers of Cyprus shall not issue a validation if they are satisfied that the holder is not a fit and proper person to hold such a validation. Furthermore, the Council of Ministers has the discretion to refuse to issue a validation if it appears to them to be inexpedient in the public interest.

Environment

The rules are mainly contained in Council Directive 92/14/EEC, as amended by Directives 98/20/EC and 99/28/EC,[27] which applies to civil subsonic jet airplanes, including civil subsonic jet airplanes fitted with engines having a by-pass ratio of less than two. Two new Community acts[28] have been adopted by the EU which concern the protection of the environment and they are examined under the heading 'The new Civil Aviation Law'. Civil subsonic jet airplanes fitted with engines having a by-pass ratio of less than two cannot operate at airports situated in their territory unless granted noise certification either:

- to the standards specified in Part II, Chapter 3, Volume 1 of Annex 16 to the ICAO Convention, or
- to the standards specified in Part II, Chapter 2, Volume 1 of Annex 16 to the ICAO Convention provided that they were first issued an individual certificate of airworthiness less than 25 years previously.[29]

All civil subsonic jet airplanes must comply with the standards specified in Part II, Chapter 3, Volume 1 of Annex 16 to the ICAO Convention. Member states shall exempt airplanes, which do not meet the standards of Chapter 3 of Annex 16 but which can be altered to meet those standards, provided that:

- suitable conversion equipment exists and is actually available for the airplane type in question
- airplanes fitted with such equipment meet the Standards of Chapter 3 of Annex 16, as determined in accordance with the technical standards and procedures accepted by the member State
- the airline has ordered the equipment by 1 April 1994
- the airline has accepted the earliest delivery date to such alteration.

Member states may permit the temporary use at airports situated in their territory of:

- airplanes whose operations are of such an exceptional nature that it would be unreasonable to withhold a temporary exemption
- Airplanes on non-revenue for the purposes of alterations, repair or maintenance.[30]

In Cyprus, Annex 16 to the ICAO Convention is applied through section 4 of the International Convention of Civil Aviation (ICAO) 1944 and its Thirteen Protocols 1947-1984 (Ratifying) Law, 1988[31] and the Air Navigation (Aircraft Noise) Regulations, 1988.[32]

Licensing

In the EU, licensing is regulated by Council Regulation (EEC) 2407/92, which is part of the Third Package of Liberalization.[33] It harmonizes the criteria for the granting of operating licences and Air Operator's Certificates (AOCs) in the member states. An air carrier established in the EU must hold a valid licence and AOC to offer commercial services. To obtain or renew a licence a carrier must be able to demonstrate that:[34]

- the provision of air transport services is its main activity
- its principal place of business is within the EU
- it is majority owned and controlled by member states or their nationals

- it has sufficient financial and other resources; and
- it fulfils technical criteria laid down by the Joint Aviation Authorities.

Start-up carriers must be able to demonstrate that they can meet their fixed and operational costs for a period of three months without recourse to income generated from their activities and that they can meet actual and potential obligations for two years.[35]

In Cyprus an aircraft cannot fly for the purpose of public transport (passengers or cargo) for hire and reward, unless it has obtained previously an operating license issued by the Air Transport Licensing Authority (ATLA), condition of which is also to obtain an air operator's certificate, certifying that the holder is competent to operate such flights. The Licensing Authority may attach conditions to any licence and also it is a condition that:

- the holder of the licence does not refuse booking facilities to any other holder of a licence and does not grant facilities on onerous terms
- the wages, salaries or other remuneration paid by the holder of the licence to all person employed in connection with the operation
- the holder of the licence performs all reasonable services as the Postmaster-General may require.[36]

Market access

Council Regulation (EEC) 2408/92 prohibits any restrictions on entry or capacity to all scheduled and non-scheduled routes between and within the member states, for licensed EU carriers. It is possible to impose restrictions on environmental, infrastructure capacity, regional development, safety or public service grounds.[37] The restrictions must be of a non-discriminatory nature and are subject to investigation by the European Commission. A member state may impose public service obligations in respect of a scheduled service to an airport in a peripheral or development region or on any thin route to a regional airport considered vital to the economic development of the area. Under certain circumstances access to such routes may be restricted to one carrier.[38]

A member state may refuse a scheduled air service by a carrier on a new route between regional airports, where one of the carriers licensed by it commenced a scheduled passenger service with an aircraft seating fewer than 80 seats and on which the capacity does not exceed 30,000 seats per annum. A member state may also limit or refuse the exercise of traffic rights for a period of three years, subject to the agreement of the European Commission, where serious congestion or environmental problems exist. Finally, a member state may not authorize a carrier to commence a new service or increase the frequency of an existing service between a specific airport in its territory and another member state whilst a carrier licensed by the other State is prevented from establishing such a service or increasing its existing services on the route as a result of slot allocation rules.

In Cyprus there is no compliance with the provisions of Council Regulation (EEC) 2408/92. The Bilateral Air Agreements adopted in accordance with Article 169.1 of the Constitution provide that the airlines shall be given equal opportunity in the operation of the agreed services on the prescribed routes. The designated airlines shall take into account the interests of the airline of the other Contracting Party to the Bilateral Air Agreement so as not to affect unduly the services which the latter provides on the whole or part of the same routes.

The ECAC International Agreement on capacity sharing, which applies between the member states which ratified the Agreement, including Cyprus,[39] provides for up to 60:40 sharing. No fifth freedom rights are expressly permitted, pursuant to the provisions of the Bilateral Air Agreements (though in the past British Airways had the right to exercise fifth freedom rights for Teheran). These rights are always subject to the condition that the carriers sign a commercial agreement with Cyprus Airways. With respect to non-scheduled services, a permit shall be granted by the Chairman of the Air Transport Licensing Authority. This requirement was contrary to Council Regulation (EEC) 2408/92 which also applies to non-scheduled services.

Fares and rates

In Cyprus there are no liberal rules in the area of fares and rates for air services. Pursuant to the provisions of the Bilateral Air Agreements, the tariffs to be charged by the airlines of the Contracting Parties to the Agreements shall be established at reasonable levels, taking into account the cost of operation, reasonable profit, characteristics of service and the tariffs of other airlines operating scheduled services over the whole or part of the same route. The agreed tariffs shall always be submitted for approval to the aeronautical authorities of the Contracting States at least thirty days before the proposed date of their introduction.

However, the position is different in the EU. Council Regulation

(EEC) 2409/92[40] provides air carries with complete freedom to determine fares and rates. The Regulation applies to fares and rates charged by EU air carriers on any air service wholly within the EU. The Regulation provides that charter fares, seat and cargo rules charged by EU air carrier shall be set by free agreement between the parties to the contact of carriage.[41] All carries operating within the EU must inform the public, on request, of all air fares and standard cargo rules. Member states may, without discrimination on grounds of nationally or identity of air carriers, require air fares to be filed with them in the form prescribed by them. Such filing shall not be required to be submitted more than 24 hours (including a working day) before the air fares come into affect, except in the case of matching of an existing fare for which no more than prior notification is required.[42]

A member State may at any time decide to:

- withdraw a basic fare which taking into account the whole fare structure for the route in question and other relevant factors including the competitive market situation, is excessively high to the disadvantage of users in relation to the long term fully-allocated relevant costs of the air carrier including a satisfactory return on capital
- Stop, in a non-discriminatory way, further fare decreases in a market, whether on a route or a group of routes, when market forces have led to a sustained downward development of air fares deviating significantly from ordinary seasonal pricing movements and resulting in widespread losses among all air carriers concerned for the air services concerned, taking into account the long term fully-allocated relevant costs of the air carriers.[43]

Air carrier liability in the event of accident

Cyprus ratified[44] the international rules governing the liability of air carriers for injury or death of their passenger and for loss or damage to baggage and cargo. These rules are contained in the Warsaw Convention, 1929, as it was amended, which were drafted at a time when aviation was a fledging industry with a dubious safety record and in need of protection from excessive claims for compensation. In the case of *Austrian Airways* v. *Cyprus General Insurances Ltd*[45] the Supreme Court of Cyprus stated that Article 26 (2) of the Warsaw Convention does not apply to complainants who are not recipients of goods or where the goods were lost.

Furthermore, Cyprus ratified[46] the Convention for the Unification of Certain Rules for International Carriage by Air signed at Montreal on 28

May 1999 (known as 'the Montreal Convention').[47] The Montreal Convention established a modernized and uniform legal framework to govern the liability of airlines for damage to passengers, baggage and cargo incurred during international journeys. It established unlimited liabilities for death and injury to passengers and higher liability limits for baggage and cargo. In respect of unlimited liability, it is compatible with the system already operating in the Community.

Council Regulation (EC) 2027/97 on air carrier liability in the event of accidents abandoned the low liability limits set out in the Warsaw system when passengers are killed or suffer injury in an accident. The Regulation established a system of unlimited liability for such cases and in addition requires EU carriers to make advance payments to accident victims and their families in order to meet immediate economic needs. In addition, for claims up to €100,000 the Regulation prevents EU carriers from using the legal defence that they took all possible measures to avoid the accident. This is designed to facilitate the resolution of smaller claims where legal fees could otherwise be a high proportion of the compensation paid. Air carriers from outside the EU are not obliged to follow this regime. However, if these carriers choose not to follow the regime, they are obliged to inform their European customers at the time the ticket is purchased.[48]

The European Commission proposed[49] the ratification the new Convention for the Unification of Certain Rules for International Carriage by Air signed at Montreal on 28 May 1999 ('the Montreal Convention'). Furthermore, the European Commission proposed[50] the amendment of Regulation 2027/97 in order to be in line with the provisions of the Montreal Convention. The EU ratified the Montreal Convention and adopted a new Regulation amending Regulation 2027/97 in order to align the latter Regulation with the provisions of the Montreal Convention.

Ground handling services

The Aerodromes (Amendment) Regulations, of 1998,[51] issued by the Council of Ministers under section 4 of the Aerodromes Law, Cap. 300, stipulate that for the provision of ground handling services, the approval of the Director of the DCA is required. Cyprus Airways and any air carrier who operates fights to Cyprus, in accordance with the provisions of a Bilateral Air Agreement, are allowed to provide ground-handling services. However, only Cyprus Airways may provide third-party handling.

There is no question that these Regulations are not compatible with Council Directive 96/67/EC. Article 6 of the Directive ensures free access by suppliers of ground handling services to the market for the provision of ground handling services to third parties. Moreover, Article 7 regulates the freedom to self-handle while Article 9 offers the possibility for exemptions for purposes of availability of space or capacity of an airport, arising in particular from congestion and area utilization rate.

Cyprus applied to TAIEX for the nomination of an expert who will assist the DCA to implement the Directive and also intends to seek technical assistance for the separation of accounts of ground handling services, as specified in Article 4 of the Directive.

Safety

Council Directive 94/56/EEC establishes the fundamental principles governing the investigation of civil aviation accidents and incidents. It imposes an obligation on member states to establish a permanent and independent body with the necessary powers of inquiry and access. It also provides for the publication of the results of the investigation. The Directive applies to civil aviation accidents and incidents:

- occurring in the EU
- occurring outside the EU, involving an aircraft registered in a member state
- involving an aircraft when there is no other state carrying out an investigation.

Annex 13 to the ICAO Convention, concerning the aircraft accident and incident investigation, is part of Cyprus's legal order through section 4 of the International Convention on Civil Aviation (ICAO) 1944 and its Thirteen Protocols 1947-1984 (Ratifying) Law, 1988.[52] The Civil Aviation (Investigation of Accidents) Regulations, 1952,[53] are compatible with the Directive, save for the following:

- there is no obligation to appoint an independent body, though they do not exclude it
- there is no provision for requesting assistance from bodies or entities from other member states or for delegating this function to another member state, though they do not exclude it
- there is no obligation to submit copies of the report and safety recommendations to the European Commission.

With respect to harmonization of technical requirements, Council Regulation 3922/91/EEC adopts the Joint Aviation Regulations (JARs) and prescribes a procedure for the adoption of new or amending JARs. Furthermore, it imposes an obligation on the member states to be full members of the Joint Aviation Authorities.

Cyprus is a phase one member of the JAA but declared its intention to become a full member. In fact, a delegation of the Joint Aviation Authorities assessed on 1 September 2000 the aviation safety standards and oversight capabilities in Cyprus. Furthermore the new Civil Aviation Law of 2002 empowers the Minister of Communications and Works to adopt by Order any Joint Aviation Regulation.

Eurocontrol

Council Directive 93/65/EEC, as amended by Commission Directive 97/15/EC, adopts the Eurocontrol Standards. These standards are mandatory and member states are under the obligation to adopt and implement them.

Cyprus is a member of Eurocontrol through the International Convention Eurocontrol (Ratifying) Law of 1990.[54] The Law has been amended in order to adopt the amendments and the new consolidated text of the Eurocontrol Convention contained in the Final Act, which was signed in Brussels on 27 June 1997. Furthermore, the House of Parliament approved the Draft Regulations,[55] which are adopting the following Eurocontrol standards:

- Flight Exchange Interface Control Point-to-Point and Limited Networking Circuits
- ATS Data Exchange Presentation (AD EXP)
- On Line Data Interchange (OLDI).

Slot allocation

The process of slot allocation in Cyprus is done in accordance with IATA scheduling committee regulations. However, this process is not compatible with Council Regulation 95/93/EEC. The Regulation established common rules for the allocation of slots at EU airports. Air carriers are entitled to keep slots granted to them in the previous corresponding season if they have used them. The available slots are put in a pool.

A member state may designate a coordinated airport provided that principles of transparency, neutrality and non-discrimination are met.[56] The member states shall ensure that a capacity analysis is carried out, having regard to commonly recognized methods, as soon as possible at the airport with the purpose of determining possibilities of increasing the capacity in the short term through infrastructure or operational changes and to determine the time frame envisaged to resolve the problems.

If the analysis does not indicate possibilities of resolving the serious problems in the short term, the member State shall ensure that the airport shall be designated as fully coordinated for the periods during which capacity problems occur.[57]

The new civil aviation law

In 1999 the Attorney General of Cyprus appointed a foreign expert to prepare, in collaboration with the competent authorities of Cyprus, new legislation adopting the Community air law and provide implementing measures for international air law in force in Cyprus. The preparation of the new legislation was completed in September 2001 and sent to the Council of Ministers for approval and then laid before the House of Representatives for enactment. The new legislation was approved by the Council of Ministers on 20 March 2002, enacted by the House of Representatives on 6 December 2002 and published in the Official Gazette on 13 December 2002.

The new legislation is referred to as the Civil Aviation Law of 2002 (Law No. 213(I)/2002). This Law regulates the following issues regarding harmonization with EU law:

- computerized reservation systems (Chapter 23)
- denied boarding compensation system (Chapter 10)
- environment (Chapter 24)
- licensing of air carriers (Chapter 17)
- market access (Chapter 18)
- fares and rates (Chapter 22)
- air carrier liability in the event of accident (Chapter 26)
- ground handling services (Chapter 12)
- slot allocation (Chapter 11)
- baggage control (Chapter 20)
- competition (Chapter 21)

- investigation of civil aviation accidents (Chapter 25)
- adoption of Joint Aviation Regulations (Article 261)

The problem with the Civil Aviation Law of 2002 is that it incorporated the provisions of Regulations which will be directly applicable upon accession under Article 249 of the Treaty Establishing the European Community. It means that whenever a new EU measure is adopted, amending existing Community Regulations, Cyprus will have to amend the corresponding provision of the Law. In fact, there is a proposal for adopting new Regulation in the area of denied boarding compensation system which will repeal Regulation (EEC) 295/91.[58] There is no provision in the Law stipulating implementing measures for new EU Regulations in air transport or, alternatively, extending the scope of application of the Law to any EU Regulations specified by the Council of Ministers. It is noted that already there are new EU Regulations on various aspects of air transport.[59]

In addition to the adoption of new EU Regulations, the EU has also adopted new Directives[60] which need to be transposed into the national legal system. For this reason the new Law needs to be amended, although it has been enacted recently, in order to incorporate the new provisions and provide implementing measures for the new EU Directives. The Law is supplemented by national regulations and orders which were adopted under sections 159 and 160 of the Law. A set of these national regulations deals with the mutual acceptance of personnel licences for the purposes of harmonization with Directive 91/679/EEC. Finally, the Law does not use marginal notes for every section and it not divided into parts, sections and subsections as it is the case with the other Cyprus laws. Instead, it was decided to use headings for every section of the Law and divide the Law into chapters, articles and paragraphs, thus adopting the same drafting style used by the EU when issuing Regulations and Directives.

Concluding remarks

Although air transport is a very important industry in Cyprus, it is clearly not liberalized since the national measures were formulated in a way which ensured that the national air carrier (Cyprus Airways) is protected from any kind of competition.

The decision taken by the Attorney General of Cyprus, to appoint a foreign expert to prepare new legislation – harmonised with Community law – was a good solution considering the fact that the competent authorities did not have sufficient experience in air transport liberalization to do it themselves. It would not have been prudent to amend the existing 1955 Air Navigation Order[61] because it is not harmonized with Community law, it is very complicated since it is old, it is not consistent with all the international rules, it has been amended at least seven times and it will be more practical if the practitioners and all those dealing with air transport have a consolidated text. An alternative solution was to draft separate bills for transposing the three EU Directives[62] into national law and at the same time amend the ratifying Law of the Chicago Convention in order to include sanctions in case of violation of any provision of the Convention and its Annexes and prepare secondary legislation for prescribing matters which were necessary for the application of the Convention.

More efforts need to be made with respect to Cyprus's obligation to become a full member of the Joint Aviation Authorities. Although JAR 145 and JAR OPS 1 and 3 may be adopted by Order of the Minister of Communications and Works, under section 261 of the Civil Aviation Law of 2002, the mandatory applicability of JARs needs to be strengthened. Although UK CAA brings contractual support through the permanent presence of an Airworthiness Inspector and inspections made by visiting Flight Operations Inspectors, DCA Staff appropriately qualified, experienced and in sufficient number should be devoted to the issuance of aviation safety standards and safety oversight tasks.

The DCA exercises minimal oversight over professional license holders operating aircraft registered in Cyprus and the necessary manpower or technical expertise needs to be introduced. Under the present arrangements, it will be difficult to introduce JAR-FCL. It is necessary to improve the structure, policies and procedures established to control professional flight crew licensers. Globally, an increased oversight would be desirable over professional licence holders operating aeroplanes registered in Cyprus and pressure should be maintained on all AOC holders to become JAR-OPS compliant. Finally, the DCA should consider reviewing the scheme of charges.[63]

It was rightly decided to implement a comprehensive action plan called 'Development of Safety Oversight Capabilities in the DCA Cyprus'. The action plan provided for services and technical assistance for the introduction of regulations, procedures and manuals as well as on the job training of personnel with a view to achieve compliance with Council Regulation (EEC) No. 3922/91 (aircraft maintenance standards and flight operation inspections). Financed by the Fourth Protocol on Financial and

Technical Cooperation between the EU and Cyprus, this action plan provides that the consultants will assume responsibility for planning, organizing and controlling the whole process on a day-to-day basis; the consultants also undertake the tasks of developing regulations, procedures, manuals and guidance material, advise on the purchase of necessary equipment, supervise for a limited time a complementary team of locally-recruited officers, develop licensing, certification and surveillance systems and provide guidance and on the job training to national personnel.

Harmonizing and liberalizing the air transport sector was a very difficult task but at the same time it was necessary, even if there had never been the intention to accede to the EU. The efforts made by the EU to establish a European Common Aviation Area with other European third states and with the USA and the fact that the EU has enlarged are indications that lead to the assumption that the air transport industry will be further developed.[64] A small island whose economy largely depends on the tourism industry, could not stay out of the open skies. The liberalization of the market and the reduction of prices will have a twofold positive impact. Firstly, on the economy because more tourists will be able to visit Cyprus and thus bring more income; and secondly, on nationals of Cyprus who will be given the opportunity to be involved in the EU air transport industry either as air carriers or as employees or experts.

Finally, Cyprus will have to assess the compatibility with EU law of bilateral air transport agreements concluded between Cyprus and third states. If it is found that they are incompatible the competent authorities should take all appropriate steps as provided for in Article 307 of the Treaty for the termination or amendment of these agreements.[65] These agreements incorporate a provision stipulating that each contracting state shall have the right to refuse or revoke an authorisation granted to an airline to exercise traffic rights if it is satisfied that substantial ownership and effective control is not vested in the contracting party designating the airline or in the national of such contracting party. In my opinion the provision incorporated in these agreements is not compatible with EU law especially Articles 10 and 48 of the Treaty[66] subject to Article 307 of the Treaty.[67]

Notes

1. This Chapter is based on information contained in:
   (a) documents provided by the European Commission during the screening

process
(b) documents provided by the Department of Civil Aviation of the Republic
(c) the study of the Cranfield University and the Cyprus Development Bank on the Harmonization of Cyprus's Air Transport Sector
(d) John Balfour, European Community Air Law (1995)
(e) Jeffrey Goh, European Air Transport Law and Competition (1997).

2. It continues to be in force pursuant to Article 188.1 of the Constitution.
3. Cap. 300 amended by Law No. 80/73.
4. Joined Cases 209-213/84 *Minister Public* v. *Lucas Asjes and others* [1986] ECR 1425.
5. See below under the comparison between Community law and Cyprus law.
6. It is not possible to analyze within a chapter rules concerning competition law and state aid and for this reason this Chapter concentrates only on issues which are directly associated with civil aviation and fall within the exclusive competence of the DCA.
7. European Commission, *2002 Regular Report on Cyprus's Progress Towards Accession*, 2002.
8. Ibid, p.29.
9. Decision of the Council of Ministers No. 48856 of 6 December 1998.
10. The committee comprises representatives from the Law Office, the Ministry of Communications and Works, the Ministry of Finance and the Planning Bureau.
11. Decision of the Council of Ministers No. 48856 of 6 December 1998.
12. The Republic of Bulgaria, the Czech Republic, the Republic of Estonia, the Republic of Hungary, the Republic of Latvia, the Republic of Lithuania, the Republic of Poland, Romania, the Slovak Republic and the Republic of Slovenia.
13. Following a relevant Decision by the Council of the EU, in December 1999, the Commission and Cyprus started negotiations on 17 January 2000, which lasted for two days. The negotiations continued on 18-19 October 2000.
14. Article 3 of Regulation 2299/89 on a 'Code of Conduct for Computerised Reservation Systems'.
15. Ibid, Article 9a.
16. Article 4a of Council Regulation No 295/91 of 4 February 1991 establishing common rules for a denied-boarding compensation system in scheduled air transport.
17. See Muller-Rostin (1980) Transp R 12; Doganis Flying Off Course 81985) Allen & Unwin; Guerreri 'Overbooking, Overselling and Denial of Boarding' (1989) Annals ASL 191.
18. Article 1 of Regulation 295/91.
19. Article 4 of Regulation 295/91.
20. Article 4 of Regulation 295/91.
21. *Official Journal* C E, 30/04/2002, p. 225.
22. Cap. 149 amended by Law No. 22(I)/95.

23. Section 73(1) and see *Hadley* v. *Baxendale* (1854) 9 Exch. 341.
24. (1984) 1 C.L.R. 0135.
25. Council Directive No.91/679EEC of 16 December 1991 on the mutual acceptance of personnel licences for the exercise of functions in civil aviation
26. Article3 of Directive 91/670.
28. See Reymond, 'Analysis and Developments of the EC Aircraft Noise Directives' (1993) Air and Space Law 2 and Davies and Goh (1993) 'Air Transport and the Environment' *Air and Space Law* 123.
29. Regulation (EC) 2320/2002 and Directive 2002/30/EC.
30. Article 2 of Directive 92/14/EEC on the limitation of the operation of aeroplanes covered by Part II, Chapter 2, Volume 1 of Annex 16 to the Convention on International Civil Aviation, second edition (1988).
31. Ibid, Article 3.
32. Law No. 213/88.
33. P.I. No. 105/88.
34. See further Crans 'The Third Aviation Package: Its impact on the Leasing Industry' (1993) *Air and Space Law* 102.
35. Article 4 of Regulation (EC) No 2407/92 on licensing of air carriers.
36. Ibid, Article 5.
37. An operator, who does not hold such a certificate, should apply using the appropriate form DCA 212. After the form has been submitted to the DCA, a file is opened and a form DCA 216 shall be enclosed giving the progress summary of the AOC. Thereafter, the DCA undertakes to carry out detailed examination of all aspects of aircraft operation, including management structure, adequacy of aircraft crews, ground staff and arrangements for their training, premises, equipment and aircraft and adequacy of arrangements and facilities for aircraft maintenance. Also, there is a scrutiny of the Operations Manual, which shall have to be written as per JAR Ops 1 (for aircraft) or JAR Ops 3 (for helicopters). Airworthiness inspectors visit the facilities of the applicant towards carrying out engineering and flight operations inspections and to complete form DCA213. The validity of the certificate is for an unlimited period, however, the DCA has the right to suspend or revoke it, if conditions warrant such an action.
38. Article 8 of Council Regulation (EEC) No 2408/92 for the operation of scheduled air services between Saint-Étienne and Nantes.
39. Ibid, Article 6.
40. Decision of the Council of Ministers No. 8211 of 17.10.1968.
41. See Haanappel, *Fares, Proceedings of European Air Law Association Annual Conference*, Sakkoulas/Kluwer, Rome 1992.
42. Article 3 of Regulation (EEC) 2409/92 of 23 July 1992 on fares and rates for air services.
43. Ibid, Article 5.
44. Ibid, Article 6.
45. 54 Supplement 2A 3 and Law No. 66/70 and 173/89.

46. (1991) CLR 764.
47. See Law No. 3(III)/2002.
48. The Montreal Convention entered into force on 4-11-2003 and by that date it has been ratified by 32 states.
49. Article 6 of Regulation 2027/97.
50. Document No. 500PC0446.
51. Document No. 500PC0340.
52. P.I. No. 110/98. Made by the Council of Ministers of Cyprus in accordance with section 4 of the Aerodromes Law, Cap. 300, as amended (see note 4).
53. Law No. 213/88.
54. They continue to be in force pursuant to Article 188.1 of the Constitution.
55. Law No. 215/90 and 22(III)/2000.
56. Date of approval: 8.2.2001, date of entry into force: 19 February 2001 (PI 92/2001).
57. Article 3.2 of Regulation No 95/93 of 18 January 1993 on common rules for the allocation of slots at Community airports.
58. Ibid, Article 4.3.
59. See the discussion above under the heading 'denied boarding compensation system'.
60. See Regulation (EC) 1592/2002. It establishes the European Safety Aviation Organization and repeals Directive 80/51/EC; Regulation (EC) 2320/2002, establishing common rules in the field of civil aviation security; Regulation (EC) 1702/2003, laying down implementing rules for the airworthiness and environmental certification of aircraft and related products, parts and appliances, as well as for the certification of design and production organizations; Regulation (EC) 1486/2003, specifying procedures for conducting Commission inspections in the field of civil aviation security; Regulation (EC) 1217/2003, laying down specifications for national civil aviation security quality control programmes; Regulation (EC) 622/2003, laying down measures for the implementation of the common basic standards on aviation security.
61. Directive 2002/30/EC Directive 2002/30/EC of the EP and of the Council of 26 March 2002 on the establishment of rules and procedures with regard to the introduction of noise-related operating restrictions at Community airports; also see Directive 2003/42/EC of the EP and of the Council of 13 June 2003 on occurrence reporting in civil aviation.
62. Ibid.
63. Directive 92/14/EEC, 94/56/EC, 91/670E/EC.
64. These are the comments made by the delegation of the Joint Aviation Authorities.
65. Thus the decision taken to start negotiations with the EU for the establishment of the European Common Aviation Area was more than justified despite the fact that the Agreement was not finally concluded.
66. Each bilateral air agreement may be amended if both contracting parties

agreed. Each contracting party has the right to terminate a bilateral air agreement and such termination takes effect 12 months after the date of receipt of the notice of termination by the other contracting state.

67. See *Commission v. Finland* Case C-469/98.

5 Harmonising Competition and State Aid Rules

VICKY CHRISTOFOROU[1]

Introduction

Competition policy is one amongst the 29 chapters of the EU acquis that, Cyprus had to negotiate in order to assume the rights and obligations of a full EU membership.

The obligation to have identical competition and state aid rules to those of the Community emanated from the Association Agreement (1973) and its Protocol (1987) signed by the Republic of Cyprus. The Agreement covered trade-related issues and various other areas of financial and technical co-operation aiming to the establishment of customs union between the European Community and Cyprus. This explains the fact that the first Law for the Protection of Competition was enacted in 1983 and generally reflected the principles provided in the Agreement.

Substantial accession negotiations on the adoption and implementation of EU legislation began in November 1998 and were concluded at the Copenhagen European Council in December 2002. It was decided that candidate countries would be eligible for full membership only if they could demonstrate that they had in place the necessary legal framework, the appropriate administrative and institutional capacity as well as the enforcement mechanisms to implement the acquis communautaire.

The competition acquis comprises the anti-trust, merger and state aid control policies. It includes rules and procedures to combat anti-competitive behaviour by companies and to prevent governments from granting state aids which distort competition in the Internal Market. Generally, competition rules are directly applicable in the whole of the EU and member States must fully co-operate with the European Commission on the enforcement of these rules.

The aim of this chapter is to give an overall picture of the existing legal framework governing anti-trust, mergers and state aid, the problems that have been encountered in the harmonisation process and the changes that took place to this end in the administrative and enforcement agencies. Last, but not least, a description of the implications of this process is given on facts and figures given by Cypriot officials and experts.

Anti-trust

The rules of anti-trust are primarily provided in the EC Treaty and in the Regulations and Directives issued by the Council or the Commission. According to the judgements of the ECJ, Treaty Articles, Regulations and Directives are directly applicable and form part of the member states' domestic law. However for Cyprus, as a candidate country, the principles of supremacy and direct applicability of EU law did not apply.

In order to comply fully with its membership requirements Cyprus had to incorporate all these provisions in its national legislation. Thus, a new law, the Protection of Competition law of 1989 (Law No.207/89), entered into force on 8 June 1990 (replacing the old 1983 Law) and it is considered to be the basic legal instrument governing competition policy. This law introduced a set of substantive and procedural rules equivalent to those of articles 81 and 82 of the Treaty and those contained in Council Regulation No.17,[2] guaranteeing effective competition in Cyprus's market. More specifically, article 4 of Law No.207/89 prohibits all agreements between undertakings, decisions by association of undertakings and concerted practices which have as their object the distortion or restriction of competition. Article 6 of the Act prohibits any abuse by one or more undertakings of a dominant position within Cyprus's market. Article 5 of the Protection of Competition law declares inapplicable the provisions of article 4 on any agreements that contribute to the improvement of the production or distribution of goods or promote technical or economic progress. Moreover, article 5 empowers the Council of Ministers of the Republic, after the Commissions' opinion, to issue orders granting group exemptions equivalent to those referred to in the relevant EC Regulations. Individual exemptions to a concerted practice may be granted by the Commission for the protection of competition. Exclusions are to be differentiated from exemptions. Exclusions from prohibition means a priori that the prohibition does not apply. Exemption means that the prohibition does apply until it is 'declared inapplicable', based on the criteria set out in article 5 of the Protection of Competition law of 1989.

An agreement may be excluded automatically if it falls within the terms set out for that particular agreement in one of the Council of

Ministers' Orders. Each Order deals with different types of agreements, e.g. exclusive distribution agreements,[3] exclusive purchasing agreements,[4] franchise agreements,[5] research and development agreements,[6] patent and know-how licences agreements,[7] agreements concerning maritime[8] and air transport services,[9] technology transfer agreements[10] and agreements for trade of agricultural products[11], agreements in insurance[12], road transport[13] and specialisation agreements.[14] These Orders are equivalent to the corresponding European Commission Regulations.

In practice most of the exemptions provided in the Orders mentioned above are of little use to the business world. The main reason for this is that full liberalisation in areas such as air or maritime transport is needed in order to promote such agreements exempted by the law. Moreover, bureaucracy, inflexible labour laws, high taxes and an uncertain political climate drive away undertakings that wish to invest in research and development, patents and know how.

In June 2000 the Protection of Competition Law of 1989 was amended in order to provide provisions equivalent to article 86 of the EC Treaty and Commission Directive[15] adopted pursuant to this article. The aim of the amendment was to extent the application of competition rules to the public undertakings and undertakings which are entrusted with the operation of services of general economic interest or having the character of a revenue-producing monopoly. However, the application of such rules should not obstruct the performance, in law or in fact, of such undertakings. In order to enjoy the exclusion from the application of the competition rules the undertakings have to prove that there were no other economic or technical means to perform the particular tasks assigned to them. To this end new definitions have been inserted to the law. Revenue producing monopolies are defined as the undertakings which enjoy a fiscal monopoly by exploiting their exclusive rights in order to raise money for the state.

Public undertakings are defined as, any undertaking over which public authorities may exercise directly or indirectly a dominant influence by:

- holding the major part of the undertaking's subscribed capital or
- controlling the majority of the votes attaching to shares issued by the undertakings or
- appointing more than half of the members of the undertaking's administrative, managerial or supervisory body.

Currently in Cyprus there are quite a few sectors of the economy that enjoy special or exclusive rights *de jure* or *de facto*. These are the postal services, telecommunications, civil aviation, ports, the shipping sector, electricity services and other public undertakings operating in the manufacturing and agricultural sectors. Regarding the agricultural sector the Cyprus Grain Commission, Cyprus Olive Products Marketing Board, Cyprus Carrot and Beetroot Marketing Board, the Vine Products Commission, the Cyprus Milk Industry Organisation and the Cyprus Potato Marketing Board share exclusive rights from the state such as tax reductions or exclusions.[16] These boards were the subject of discussions in accession negotiations under the Chapter of Agriculture and their status was reformed in order to comply with requirements of the relevant acquis.

The above mentioned amendment is considered to be very important since it enables the Commission for the Protection of Competition to intervene in the above sectors if abuse of the market is identified. However, it will take a while for these sectors to get accustomed in operating under the new rules given that they learned to operate in their protectionist environment shielded from the notion of competition.

The harmonisation process with the acquis communautaire is a moving target. So, with the adoption of the new Council Regulation (EC) No. 1/2003[17] on the implementation laid down in articles 81 and 82 of the Treaty, the Protection of Competition Law had to be amended again. The new amendment will be enacted upon accession of Cyprus to the EU. This Council Regulation aims to replace Council Regulation No.17[18] and the creation of a directly applicable exemption system in which competition authorities and courts of the member states have the power to apply directly article 81(3) of the Treaty. This means that the notification and exemption system for the application of article 81(3) provided in Regulation No.17 is abolished and there is no need to notify the European Commission about agreements in order to qualify for an exemption. More importantly the exemption rule of article 81(3) may be invoked as a defence in proceedings against any undertaking, conducted by the European Commission, national competition authorities and national courts. The undertakings have to ensure in good faith that agreements do not affect free competition and do not infringe EU competition rules.

Council Regulation 1/2003 is directly applicable which means that member states have to introduce legislative and administrative measures in order to make their implementation feasible. To this end, the Protection for Competition law had to be amended in order to ensure that the increasing tasks of the national competition authority and the Cyprus Courts, provided in Council Regulation 1/2003, were met. Under the new Protection of Competition law the Commission for the Protection of Competition (CPC) has the power to apply articles 81 and 82 of the Treaty in individual cases. For this purpose acting on its initiative or on complaints, CPC may:

- require the undertakings that an infringement be brought to an end
- order interim measures
- accept commitments
- impose fines and periodic penalty requirements.

This relates to agreements that abuse fair competition of the internal market and the Cyprus market. Council Regulation 1/2003 allows member states to provide in their territory stricter national laws or sanction unilateral conduct engaged in by the undertaking. The government of Cyprus chose to retain the standards of the Regulation.

Its very important to note that despite the fact that the burden of the European Commission concerning notifications and exemptions has been alleviated the European Commission still retains its powers to intervene and initiate proceedings against undertakings that infringe completion rules at any given time. Under Council Regulation 1/2003 the European Commission may initiate proceedings for cases where national authorities have already initiated proceedings against undertakings after consulting them.[19] For this reason a co-operation mechanism is provided in the Regulation where the national authorities and the national courts co-operate with the European Commission in order to attain proper enforcement of EU competition law.

Under article 12 of Council Regulation 1/2003 the European Commission and the competition authorities of the members states have the power to provide each other with evidence in any matter of fact or of law, including confidential information. Implementation of this particular article of the Regulation was difficult since under Article 17 of the Cyprus Constitution every person has the right to respect for, and to the secrecy of, his correspondence and other communication if such other communication is made through means not prohibited by law. Moreover interference with the exercise of this right may be feasible only in cases of convicted and remand prisoners and business correspondence and communication of bankrupts during the bankruptcy administration.

The new law has similar provisions to those of Council Regulation 1/2003 for the exchange of information. However, there is a thought to draft a Ministerial Council Order for the provision of more detailed rules as to how in practice the information will be collected and exchanged. As the Cyprus Constitution is the supreme law of the Republic it remains to be seen how this law will be interpreted. There are two schools of thought on this issue. The first argues that upon accession to the EU the EC Treaty prevails over the national law including the Constitution. Thus, if a certain issue is regulated by EU law – i.e. Council Regulation 1/2003 – supersedes any other national law which is in conflict. The second school of thought deems necessary the amendment of the Constitution in order to make the EU law supreme.

Similar difficulties concern the implementation of article 15 of Council Regulation 1/2003 where the European Commission has the right to submit written observations to Courts of the member states and with the permission of the Court in question the European Commission may also make oral observations, the so called *amicus curiae* procedure. Under Cyprus's Constitution the only person that can conduct such an action is the Attorney General of the Republic. A provision has been provided in the new law to make this right available to the European Commission but again it remains to be seen how the law is going to be interpreted after all.

Mergers

The legal instrument controlling concentrations of undertakings with a national dimension is the Control of Concentrations Between Undertakings Law of 1999 (Law No.22(1)/99) providing for the application of measures within the territory of Cyprus equivalent to those referred to in the relevant Council Regulations of the EU.[20] Under Article 4 of Law No.22(I)/99, a concentration shall be deemed to occur where:

- two or more previously independent undertakings merge, or
- one or more persons already controlling at least one undertaking, or one or more undertaking acquire, whether by purchase of securities or assets, by contract or by any other means, direct or indirect control of the whole or part of one or more other undertakings.[21]
- two or more independent undertakings create a joint venture performing on a lasting basis all the functions of an autonomous economic entity.

Concentrations of major importance must be communicated in writing to the Competition Service of the Commission for the Protection of Competition at the latest one week from the date of the conclusion of the merger agreement or the announcement of the relevant market offer or the acquisition of control.

A concentration is considered to be of major importance when:

- the aggregate turnover of at least two of the undertakings concerned exceeds CY£2 million; and at least one of the undertakings concerned is occupied with commercial activities within the Republic of Cyprus; and at least CY£2 million from the aggregate amount of the turnover of all the undertakings concerns the supply of goods or the provision of services within the Republic of Cyprus;
- it is declared of such a major importance by an order of the Minister of Commerce, Industry and Tourism. It is considered to be of major importance when the effects of such concentration are harmful to the social and economic development of the state or its public security.

The criteria taken into consideration by the Commission for the Protection of Competition in order to establish whether the above mentioned concentrations are compatible with the requirements of the competitive market are:

- the structure of all the markets concerned
- the position of the undertakings in the market
- the economic and financial power of the undertakings
- supply and demand trends for the relevant goods and services
- any barriers to entry in the affected markets
- the interests of the intermediate and ultimate consumers
- the alternatives available to suppliers and users.

According to the above if a concentration does not create or strengthen a dominant position as a result of which effective competition would be significantly impeded in the local market, it is declared compatible with the requirements of competitive market.

Administrative and enforcing bodies

The authority entrusted with the enforcement of Cyprus's Competition rules is the Commission for the Protection of Competition (CPC). The CPC was established by virtue of Law No.207/89 in June 1990. It is an independent authority vested with extensive investigative and enforcement powers, which have been increased with the enactment of The Protection of Competition (Amendment) (No.2) Law of 2000 (Law No.155(I)/2000). The CPC's duties are to conduct investigations for suspected infringements of articles 4 and 6, to offer decisions upon complaints and notifications and to give opinions on any matter prevailing the application of the law. Moreover the CPC, whose decisions are published in the Official Gazette of the Republic of Cyprus, is responsible for granting individual negative clearances.

The CPC within its extensive investigative power may order the Competition Service (CS) officials to enter the undertakings' premises without prior notice for on the spot investigations for a suspected infringement of the Law. According to the new amendment law in progress (which implements Council Regulation 1/2003 for cases that involve abuse of the internal market's fair competition) the European Commission may conduct inspections on business and non-business premises. More specifically the European Commission may inspect without prior notice the homes of directors, managers and other members of staff of the undertaking or association of undertakings suspected of being involved in violations of articles 81 and 82 of the Treaty. Such inspection is ordered by a European Commission Decision following consultation with the CPC and the authorisation of the Supreme Court of Cyprus. Council Regulation 1/2003 lays down the principles that enable the constant exchange of information and consultation between the European Commission and national authorities. For this purpose the European Competition Network (ECN) is set up in order to create closer co-operation between the European national authorities and the European Commission. The officers of the CPC participate in all the ECN meetings and activities. The experience gathered from their attendance of these meetings has proved valuable to the process of drafting the new amendment law.

Stringent provisions for the enforcement of the CPC decisions are also provided. In particular, the application of a prohibited agreement or abuse of dominant position in contravention of a decision of the CPC, is a criminal offence punishable with imprisonment of up to one year or a fine that can be as high as 10% of an enterprise's annual turnover or both of these penalties.[22]

The provision of false or the withholding of true information is a criminal offence, punishable with imprisonment of up to one year or a fine from CY£100 to CY£50,000 (€85,000).[23] In February 2003, the CPC established a 'cartel immunity programme' which aims to the detection and successful prosecution of unlawful cartels. So, if an undertaking, which is part of a cartel, provides information to the CPC that proves to be valid evidence as to an infringement of the law by that cartel, that undertaking will be immune from any fine imposed to the rest of the members of the cartel. Under other circumstances total immunity will not be granted but substantial reduction of the fine will be provided instead.

The Control of Concentrations Between Undertakings Law No. 22(I)/99 also provides for equivalent legal means of enforcement of the CPC decisions. Omitting to notify a concentration is punishable with a fine up to CY£50,000 (€85,000) plus up to CY£5,000 (€8,500) for each day the infringement continues. The provision of inaccurate or misleading information is also punishable with a fine up to CY£50,000 (€85,000). Omitting to provide the required information is punishable with a fine up to CY£30,000 (€43000) plus fine up to CY£5,000 (€8,500) for each day the infringement continues. In addition a fine up to 10% of the enterprises annual turnover in case of failure to comply with an obligation imposed by a decision of the CPC, plus fine up to CY£5,000 (€8,500) for each day the infringement continues. Finally cases where the concentration is put into effect without satisfying a condition imposed by the CPC, are punishable with a fine of an amount up to 10% of the enterprises annual turnover.

In order to accomplish its mission the CPC is assisted by the staff of the CS, the main duties of which are:

- keeping a public Register of Notifications of Consortiums and a public Register of Decisions of the Commission and the Supreme Court on Consortiums and Actions
- collecting and checking information necessary for the carrying of the function of CPC
- introducing complaints and submitting suggestions to the CPC
- taking action for the necessary notifications and publications.

Before the enactment of Law No.155(I)/2000 in November 2000, the above duties were given to the Competition and Consumer Protection Division of the Ministry of Commerce, Industry and Tourism. This Division will continue to assist the CS until the completion of the recruitment of the CS permanent staff takes place. In addition the personnel of the Division will also remain responsible for the drafting of the laws and implementing regulations of competition policy.

The Commissioner of the CPC is employed on a full-time basis for a period of five years and he or she must be a 'jurist of recognised competence'. The members of the CPC are appointed on a part-time basis and must possess specialised knowledge and experience in the fields of law, economics, commerce or industry and at least two of them must be from the private sector. The appointment of a Commissioner on a full-time basis and for a longer period of time enabled better co-ordination of the CPC's actions.

The reason for the establishment of the CS was the creation of an independent service outside the auspices of the Ministry of Commerce, Industry and Tourism. Consequently, this amendment changed the philosophy of the system of enforcement of competition rules. The division of powers became more apparent and the exercise of authority by the institutions involved became more transparent. However, in order to achieve greater efficiency on the application of competition policy the judiciary and the business community need to become more aware of the concepts of EU competition policy and its application in Cyprus's market. In the case of Cyprus courts, they have to get more expertise in the area of EU competition policy because under the new Council Regulation 1/2003 they are called upon to implement directly articles 81 and 82 of the Treaty, at least alongside national law. Furthermore, they need to speed-up their procedures and create co-operation mechanisms with the European Commission and the courts of other member states.

The consequences of infringement of Law 207/89 and Law 22(I)/99: some facts and figures

The immediate consequence for agreements that infringe the prohibitions set out by Law No.207/89 is that they are void. If particular clauses in agreements are responsible for the infringement then those clauses alone will be void. Between 1990, when the CPC was established, and 2004 the CPC has examined 94 possible infringements of article 4, 63 possible infringements of article 6 of Law No.207/89 and 10 negative clearances.[24]

Up until the year 2000 most of the proceedings have been initiated upon the CPC's initiative. However, since 2000 investigations have been initiated following complaints to the CPC. During 2003, the service of the CPC received 14 complaints, 12 of which were in relation to abuse of dominant position in various sectors of the economy and 2 in relation to concerted practices between undertakings. Overall in 2003, the complaints filed within the CPC, where 18% less than in 2002.[25]

Although the most recent figures show that there has been a decline in the number of complaints, their overall increase through the years (1990-2004) shows that the private sector has familiarised itself with the institution of the CPC. In fact, the recent drop in the number of complaints might even indicate that the business world is slowly changing its practices. During this period of time CPC had as its primary purpose to examine specific sectors. As a result it initiated investigation and actions in various sectors, such as airlines, transportation, telecommunications, production and distribution of bricks, entertainment, even the production of mushrooms, all of which were completed during 2003.

One of the most important cases that really shook the legal and business world is the case of the Cyprus Telecommunications Authority (CYTA). CYTA is a semi-governmental organisation, governed by the Telecommunications Service Law Cap 302 as amended, and enjoys a monopoly in the supply of telecommunication services. According to Cap. 302, the charges for telecommunication services supplied by CYTA should be fixed at such level that revenues simply cover its operational expenses, the repayment of capital and the interest on loans. Moreover, its reserves should be such as CYTA considers sufficient for depreciation, extensions, renovations etc. Following the publication of CYTA's financial statements for the year 2000 and the submission of a report by the Auditor General to the House of Representatives, the CPC instructed the CS to carry out investigations into possible abusive exploitation of the dominant position it enjoys in the telecommunications sector. Following the investigation by the CS it was found that CYTA abused its dominant position in the market by fixing unfair prices for the sale of telecommunication services. According to the analysis of the evidence found by the CS income from subscriptions and call charges constituted the main source of income of CYTA: CY£172 millions or 82.4% of CYTA's total income (CY£208.7 millions) for the year 2000. According to CYTA's budgets the net profit for the years 1998-2001 should have amounted to CY£117.12 millions; instead it amounted to CY£218 millions i.e. an extra CY£111 millions (or 85% more than CYTA was entitled to have).

During the hearing before the CPC it was argued that CYTA enjoyed by law special and exclusive rights and in order to attain its objectives it had to be allowed to operate under 'financially acceptable conditions'. The CPC rejected the arguments of the defence and imposed a fine of CY£20 millions for abusive exploitation of its dominant position in the telecommunications sector in violation of section 6(2)(a) of Law No.207/89 for the period of July 2000 – 31 December 2001. The CPC also ordered and recommended that:

- by 1 January 2003 CYTA should take all appropriate measures and act in such manner that any possible violations of the provisions of section 6(2)(a) of the Law, may be removed;
- CYTA should immediately stop abusing its dominant position in the telecommunication services sector and that the Commission for the Protection of Competition monitors closely the whole behaviour of CYTA and acts according to the financial results of 2002.
- in the event that the Commission finds that until 1 January 2003 CYTA continues to abuse its dominant position and has not taken any measures or has not taken the necessary actions so that the above violation – especially regarding the pricing policy – may be removed, in addition to the above penalty a fine of CY£5,000 will be imposed for each day the violation continues.

After the decision of the CPC CYTA decided to recourse to the Supreme Court for the annulment of the CPC's judgement. Amazingly enough the Supreme Court annulled the decision on procedural matters and did not really analyse or had to explore more substantial issues.[26] The result of the above case is very disappointing since the case offered prosperous ground to both sides to argue about. Nevertheless, one positive conclusion that can be reached is that an amendment of the Law is needed in order to make the CPC's decision making process more efficient either by limiting the members to 3 and make their appointment full-time or by introducing rules of conduct for the meetings in order to avoid procedural errors.

In some of the cases fines have been imposed for failing to provide sufficient information to the CPC. A good example is the case where the Gravel Industries Association stopped selling gravel and sand because they did not want to pay 10 cents per ton environmental fee. They argued that this fee should be included in the selling price of the materials – so the consumers would pay for it. The CPC found that the Associations' decisions were effectively limiting production and that the Association used its dominant position to limit that particular market to the prejudice of consumers – thus they were in breach of articles 3, 4 & 6 of Law No.207/89. The CPC imposed a CY£4,000 fine but the Association failed to pay. The CPC proceeded by suing them and the District Court decided on 24 January 2001 that the Association was liable to pay CY£4,000 plus 8% interest since 1995 when the first decision came out.

Since the enactment of Law No.22(I)/99 there was only one merger reported to the CPC in 1999, 16 in the year 2000, 7 in the year 2001, one in the year 2002, one in the year 2003 and one in the year 2004. Eleven of these mergers were not considered to be of major importance, i.e. their aggregate turnover did not exceed CY£2 millions. The CPC has not decided upon the rest. However a fine of CY£2,000 for repeated failure to provide sufficient information to the CPC was imposed upon a concentration of two stock broking companies.

During 2003, the CPC received 6 notifications for concentrations between undertakings, compared to 9 in 2002. The majority of the notifications for concentrations between undertakings received in 2003 were in relation to services. The small numbers shown above are possibly the result of the lack of competitiveness due to the protectionist philosophy exercised so far by the state and the small-scale economy of Cyprus. With the establishment of the CS and the appointment of expert permanent staff working in co-operation with the Ministry of Commerce, Industry and Tourism officials, it is expected that there is going to be an increase in the number of investigations and a possible increase in the number of cases.

Finally, because of the recent establishment of Cyprus's Stock Market an increase of concentrations is expected. The reason for this is that Cyprus's Stock Market suffered a crash at the end of 2000, after a boom in 1999, and the companies will tend to merge in order to cope with the market pressures. In addition a prolonged decline in equity prices since 2000 and the reluctance of target companies to accept equity for giving up control, and insisting on cash only, has brought a decline in mergers and acquisition activity. Many analysts expect the mergers and acquisitions market to liven up in 2004 as incentive tax reforms took effect on 1 January 2003. Upon Cyprus's accession to the EU renewed interest is expected from abroad, especially from Greece. However, it remains to be seen whether these mergers would be considered to be of major importance due to the small scale of Cyprus's economy.

State aid

The general principle laid down in the EC Treaty is that any aid granted by a member state – favouring certain undertakings or the production of certain goods – which distorts or threatens to distort competition within the common market is prohibited. However, this prohibition is not an unqualified one. Under the Treaty the European Commission has the exclusive competence to declare these aids compatible with the common market according to specific circumstances (article 87 of the Treaty). Thus, any aids of a horizontal nature (SME's, environmental protection, research and development, etc), regional aids (aid to facilitate development of the EU's least developed areas), sectoral aids (textile, clothing and synthetic fibre industries, aid to motor vehicle industry), aids to promote cultural and heritage conservation, can be considered compatible with the common market. However, the Commission has no power to refuse aids that aim to restore damages caused by natural disasters or exceptional occurrences or which have a social character granted to the individual consumers.[27] Finally any aids up to €100,000 granted over a period of three years to any undertaking are also considered compatible with the common market.

The EU's State Aid policy is vital for the creation and maintenance of a unified common market. It controls directly the exercise of granting power of the member states, guaranteeing the utilisation of competition rules with the primary goal of market integration. The accession countries were obliged to adjust their economies to be able, upon accession, to integrate smoothly into the common market. For this reason in the pre-accession stage the candidate countries were obliged to introduce the above mentioned principles and to set up the proper infrastructure to be able to identify and monitor the aids granted by their governments. These authorities assumed temporarily the European Commission's duties regarding granting or refusing state aids. Their decisions were based on the same criteria set out in the Commission's codes or frameworks.[28] Moreover, in order to monitor state aids in the EU, increase transparency and encourage the exchange of information between itself and the member states, the Commission launched a 'scoreboard' in July 2001. The scoreboard contains information on the overall state aid in the EU and on the Commission's current state aid control activities. Acceding countries were included in the scoreboard for obvious reasons, i.e. to enable the European Commission to discipline the acceding countries to granting aid and to improve quality and comparability of data, with the ultimate purpose to fully integrate them upon their accession.

In an attempt to set up a legal framework for the control of state aids in Cyprus the Public Aid Control Law of 2001 (Law No.30(I)/2001) was enacted. It incorporates the principles enshrined in the EC Treaty (articles 87 and 88(1)) and empowers the Council of Ministers to adopt regulations and issue orders[29] for the implementation of the acquis, codes and frameworks of the Commission concerning horizontal, regional and sectoral aid. The Public Aid Control law rectified the drawbacks of the old system of state interventions, which was based on a bundle of discretionary policy decisions taken to promote a multiplicity of objectives affected by the characteristics of Cyprus's market economy at the given time. Accordingly under the law the State Monitoring Unit, was created in order to monitor any existing or new aid given by the granting bodies. No aid can be authorised unless analytical data is given about the project for which the aid is granted and its means of realisation. These measures inevitably make the current system more efficient and transparent.

It is interesting to note that aids concerning agriculture, stock-breeding and fisheries do not fall within the ambit of this law. There are special rules in the acquis applying to aid in these sectors, which were the subject of discussions for the Chapter of Agriculture. Moreover, any aid granted to international business enterprises is exempted from the application of the Public Aid Control law. These enterprises are established in Cyprus but their income is derived from resources outside Cyprus. Such exclusion has been criticised by the EU during the accession negotiations but in the end a transitional period of five years was granted. The EU considers that the favourable regime of international business enterprises, i.e. income tax exemptions, export aids and other forms of operating aids, need to be brought into line with the state aid acquis. The contribution of the international business enterprises to Cyprus's economy is substantial especially in the service sector, which accounts for 75% of the GDP. The reform of their regime has been the subject of a gap analysis undertaken by a committee of experts especially created for this purpose. The aim of the committee was to strike a balance between the necessary alignment with the acquis and the best possible way of preserving their favourable regime. To this effect the process of reform of the regime of business taxation and the abolition of the harmful measures is being initiated.

Another burning topic in the accession negotiations concerning elements of a favourable tax regime was the exemption of co-operative societies from the payment of corporate income tax. These co-operative societies are non-profit organisations that operate near cost and aim to provide services that have as their object the promotion of economic, social and educational interests of their members. They are mainly engaged with the marketing of agricultural products, manufacturing, trade and financial services. The main concern of the EU in the accession negotiations was the provision of financial services of the Co-operative Credit Institutions to non-members mostly SME's and local authorities. The provision of financial services to non-members effectively places Co-operative Credit Institutions in competition with commercial banks. For this reason the EU demanded that the products or services to non-members should become subject to normal corporate income tax. In this respect with the reform of the tax regime upon accession this problem will be solved. In addition, the Public Aid Control law of 2001 provides that any aids granted to undertakings entrusted with the operation of services of general economic interest or services that have the character of a revenue-producing monopolies are held to be compatible with the rules of competition and are immediately approved if such aids are considered necessary for the performance of the particular tasks assigned to them. This provision hits the nail on the head since any existing or future aid, granted by the state to these bodies, must be well justified and supported by facts and figures that prove that there were no other means available to accomplish the special mission assigned to them.

Currently in Cyprus there are approximately 39 statutory public bodies, which have been established by law and cover a wide spectrum of activities concerning mainly the exercise of regulatory functions, the provision of public utility services and some public undertakings operating in the manufacturing sector or the marketing of agricultural products. Their financial relationship with the government is relatively extensive and takes mainly the form of grants, government guarantees, government loans and import duty exemptions. In addition the government is involved in the private economic activity on a limited scale. There are approximately 9 private companies in which the government maintains capital holding.

The introduction of measures for the control of state aid came at the right time to complement the Strategic Development Plan[30] introduced by the government in 1999. The plan covered the period of 1999-2003 while its objectives were based on three values: development, stability, and social cohesion. A great part of this plan concentrated on the reconstruction of the protected sectors of the economy, and the modernisation of business units. This was achieved by strengthening the existing and by attracting and developing new high technology industries, by reforming and supporting the traditional manufacturing industry and by attracting foreign capital investments.

It is interesting to note that the strategic plan aimed at public sector reform. The governments' policy focused on the modernisation of semi-governmental organisations and state-owned firms so as to render them more flexible to face the globalisation of the economies, without pursuing privatisation. State monopolies have also been subject to reform in order to comply with the acquis and continue their positive contributions to the economy.[31] For example, in the telecommunication sector, an independent National Regulatory Authority regulating telecommunications and postal services, was established. This Authority surveys the market aiming at its gradual liberalisation and carries out the essential task of drafting implementing regulations. The same applies to the Electricity Authority, which is currently the sole producer and distributor of electricity in Cyprus. An Energy Regulator has been appointed who surveys the market and is responsible for the placement of electrical equipment on the market.

With the establishment of the regulatory authorities the government's role is limited to the drafting of primary and secondary legislation implementing the relevant acquis. However, the participation of the regulatory authorities in the drafting process is of primary importance since most of the related issues are technical and demand good knowledge in the commercial practices. Of course, these reforms are not enough. In order to promote effective reform additional elements are necessary, such as: the promotion of internal control systems in individual organisations, the recruitment of permanent employees, the greater involvement of NGO's and the creation of an independent anti-corruption watchdog agency, using leadership and political will to give impetus to change, initiating policy reforms including the effective application of the anti-corruption legislation and other reforms to promote competition.[32]

Another important feature of the Public Aid Control law of 2001 is the introduction of the *de minimis* rule. According to this rule any aid, given to any kind of enterprise during a three year period, whose aggregate value amounts to CY£57,000 is considered to be of minor importance (*de minimis*) as it does not have appreciable effect on competition. Cyprus is characterised by its small-size economy where most of the SME's are family owned business. The existence of the *de minimis* rule will safeguard their survival in the fierce competition which they are shortly going to experience with the opening of the market.

The new legal order encourages the development of previously undermined areas like environmental protection, measures taken in the areas of health and education, the promotion of research and development and the investment in patents and know-how. The support of such projects will play an important role for sustaining better quality of life to Cypriot citizens.

Regional aid

Despite the small size of Cyprus, there are differences in the level of development and welfare of the population between the different administrative Districts and even within individual Districts. The most profound disparities exist between urban and rural areas. Currently certain state aid schemes with a regional orientation exist in the agricultural and non-agricultural sectors. For example the 'Scheme for Encouraging the Establishment of Industrial Units in Rural Areas' which provides investment grants for buildings (up to 15%), machinery (up to 25%) and investments for infrastructure services or utilities (up to 100%). The amount of the grant is limited to CY£50,000 (€85,000) per establishment. For the purposes of the scheme specific eligible areas have been designated.

In order to strengthen the administrative capacity to implement the acquis and to maintain stability as regards the current structures and systems of Cyprus the government introduced a new Development Plan. The new Development Plan 2004-2006 will constitute the basis for the preparation of the Programming Documents, which will include actions and projects proposed for co-financing from the Structural Funds, the Cohesion Fund and other EU Community Initiatives. As a result, the new plan should take into account the EU's timetable for its structural actions, and, therefore, its duration is limited up to 2006, so as to cover the remaining programming period of the EU's current structural actions.

The primary objective of the new Development Plan is to achieve a satisfactory rate of sustainable growth and the utilisation, to the greatest possible extent, of the opportunities offered through the accession, thus contributing substantially to a greater real convergence with other member states. Other objectives of the Plan are the following:

- Enhancing the competitiveness and macroeconomic stability of the economy, primarily in expanding and upgrading the infrastructure in the sectors of transport, linking Cyprus with the Trans-European Networks, energy and telecommunications,
- Achieving balanced regional development, in particular by strengthening the small and medium-sized firms, encouraging research and development, and utilising the possibilities opened up by information technology society. In addition the aim is to strengthen the underdeveloped areas,
- Embedding social cohesion and full employment conditions, especially promoting equality between the sexes, and the social exclusion of vulnerable social groups,
- Protection of the environment and improving the quality of life.[33]

The expansion and upgrading of the infrastructure will rectify existing weaknesses and secure the necessary preconditions for continuous and sustainable growth, given the complementary nature between private sector investments and investments in infrastructure.

Enforcement body

The Commissioner heads the State Aid Monitoring Unit, which operates within the Ministry of Finance, and he is responsible for the enforcement of the Law No.30(I)/2001. His actual duties are:

- to investigate a priori any state aid provided or to be provided by the government and to approve the grant of that aid
- to follow up and monitor the aid granted ensuring that it has been utilised for that particular purpose
- to prepare and keep an inventory of all existing and new aids granted
- to gather and analyse any records or particulars of aid schemes
- to obtain all the reports and particulars of the aid scheme from the granting bodies
- to verify that the aid granted under a particular scheme has been used for that particular scheme only
- to prepare and submit an annual report of his activities to the President of the Republic of Cyprus
- to co-operate with other international bodies and committees relating to state aids and to ratify any multilateral or bilateral agreements concerning state aids.

The Commissioner is assisted by the officials of the Ministry of Finance. These officials already have the experience of preparing the first inventory of all existing support schemes and ad hoc measures at central and local government levels. This was an enormous project undertaken upon the accession negotiations. These officials, as staff of the State Aid Monitoring Unit, are going to continue the assessment of the compatibility with State Aid rules of each scheme/measure.

Transitional measures have been undertaken in order to keep track and pinpoint unlawful aids granted. The Public Aid Control law of 2001 demanded that any existing aid schemes must be communicated to the Commissioner, within four months from the date of the enactment of the

Law. The Commissioner had to decide within 18 months from the enactment of the Law, whether the aid schemes were compatible. Having regard that there were approximately 380 support schemes to be examined within a short period of time the State Monitoring Unit right from its infancy faced a great challenge. Moreover due to the tight time limits of the examination of all support schemes there was a great risk for unlawful projects to be rendered automatically compatible. In order to tackle any unwanted occurrences, three qualified professionals as well as two supporting staff were appointed. In addition technical as well as professional support (twinning projects with the officers of EU Commission, training projects) took place.

According to the Public Aid Control law the decisions of the Commissioner are published in the Official Gazette of the Cyprus Republic, and communicated to the granting body. The publication of the Commissioners' decisions plays an important role in the efficiency and transparency of the granting system. On one hand the Commissioner maintains his status of independence and impartial decision-making; on the other hand the non-beneficiary undertakings or regions whose interests are negatively affected can challenge the Commissioners decisions. In order to ensure the implementation of the law additional financial and other sanctions are provided. Thus, it is an offence if someone:

- fails on purpose to provide any information regarding the investigation exercised by the Commissioner upon an aid scheme
- fails to provide facts and figures required by the Government
- obstructs the investigation carried out by the Commissioner
- provides the Commissioner with material that he believes is incorrect or false.

This offence is punishable with imprisonment not exceeding six months and with a fine of CY£10,000. In addition, proper monitoring of new aid schemes is ensured under article 12 of the law where the granting body must report to the Commissioner, every three months, in detail the stages of the realisation of the aid scheme. If the Commissioner identifies any inconsistencies in the approved aid scheme he notifies the granting body in order to act in due time to rectify those inconsistencies. Finally if the granting body continues to act contrary to the Commissioner's decision then it is in breach of the law and any aid granted has to be returned.

Upon accession, the acquis will supersede any national rules in force in the field of state aid. Consequently, no national legislation enacted under the obligations arising from the Association Agreements may impede the direct application of the acquis as of 1 May 2004. An amendment of the law has been recently prepared and will be put into force upon accession. According to the new law the State Aid Monitoring Unit will remain responsible for the general co-ordination in the field of state aid within Cyprus, in order to be able to submit and prepare notification of aid schemes to the European Commission. Moreover, the Commissioner's powers for the approval of aid schemes will be surrendered to the European Commission, except for cases of aids granted under the Block Exemption Regulations regarding state aid to small and medium enterprises,[34] training aid[35] and employment aid.[36] For these cases the same procedure analysed above will apply.

It should be noted that from the 113 cases before the state Monitoring Unit 50% concerned state aid falling under the scope of the Block Exemptions. For other types of state aid the Commissioner's task will be to issue opinions irrespective of whether such state aid scheme is noticeable. If it is considered noticeable all the relevant information will have to be sent to the European Commission and the scheme will not be put into effect until the European Commission decides that it is compatible according to the Treaty Rules.[37]

Concluding remarks

In the light of the above analysis one might conclude that Cyprus's effort to harmonise with the acquis in competition and state aid area has proved, so far, to be successful. The sole aim of Cyprus as an acceding country was to prepare its economy for the demands of the common market and EMU.

In order to achieve this, national legislation is still being introduced providing for measures equivalent to those provided in the competition and state aid acquis. The undergoing liberalisation of the protected sectors of the economy as well as the control of public aid aiming to the reduction of public expenses and public deficit is also a step forward. These measures will facilitate to the smooth direct application of EU law upon Cyprus's accession.

Setting up the appropriate administrative structure and creating the monitoring and regulatory authorities is also very important. The current trend of decentralisation of the European Commission's powers regarding the application of competition and state aid rules is a fact that nobody can afford to ignore. The policy of the European Commission seems to be the creation of efficient national authorities. The national competition authorities must be able to apply the acquis efficiently and co-operate with the European Commission with the sole aim of harmonised actions both on national and European level.

The aim of the Republic of Cyprus is to sustain functional administrative and regulatory authorities of a high standard, which in the future will be able to assist the European Commission's work. To this end strengthening the CPC and creating a State Aid Monitoring Unit is definitely a step towards the right direction. The enactment of the legal framework and the recent amendments awaiting to come into effect provide valuable means for the judiciary, the administrative and regulatory authorities to enforce Competition and State Aid policy.

The overall picture looks very positive, it remains to be seen how it will be formed in the European environment having always in mind that, the challenges are endless.

Notes

1. The views expressed in this Chapter are the personal views of the author.
2. EEC Council Regulation No.17: First Regulation Implementing Articles 85 and 86 of the Treaty.
3. The Exclusive Distribution Agreements (Block Exemptions) Order of 1995, in force since 26 January 1996, which is in accordance with Commission Regulation (EEC) 1983/83 on 'the application of Article 85(3) of the Treaty to categories of exclusive distribution agreements'. Repealed in December 2000.
4. The Exclusive Purchasing Agreements (Block Exemptions) Order of 1995, in force since 26 January1996, which is in accordance with Commission Regulation (EEC) 1984/83 on the application of Article 85(3) of the Treaty to categories of exclusive purchasing agreements.
5. (a) The Exclusive Franchise Agreements (Block Exemptions) Order of 1996, in force since 26 January 1996, which is in accordance with Commission Regulation (EEC) 4087/88 on the application of Article 85(3) of the Treaty to categories of franchise agreements. Repealed in December 2000.
   (b) The Block Exemption (To Categories of Vertical Agreements and Concerted Practices) Order of 2000 in force since 15 December 2000, which is in accordance with Commission Regulation (EC) 2790/1995 of 22 December 1999 on the application of the Article 81(3) of the Treaty to categories of vertical agreements and concerted practices.
6. The Block Exemptions (Research and Development Agreements) Order of

1997, in force since 24 January 1997, in accordance with Commission Regulation (EEC) 418/85 on the application of Article 85(3) of the Treaty to categories of research and development agreements, as amended by Commission Regulation (EEC) 151/93. The Order was replaced in February 2002 by a new Order in accordance with Commission Regulation (EC) 2659/2000.

7. The Block Exemption (Patent and know How Licences Agreements) Order of 1996, in for since 21 June 1996.

8. (a) The Block Exemption (Maritime Conferences) Order of 1997, in force since 18 July 1997, which is in accordance with Council Regulation (EEC) 4056/86 laying down detailed rules for the application of articles 85 and 86 of the Treaty to maritime transport.
(b) The Block Exemption (Agreements, Decisions and Concerted Practices between Liner Shipping Companies-Consortia) Order of 1997, in force since 18 July 1997, which is in accordance with Commission Regulation (EC) 870/95 on the application of Article 85(3) of the Treaty to certain categories of agreements, decisions and concerted practices between liner shipping companies (consortia), pursuant to Council Regulation (EEC) 479/92. Amended in February 2002 by the Block Exemption (Agreements, Decisions and Harmonised Practices among Shipping Camers, Regular Lines-Joint Enterprises) Order of 2002, in accordance with Commission Regulation (EC) 823/2000.

9. The Block Exemption (Agreements between Undertakings Relating to Computerised Reservation Systems for Air Transport Services) Order of 1997, in force since 18 July 1997, which is in accordance with Commission Regulation (EEC) 3652/93 on the application of article 85(3) of the Treaty to certain categories of agreements between undertakings relating to computerised reservation systems for air transport services. Abolished in February 2002, in accordance with council Regulation (EC) 365/2. The Block Exemption (Technical Co-operation in the Air Transport Sector) Order of 1997, in force since 12 December 1997, which is in accordance with Council Regulation (EEC) 3976/87 on the application of article 85(3) of the Treaty to certain categories of agreements and concerted practices in the air transport sector. The Block Exemption (Agreements between Air Transport Undertakings Concerning Joint Planning and Co-ordination of Schedules, Joint Operations, Consultations on Passenger and Cargo Tariffs on Scheduled Air Services and Slot Allocation at Airports) Order of 1998, in force since 20 February 1998, which was in accordance with Commission Regulation (EEC) 1617/93 on the application of article 85(3) of the Treaty to certain categories of agreements and concerted practices concerning joint planning and co-ordination of schedules, joint operations, consultations on passenger and cargo tariffs on scheduled air services and slot allocation at airports. The Order was repealed in July 2000 and has been replaced by a new Order in

accordance with Commission Regulation (EC) 1083/99.

10. The Block Exemption (Technology Transfer Agreements) Order of 1998, in force since 30 April 1998, which is in accordance with Commission Regulation (EC) 240/96 on the application of article 85(3) of the Treaty to certain categories of technology transfer agreements.
11. The Block Exemption (Agreements, Decisions and Concerted Practices Concerning the Production or Trade in Agricultural Products) Order of 1998, in force since 23 january 1998, which is in accordance with Commission Regulation (EEC) 26/62 applying certain rules of competition to production of and trade in agricultural products.
12. The Block Exemption (Agreements, Decisions and Concerted Practices in the Insurance Sector) Order of 1997, in force since 31 October 1997, which is in accordance with Commission Regulation (EEC) 3932/92 on the application of article 85(3) of the Treaty to certain categories of agreements, decisions and concerted practices in the insurance sector. Replaced by a new Order in November 2003 in accordance with Commission Regulation (EC) 358/2003.
13. The Block Exemption (Exclusive Motor Vehicle Distribution and After Sales Servicing Agreements) Order of 1998, in force since 20 February 1998, which is in accordance with Commission Regulation (EEC) 1475/95 on the application and servicing agreements. Replaced by a new Order in November 2003 in accordance with Commission Regulation (EC) 1400/2002. The Block Exemption (Agreements, Decisions and Concerted Practices in the Road Transport Sector) Order of 1997, in force since 12 December 1997, which is in accordance with Commission Regulation (EEC) 1017/68 applying rules of competition to transport by rail, road and inland waterway. It should be noted that transport by rail and inland waterway are non-existent in Cyprus.
14. The Block exemption (Specialisation Agreements) Order of 1997. The said order was replaced in February 2002 by a new Order in accordance with Commission Regulation 2658/2000.
15. Commission Directive 80/723, OJ 1980 L195/35, on the transparency of financial relation between member states and public undertakings.
16. These marketing boards are state monopolies of a commercial character under the meaning of article 31 (ex 37) of the Treaty, and deal with products, which are traded and marketed by the Common Market Organisations.
17. Council Regulation (EC) 1/2003 of 16 December 2002 L1/1, 4 January 2003.
18. Ibid, p.2.
19. Article 11 of the Regulation 1/2003, see Ibid, p.17.
20. Council Regulation (EEC) 4064/89 on the control of concentrations (as amended by Council Regulation 1310/97) and to the Council Regulation (EC) 447/98.
21. For the purposes of the act ‘control’ shall be constituted by rights, contracts, or any other means which, either separately or in combination and having regard to the considerations of facts or law involved, confer the possibility of

exercising decisive influence on an undertaking, in particular by: ownership or the right to use all or part of the assets of an undertakings rights or contracts which confer decisive influence on the composition voting or decisions of the organs of an undertaking.

22. In case the infringement continues, the CPC can impose a fine of an amount of CY£20 up to CY£500 (€35-€850), for each day. With the second amendment to the Protection of Competition Law No.207/89 these fines are increased to up to CY£5000 (€8,500) for each day.
23. In case of omission to provide the required information within the fixed time limit or of intentional or negligent provision of inaccurate or misleading information, the CPC has the power to impose a fine In case of omission to provide the required information within the fixed time limit, the CPC can impose a penalty of up to CY£5,000 (€8,500) for each day.
24. Statistical data given by officials of the Ministry of Commerce Industry and Tourism.
25. Statistical data given by officials of the CS.
26. The Supreme Court found that the meetings which took place were not conducted properly, since the composition of the CPC was not the same and different members did not attend for some reason all the meetings. Furthermore, the notes taken at the meetings did not refer to the fact that the members missing from the previous meeting were informed about the facts of that meeting of the CPC. The Supreme Court found that since the members of the CPC did not attend the whole hearing process and there was no evidence to show that they were informed about the meetings which they missed there was no legal composition of the CPC in order to be able to reach a legal decision, and annulled CPC's decision.
27. Articles 87 & 88 (ex 93) of the EC Treaty.
28. These codes or frameworks constitute guidelines setting out the course of conduct which the Commission intends to follow and with which it requests member states to comply but they do not derogate from the provisions of articles 87 and 88 of the EC Treaty.
29. (a) The Control of Public Aid (Small and medium sized enterprises) Regulations of 2001 which entered into force as from 4 May 2001 implementing the Commissions Regulation (EC) 70/2001.

    (b) The Control of Public Aid (Professional Training) Regulations of 2001 which entered into force as from 4 May implementing Commission Regulation (EC) 68/2001 of 12 January 2001.

    (c) The Control of Public Aid (Research and Development) which entered into force as from 4 May implementing Community Framework for State Aid for (96/C45/06).

    (d) The Control of Public Aid (Notification Procedure) Order of 2001 which entered into force as from 15 June 2001 incorporating in particular the Commission Standard Notification Form.

30. Address by the Minister of Finance Mr. T. Clerides before the Parliament on the occasion of the debate on the Budget for 2000.
31. Ibid, p. 24.
32. D. Gill, 'Public Sector Reform' Government of New Zealand, Vasos Pyrgos, Lazaros Savvides and Alecos Michaelides, Government of Cyprus for a seminar 'Towards a vision and a strategy for Cyprus in the 21st century', June 2001.
33. *On the Way to EU Membership*, Press and Information Office, Republic of Cyprus, 2003.
34. Commission Regulation (EC) 70/2001 of 12 January 2001 on the application of Articles 87 and 88 of the EC Treaty to state aid to small and medium-sized enterprises, Official Journal L 10, 13 January 2001.
35. Commission Regulation (EC) 68/2001 of 12 January 2001 on the application of Article 87 and 88 of the EC Treaty to training aid, Official Journal L 10, 13 January 2001.
36. Commission Regulation (EC) 2204/2002 of 12 December 2002 on the application of Articles 87 and 88 of the EC Treaty to State aid for employment, Official Journal L 337 of 13 December 2002.
37. Council Regulation (EC) 659/1999 laying down detailed rules for the application of Article 93 of the EC Treaty (at present Article 88).

6 The Environment

CHRISTINA HADJIDEMETRIOU[1]

Introduction

Cyprus's commitment to harmonize its legislation with the environmental policy of the EU has been an enormous task involving the drafting of a substantial amount of legislation and the challenge of implementing and enforcing it. The process of transposition requires setting up new mechanisms and strengthening the infrastructure in those areas of environmental protection where it already exists. This article discusses the protection of the environment prior to the harmonization process and the efforts undertaken to upgrade it to EU standards.

EU legislation takes the form of Directives (the vast majority of the legislation), Regulations and Decisions. Regulations are directly applicable in the legal system of the member states. Since this principle does not apply in the case of acceding countries, legislation is indeed drafted for the purpose of transposing the provisions of Regulations in the national legal system. Decisions, on the other hand, refer to specific measures taken for the enforcement of an environmental policy, which is already in place – and thus most of them were not applicable in the case of Cyprus during the harmonization stage. Cyprus, therefore, was mainly concerned with the transposition of legislation in the form of Directives and Regulations.

EU environmental legislation is divided into sector-specific and horizontal effect. The former is concerned with limiting and preventing pollution in areas such as waste management, air pollution, water pollution and exposure to noise. There is also a series of Directives and Regulations adopted on the basis of the Euratom Treaty setting the standards for nuclear safety and radiation protection (for the workers and the population at large). Horizontal legislation indicates the recent trend in the EU to integrate environmental concerns in the implementation of all other policies. It follows that national administrations have to adopt the principle of integrating environmental concerns when formulating their policy in an area that might affect the environment mainly, energy, transport, agriculture and tourism.

The commitments undertaken by Cyprus vis-á-vis the EU come at a time when the protection of the environment is becoming a major priority in the agenda of the government. For a small island heavily relying on tourism there were compelling reasons for investing on environmental infrastructure in this sector, irrespective of the accession process. Over the last two decades the island has developed into one of the most visited tourist destinations of the eastern Mediterranean and tourism is one of the country's most profitable industries; with a surface of 9,251 km and a population of 666,800 it receives 2.7 millions tourists per year, a figure, which according to government estimates, is going to rise. One might say that this contradicts the strategic development plan of the government for 1999-2003 that incorporates sustainable development as one of its main goals. The small size of the country exacerbates other problems that have to be tackled effectively in the near future, more notably waste management, water shortages and urbanization – the latter becoming a major factor as the number of people living in towns is rising.[2]

The initial stage: assessment of the work ahead and need for new working methods

At the first phase of the accession process an extensive effort was undertaken in the form of 'gap analysis', which predictably showed that there were big gaps in the legislation in force. The legislative gaps to a certain extent contrasted with administrative practices. The civil servants who oversee the implementation of the legislation in the various ministries were quite well informed about the EU requirements and in many cases they were implementing them even in the absence of an obligation in the law to do so. However, most of the legislative provisions relating to environmental protection were outdated and were scattered in a piecemeal fashion in other legislation. The notable exceptions were the framework laws on atmospheric pollution and water pollution, which were drafted in the early 1990s and took into consideration the relevant acquis. In some areas such as biotechnology there was no legislation.

At the administrative level it has proven to be very challenging for the public administration to adjust to a new way of reaching policy decisions and carrying them out. The environmental policies require from the administration coordinated and comprehensive methods of implementation and enforcement. The most fundamental characteristic of the acquis on environment is that it calls upon the member states to take an integrated approach in preventing the creation of sources of pollution and in limiting the pollution caused by existing sources.

Although the vision of adopting an 'integrated system approach' was welcomed by the different government departments involved in the transposition process, it has proven in practice to be a major stumbling block for the initiation of harmonizing legislation. By and large, in Cyprus each piece of legislation is written specifically in relation to the particular domain of the ministry that is responsible for its implementation. Attempting to get an administration that is used to a compartmentalized way of governing, to adopt a holistic approach has proven to be a time consuming exercise, involving long negotiations and adaptation to new practices.[3]

The Law Office and other lawyers in charge of drafting the harmonizing legislation were also faced with various challenges, mainly with regard to: a) the new approaches and legal methods for applying the environmental policy, b) the use of different type of terminology, c) conceptualizing the legal framework for the transposition of complex legislation and d) the need to proceed in a swift manner in spite of the administration's initial difficulties.

New legal frameworks

The impact of the acquis on the protection of the environment is becoming obvious when one sees that national legislation extends to areas that were completely unregulated or that new sophisticated legislation involving the use of new technology replaces existing laws. To illustrate this point some examples are cited in the following paragraphs.

Waste management

The sector of waste management will benefit enormously from the transposition process. Until very recently, the waste sector was characterized by lack of up to date legislation, which contrasts public awareness regarding the degradation of the environment and the standard of living especially of those who are living close to landfills. The main form of disposal is landfills where the bulk of the municipal waste was disposed of without prior segregation of the various types of waste and there were no schemes in place with regard to the operation of existing landfills in accordance with the EU standards and the specifications of the landfill Directive.[4]

As far as recycling and re-use of waste is concerned, there are very few programs at this stage and they mainly consist of collection of waste and exporting it for treatment.

For the purpose of transposition a comprehensive law on waste management incorporating the provisions of the Directives on waste management and on dangerous waste such as the management of batteries and accumulators, came into force in 2002. In addition a separate law was enacted for the recycling of packages and packaging waste. These laws set up complex requirements and use technological solutions for the purpose of minimizing waste so that a smaller amount of it ends up in landfills and set up the appropriate procedures for the disposal and treatment of dangerous waste. For the purposes of correct implementation of these laws the cooperation of the individual citizens, the business sector, the municipalities and the local communities is indispensable. This introduces a novel concept which increases the awareness of the general public and is already affecting the behaviour of the citizens and the economic factors.

Nature protection

The main EU Directives that deal with biodiversity are the Birds Directive[5] and the Habitats Directive.[6] The Habitats Directive aims to 'protect wildlife species and their natural habitats. The member states are required to identify sites of European importance and put in place a special management plan to protect them'.[7] These Directives together with other relevant Community legislation were very recently transposed by way of two separate laws[8].

Nature protection has traditionally been the thorniest environmental issue for governments on all sides of the political spectrum. Questions on how and to what extent to protect biodiversity in sensitive natural areas are usually highly controversial. In some cases attempting to reach a consensus between the government sectors, the ecological movement and the distinct groups affected by the application of environmental policies leads to intractable problems. It is thus hard to speculate on the pace of any progress in this field had it not been for the pressure exercised by the EU.

In addition to the general policy issues there were also obstacles at the administrative level. The pre-existing system was governed by fragmented legislation implemented by different ministries which prevented the smooth and quick transposition of the environmental legislation. Indeed, the new laws enacted this year for transposition purposes, maintain the division of authority between government sectors over the protection of nature on the one hand and the protection and management of wild life on the other.[9]

A clear illustration of the obstacles for striking the right balance which would be in line with the European environmental law is provided by the controversy concerning the protection of the Akamas peninsula. This debate has been going on for the last two decades. Even before the approximation phase begun, Cyprus, being a member State to the Bern Convention[10] had international obligations concerning the conservation of wild fauna and flora and their natural habitats.

In the case of Akamas successive governments were caught between on the one hand the need to take the appropriate measures to protect the environment and on the other, to please the local communities who together with developers are claiming they should have the right to use their property as they like. 'Akamas is an area with rare endemic plants and many types of migratory birds. ... The large unspoiled coastal area is one of the very few important sea turtle nesting areas in the Mediterranean. In fact the Green Turtle depends on the Akamas beaches for its very survival in this region'.[11]

The Ministry of Agriculture and Natural Resources has been considering since 1986 the possibility of a policy of preservation of the Akamas peninsula. Governments have taken various measures such as freezing development in some parts of it. Throughout the years the developers and local villagers aiming to create a different situation on the ground have been engaging in various types of illegal activities such as removal of natural vegetation, bulldozing areas to set up tourist facilities, putting up illegal restaurants, etc.

It is worth mentioning the decision of the High Court in the case of *Demetriades and Others*[12] where owners of land in the Akamas peninsula and developers appealed to the Court against the government refusal to grant them a permission to build. The Court dismissed the argument of the appellants that the refusal violates their right to enjoy their property. According to the Court the appellants remain the owners of the land in question irrespective of the limitations on development. They are free to make use of their property as long as their activities are in harmony with the natural environment and within the restrictions imposed by the law.

In 1995 the World Bank following an earlier request by the Cyprus Government, produced a Conservation Management Plan for Akamas. This report was financed by the World Bank the EU and the UNDP.[13] The Plan classifies specific areas into areas to be strictly protected, areas where some agriculture is allowed and areas for mild development. Also in 1997 the Standing Committee of the Bern Convention on the European Wildlife and Natural Habitats of the Council of Europe issued a series of recommendations, asking the Republic of Cyprus to inter alia, declare the peninsula a national park.[14]

The Council of Ministers of Cyprus decision of 2000 on the Management Plan of the Akamas Penisnula, designated an area for the proposed national park which was smaller than the area mentioned in the report of the World Bank.

In recent years the ecological Non Governmental Organizations (NGOs) have been conducting a campaign to secure the appropriate management scheme for the Akamas penisnula. They have been lobbying Members of the European Parliament and have found support from the EU in their efforts. A year after the Council of Ministers decision, the Joint Parliamentary Commission in its resolution on Akamas urged the government to adopt the Management Plan of the World Bank and to give special emphasis on the Habitats Directive, the Berne Convention and the Rio Convention.[15]

Currently the government is about to adopt a comprehensive management plan, which will foster effective protection and will take account of the needs of the local communities. Mainly it purports to: outlaw any kind of development in designated areas, rehabilitate the environment, set out strict conditions for all legal development and shift the development inland as opposed to the coastal areas. At the same time the living conditions of the local communities will be improved with publicly funded projects and they will not be excluded from the possibility of engaging in profitable activities, such as agro tourism and environmentally friendly agriculture.

In view of the date of final accession coming closer one would expect that any plan adopted now will be in line with the acquis and with the country's international obligations.

Biotechnology

This area was new for Cyprus and there was no legislative framework to comprehensively regulate release of genetically modified organisms (GMOs) into the environment.

This field is concerned with regulating: a) the cultivation of genetically modified crops, b) placing on the market of food and food ingredients produced from genetically modified organisms like plants or other organisms or which contain such organisms and c) the contained use of genetically modified micro organisms. The objective of the acquis is to lay down the conditions for the deliberate release of GMOs into the environment for the purposes of protecting human health and the environment. This is also the case with regard to the contained use of micro organisms. The placing on the market of food containing GMOs is subject to requirements concerning public health, environmental safety and promoting consumer choice through labelling.

Genetically modified organisms are the result of gene splicing, the combination of DNA from one organism to another.[16] Combining genes from different organisms is known as recombinant DNA technology and the resulting organism is said to be genetically modified. GM products include medicines and vaccines, food and food ingredients.[17] There is no agreement between scientists that GMOs are completely safe for consumption. The ecologists world wide and particularly in the EU are opposed to the use of GMOs and the same position was taken by the NGOs and the green party in Cyprus.

The concerns of the NGOs were thoroughly discussed before the enactment of the law drafted for the purpose of transposing the provisions of Directive 2001/18/EC on Genetically Modified Organisms. The law aims to protect the environment and human health when there is deliberate release of GMOs into the environment or when placing on the market products containing GMOs. The green party and the environmental NGOs, opposed this law and demanded that Cyprus be excluded by way of a derogation from the Directive.

The aim of the Cyprus Green Party is to declare Cyprus a GMO free zone. Their arguments which are similar to those of other green parties in the European Union refer mainly to the risks to human health and the risks to the environment, such as the risk of cross pollination and the serious risks to the biological diversity of Cyprus. It is also argued that it will be hard for farmers and food processors to sustain purity of seeds and segregation of processed GM and non GM food.

The position adopted by the government was to proceed with the law not only for the purpose of harmonization but also to set up a legal framework to regulate this area of biotechnology. This line of thinking was also adopted by some NGOs of the ecologist movement who nevertheless scrutinized the draft law and proposed many changes such as providing for effective information of and active consultation with the public. The Parliamentary Committee on environment engaged in the difficult task of accommodating as far as possible the demands of the environmentalist movement. One should bear in mind that the law was drafted in order to transpose Directive 2001/18/EC and therefore, there is very limited room for adjusting the legislation to local needs.

The outcome was to produce a law which in some ways is more prohibitive than the Directive. The procedures for approval of placing GM products on the market or for the deliberate release into the environment are the same as those spelled out in the Directive. However, the parameters are stricter, especially in relation to the proximity of GM crops to sensitive areas or wetlands.

While these parameters might protect native plants in the short run, given the small size of the island, there seems to be a strong case for concern with regard to contamination of fields with native crops. It is also fair to say that in spite of regulating the deliberate release of GM organisms, the use of GM crops might eventually affect the biodiversity. Assuming that many Cypriot farmers will be using GM plants and less local varieties then there is a chance of decreasing the biodiversity of Cypriot plants which have been adapted to local conditions for centuries. However, these questions, namely what is the effect to the endemic plants and the speed with which they will be affected, are beyond the scope of this chapter.

In order to make an informed opinion one should also examine the benefits of GM organisms and products. The yields from GM crops are usually higher and at the same time they can contribute to a decrease in pollution as they require the use of less pesticides and insecticides. GM crops may improve the quality and health benefits of plants by increasing the protein, mineral and vitamin content in some crops which naturally have a deficiency in these ingredients. Such an increase will improve the public health in countries where the population consumes an unbalanced diet, for example, population consuming a lot of corn may have a deficiency of protein and incorporating genes that increase protein content of corn will greatly benefit corn consumers in Central and South America. Likewise consumers of rice in Asia will benefit from the incorporation of genes that will increase the concentration of beta-carotene (a precursor of vitamin A) and iron.[18]

Surely a balanced policy that considers risks and benefits, that will enable both to reap the fruits of this scientific new technology and attempt to reduce possible risks is the right policy. Unfortunately commercial considerations blur the issue in a way that might jeopardise the long term benefits of producers and consumers.

Genetic modification is also a powerful tool to develop new medicines and vaccines. It is virtually very difficult not to deal with this field at least on a scientific and technological level. Thus it is important for legislation to keep up with the advances of technology and set up the appropriate regulatory frameworks.

Horizontal legislation

Access to information

The adoption of the law on Freedom of Access to Environmental Information,[19] harmonizing the national legislation with the Environmental Information Directive[20] is a very positive development, enhancing the position of the individual vis-á-vis the administration. It increases transparency and contributes to the participation of individuals and the civil society in environmental issues. It should be noted that before the enactment of this law, citizens who requested information on government decisions relating to the environment were requested to show a vested interest in the matter.

The law imposes a general obligation on all government departments to keep record of information on their decisions and actions so that they are easily accessible to the public. The various departments are under the obligation to have the necessary facilities for the public to apply for and receive any kind of information. The law also provides for the publication of a state of the environment report every two years.

While the transposition of the Environmental Information Directive was the first step in this direction, the most notable development in this field is the ratification of the Aarhus Convention on Access to Information and Justice.[21] The Convention aims to (a) enhance public awareness to information, (b) develop participation in decision-making concerning the environment and (c) extend access to justice to any person who considers that his/her request for information under the Convention has been ignored, or wrongfully refused, etc.

It is foreseeable that this Convention will have a significant impact in reshaping the position of the individual, the civil society and the public at large before the executive and the judiciary. It will be interesting to see whether the participation of the public in plans, programmes and policies relating to the environment will lead to any substantial changes in the process leading to and in the context of decisions. Public participation will certainly increase the legitimacy of these decisions. This will in turn have a positive effect in their implementation as by and large environmental law requires the active contribution of the public for its correct application.

Regarding access to justice, article 9 (2) of the Convention grants members of the public the right to a review procedure before a court of law to 'challenge the substantive and procedural legality of any decision, act or omission .... where so provided for under national law',[22] as long as they have a sufficient interest or maintain impairment of a right. As for what constitutes 'sufficient interest and impairment of a right' this 'shall be determined in accordance with the requirements of national law and consistently with the objective of giving the public concerned wide access to justice within the scope of this Convention'. The Convention also grants this right to ecological NGOs. For the purposes of Article 9 (2) (a) and (b), the interest of NGOs 'promoting environmental protection and meeting any requirement under national law'[23] shall be deemed to be sufficient.

This will probably expand the scope of action of the ecological movement in Cyprus. In the absence of any law granting the public at large or the NGOs in particular, a right to challenge decisions of the the administration on environmental matters, the High Court has been quite reluctant in recognizing such a right to NGOs or other associations. According to the case law of the High Court of Cyprus, organizations that have the protection of the environment as one of their objectives and purposes in their founding document are not granted a vested interest to challenge administrative/executive decisions under article 146 of the Constitution.[24] In the case of *The Local Community of Pyrgos v The Republic*,[25] the High Court recognised the right of the local community to a review procedure under article 146 for issues related to the environment in the specific geographical area of the community in question but did not grant such a right to any association/organization. In order to recognize a vested interest to the local community, the Court resorted to Article 7.1 of the Constitution which safeguards the right to life and physical integrity. The Court also indicated that Article 9 which safeguards the right to a decent existence could arguably provide the basis for challenging decisions that influence the environment in which the individual lives and therefore might affect his/her health.

It is interesting to note that the Court seems to be determined to go a long way to hear cases on environmental issues. However, it is calling for a broader legal basis that will enable it to do so. This was clearly stated by the Court in the decision on appeal of the above mentioned case: 'We indicate that the issue of the environment has acquired internationally and in Cyprus huge importance and that its protection is directly related to the high quality of life of the individual. It is therefore necessary that an environmental policy be adopted which will be expressed by means of the relevant legislation'.[26]

In spite of the gaps in the legislation, the High Court concluded in the case of *ETEK v The Republic*,[27] that legal persons of public law or groups of people whose objectives include the protection of the environment are entitled to claim a vested interest in environmental matters. The Court having clarified that the Constitution does not provide for an actio popularis, and that defending the public interest in a rightful public practice is not a sufficient ground to challenge an act/decision, it went on to say that: 'The issues that affect the environment and the quality of life, affect a much bigger group than the one that is directly affected *from the act in question*... Intrusions into the environment which adversely affect a very large group of people create a vested interest and give to various natural and legal persons the right to claim such an interest...'. This decision could arguably strengthen the role of the environmental movement and anticipate the changes that will now come about following the ratification of the Aarhus Convention. However any speculation into that direction is futile since the decision on the vested interest of a legal person of public law or of other associations was reversed on appeal.

Concerning this question, the Court's decision on appeal was as follows: An association cannot have in relation to the environment a status that is superior to that of the individual. Neither the fact that an association comprises of a number of individuals nor its constitutional document can confer to it rights that are not enjoyed by individuals. A general right would lead to an acknowledgment of an actio popularis. On the other hand a vested interest can be recognized for a neighbor assuming that his/her living conditions and right to property are affected by the act/decision in question.[28] In view of the Court's decision it is expected that interesting developments will occur following the ratification of the Convention. At the moment it does not form part of the acquis but there is a general understanding that it will soon be ratified by the EU.

Environmental impact assessment

The Environmental Impact Assessment Directive has been transposed into the Cypriot legal system by way of a new law.[29] This law rectifies the weaknesses of the old system concerning assessments of environmental impact. According to a 1991 Decision of the Council of Ministers of the Republic the procedure followed before the adoption of the law had as follows:[30] With regard to the projects listed in the Annex (private and large public projects), a preliminary environmental assessment (PEA) was submitted to the Town Planning Authority which in turn, forwarded it to the Environment Service of the Ministry of Agriculture, Natural Resources and the Environment. A technical committee chaired by the Environment Service examined the PEA and a decision was reached, which could be one of the following:

i. the PEA was approved and sent back to the Town Planning
ii. further information or a full EIA was required
iii. the PEA was not approved and the Technical Committee's suggestion was for the project not to be implemented.

The weakness of the old system was that the role of the Environment Service and of the technical committee was purely consultative. The Town Planning Authority (a department of the Interior Ministry) was not bound by their decision.

Under the new law, whenever there is a disagreement between the Town Planning Authority and the Environment Service, the matter is taken to a committee comprised of the minister of agriculture, natural resources and the environment and the minister of interior. If these two cannot reach an agreement the matter is forwarded to the Council of Ministers for a final decision.

Concluding remarks

The environmental acquis consists of sophisticated legislation, the underlying objective of which is the prevention and the reduction of pollution caused by traditional and high tech activities – even though the distinction between the two is eroding as the former is becoming industrialized at a swift pace.

The measures to be adopted will bring about drastic improvements to the quality of life of the citizen. The environmental acquis deals with such diverse issues as town planning, organization of industrial units, fuel quality, storage of petrol and distribution terminals, protection of the marine environment, preservation of the fauna and flora, deforestation, as well as nuclear safety. It is apparent that in the context of environmental protection, member states are delegating a substantial part of their sovereignty to Brussels. This may prove to be very beneficial especially for the environment and the citizens of the southern European states where environmental protection was often ignored for the sake of economic development.

Acceding countries are also beginning to realize that when applying environmental law or other Community policies they are being monitored not just by their own citizens but by the wider European public. In the case of Cyprus, this promotes environmental protection in many ways.

The pressure exercised by the Commission as well as the European Parliament on the Cyprus Government to complete the harmonization and implementation process has proven to be a very useful tool for the Government itself. The Government has successfully gathered the political consensus needed to proceed with projects that otherwise would have taken years to be realized.

The adaptations made to the environmental policies are expected to bring forth-immeasurable benefits resulting from a higher quality of life and long needed improvements and technological solutions for the environment and the population of Cyprus.

Notes

1. I would like to thank Michalis Raftopoulos, Nicoletta Ioannou, Elena Papageorgiou and Amy Klem for their generous assistance and Christina Pantazi for her critical reading of this chapter.
2. In 1982 63.6% of the population were living in urban agglomerations, in 1992 the number was 67.7% and in 1999 it was 69.9%. In the last two years (2001 and 2002) the numbers seemed to be stable.
3. For more on administrative reform for the purpose of applying the European environmental law see: Christoph Demmke, *Towards effective environmental regulation: Innovative approaches in Implementing and Enforcing European Environmental Law and Policy*, European Institute of Public Administration, October 2000.
4. Directive 1999/32/EC on the landfill of waste.
5. Birds Directive 79/409/EEC.
6. Habitats Directive 92/43/EEC.
7. See *http://europe.eu.int/comm/environment/nature_biodiverity/index_en.htm.*
8. The Protection and Management of Nature and Wild Life law and The Protection and Management of Wild Birds and Game Law. These laws have only been adopted very recently and their numbers of publication are not yet available.

9. The competent authority for the implementation of the law transposing the Habitats directive is the Ministry of Agriculture, Natural Resources and the Environment, whereas the competent authority under the law transposing the Wild Birds directive is the Ministry of Interior.
10. Convention on the Conservation of European Wildlife and Natural Habitats, Bern, 1979.
11. See the report of the Cyprus Conservation Foundation at: http://www.conservation.org.cy/akamas/akamas_history.htm.
12. Demetriades and Others v Council of Ministers, 1029/1985.
13. Conservation Management Plan for the Akamas Peninsula 'Mediterranean Environmental Technical Assistance Programme, World Bank, UNDP, September 1995.
14. Recommendation No.63 on the conservation of the Akamas peninsula, Cyprus, and, in particular nesting beaches of Caretta caretta and Chelonia mydas, 'Council of Europe-Standing Committee, Convention on the Conservation of European Wildlife and Natural Habitats', 1997.
15. Resolution on Akamas, 19th meeting of the EU-Cyprus Joint Parliamentary Committee, March 2001.
16. See http://sciencefairtopic.com/life_sciences/sf-GENETICS.htm.
17. See www.ornl.gov/sci/techresources/Human_Genome/elsi/gmfood.shtml.
18. Ibid.
19. Freedom of Access to Information Law 125(I) 2000.
20. Access to Information Directive Directive 90/313/EEC.
21. UN/ECE Convention on Access to Information, Public participation in decision making and access to Justice in Environmental matters, Aarhus, Denmark, 1998.
22. Ibid, Article 9 (2)(b).
23. Ibid, Article 2 (5).
24. Article 146 of the Constitution of the Republic of Cyprus grants the right to any individual to make a complaint to the Supreme Constitutional Court for a decision, an act or omission of any organ, authority or person exercising any executive or administrative authority which is contrary to the Constitution or made in excess of powers. Such a recourse may be made only by a person whose any existing legitimate interest was adversely and directed affected.
25. *Community of Pyrgos v The Republic*, 1991 4 AAΔ 3498
26. *The Republic v The Local Community of Pyrgos*, (1996), 3 AAΔ 503, p.508.
27. *ETEK v The Republic* 358/96.
28. *Thanos Club Hotels Ltd v Επιστημονικού Τεχνικού Επιμελητηρίου Κύπρου, AE* 2710.
29. The Environmental Impact Assessment Law 57(I)2000.
30. Council of Ministers, 'Decision on an Integrated System for Environmental Impact Assessment' (1991).

7 Harmonization with the Acquis Relating to EMU and Free Movement of Capital

ALEXIA KALISPERA

Introduction

January 1, 1999 is considered a landmark and a historic event in the process of European integration, as it was the date when the third and final stage of EMU was launched and its common currency the Euro was born, in an accounting form,[1] with fixed and irrevocable bilateral exchange rates with the national currencies of the participating countries.[2] This monumental development, which has no parallel in history, builds upon the already achieved progress in strengthening political, economic and monetary ties within the EU and provides, *inter alia*, for unified monetary and exchange rate policies and for the replacement of national currencies with a single common currency. There is no doubt, that the impact of this momentous change is not confined within the Union but beyond the latter's boundaries: new member states such as Cyprus, are affected by EMU and free movement of capital not only in terms of experiencing a direct economic impact through economic linkages, but also in terms of having to reform and adjust their structural and macroeconomic policies with the ultimate goals of meeting the Maastricht criteria.[3]

The Copenhagen Council concluded that membership requires that a '...candidate country has the ability to take on the obligations of membership, including adherence to the aims of political, economic and monetary union'. Within this context, there are no possible opt-out clauses from any obligations given to new member states. Thus, accession to the EU means acceptance of the EMU acquis and ultimately the adoption of the Euro when new member states have reached the required and necessary state of readiness (i.e. the Maastricht criteria for Eurozone membership).

Treaty provisions leading to the adoption of the Euro apply only to member states. This means that candidate countries must first join the EU, i.e. become full member states, and then be eligible for the adoption of the Euro. In fact, for reasons of procedure and substance they are not supposed to join the Euro upon accession. Consequently, no transitional period for the adoption of the Euro needs to be negotiated. However, the Accession Treaty may deal with the practical and technical modalities of adopting the Euro or provide for a derogation. In any case, upon accession, a new member state is required to prepare actively to fulfil all EMU obligations. According to the Treaty, following the assessment of the attainment of a high degree of sustainable convergence, the new member state will either continue to have a derogation or will fulfil the necessary conditions for the adoption of the Euro.

The financial sector in Cyprus, is steadily proceeding on the path of modernization and deregulation, with a view to adapting timely and smoothly the aquis in this area. With emphasis on the harmonization of the Cyprus laws and practices with the EMU and Capital movements acquis, this chapter will focus on the changes in the laws, the difficulties encountered in the process and the implications emanating from the transposition of the aquis.

The EMU acquis

Three distinct preparatory phases on the adoption of EMU acquis can be identified, namely: (i) pre-accession phase, covering the period up to accession; (ii) accession phase, covering the period from accession up to the adoption of the single currency; and (iii) final Euro phase, with the adoption of the Euro. Each one of the phases entails a specific acquis.

Pre-accession phase

During this phase, candidate countries must carry out the economic reforms needed to fulfil the Copenhagen economic criteria, requiring the existence of a functioning market economy and the capacity to cope with competitive pressure and market forces within the Union. Specific parts of the EMU acquis which need to be implemented are, the completion of the orderly liberalization of capital movements; prohibition of any direct public sector financing by the central bank of a member state and of privileged access of the public sector to financial institutions; alignment of the statute of the national central bank with the relevant Treaty provisions and the Statute of the European System of Central Banks (ECSB).[4]

Accession phase

During this phase, new member states participate in EMU with a derogation and have to comply with Title VI of the Treaty which includes the following obligations: adherence to the aims of economic and monetary union; treatment of exchange rate policy as a matter of common interest and eventually, participation in Community procedures; avoidance of excessive government deficits and adherence to the relevant provisions of the stability and growth pact; further adaptation of the national central bank's statutes, with a view to integration in the ESCB, progress towards the fulfilment of the Maastricht convergence criteria.

Final Euro phase

Participation of new member states in the Eurozone will be decided upon compliance with the conditions for the adoption of the single currency, following the assessment of the attainment of a high degree of sustainable convergence. Fulfiling the Maastricht nominal convergence criteria will be the final key to open, full participation in the Eurozone. It should be clarified though, that his does not mean that the convergence criteria are of no significance for the acceding countries. In due time, their participation in the Eurozone will be judged on the basis of these criteria and, therefore, the acceding countries should take the convergence criteria as medium-term references for their stability-oriented macroeconomic policies.

In general, the EMU acquis is governed by Article 3a and Title VI (Article 102a to 109m) of the Treaty and by relevant implementing legislation. It consists mainly of Treaty provisions and protocols, Regulations and Decisions that do not require transposition into national legislation. However, what requires adaptation is the statute of the national central bank of a member state (even a member state with a derogation) to be made compatible with the provisions of the Treaty and the Statute of the ECSB. As it was mentioned before, Treaty provisions relating to the adoption of the Euro do not apply to member states with a derogation.[5]

Moreover, it is worth mentioning, that according to paragraph 2(a) of Article 109e of the Treaty, a pre-condition for EMU participation is the compliance with the acquis on free movement of capital.

Convergence of laws in EMU related issues[6]

According to the Treaty, a member state is either a member state that has adopted the Euro or a 'member state with a derogation'. Cyprus will participate in EMU with the status of a country with a derogation, from the date of accession, and will have to act in accordance with the objective of adopting the Euro. As a result, Cyprus will need to implement the necessary changes to its institutional and legal framework.

Regarding the administrative capacity in the field of EMU, the infrastructures responsible are: the Ministry of Finance, the Central Bank of Cyprus (CBC) and the Planning Bureau. For an overview of alignment with the acquis, three broad sectors can be identified, namely: (i) fiscal policy and economic policy co-ordination; (ii) monetary policy; and (iii) exchange rate policy. It must be noted, however, that legislative adjustments have been made only in relation to monetary policy.

Fiscal policy and economic policy co-ordination

A five-years Strategic Development Plan 1999-2003 is followed – based on the EU's broad economic policy guidelines – aiming towards full compliance with the convergence criteria.[7] Cyprus has adopted the methodology required by the acquis as far as the compilation of fiscal accounts is concerned. In particular, the finances of local authorities have been incorporated in the consolidated fiscal accounts. Previously, the methodology followed was that of the IMF Manual.

Monetary policy

The CBC, in an attempt to modernize the operational framework of monetary policy and adjust to EU norms, has moved away from the use of direct instruments for controlling liquidity in the economy in favour of market-based tools. More specifically, the liquidity ratio was abolished and replaced by reverse transactions as the primary tool for liquidity management. In addition, minimum reserve requirements were reduced significantly and two standing facilities aiming at providing and absorbing overnight liquidity were introduced (a lombard-type short term facility and an overnight deposit facility[8]). Divergences[9] existing in this area concern Central Bank independence, Central Bank financing of the government as well as a fixed legal interest rate ceiling. Specifically, legal adjustments were made in the following areas.

Interest rate regime Until 31 December 2000, Cyprus had a ceiling on interest rates of 9% per annum, stipulated by Law No.2/1977. This anachronistic legislation was imposed at a time when the economy and the financial system were underdeveloped, aiming to protect the public from exploitation by money lenders. This regime, constituted one of the major distortions in the financial system and contrasted starkly with the acquis which requires a system of flexible interest rates varying in accordance with changing economic conditions. As a consequence of the inflexible interest rate structure, money and capital markets have not developed and the financing of government from the private sector on market-related terms was limited. Consequently, the government had to rely heavily on financing from the CBC. The Law liberalizing interest rates was enacted in December 1999 and came into force on 1 January 2001. The main provisions of the new Law are the following:

- repeal of the 1977 Interest Rate Law
- the obligation of credit institutions for transparency on the interest rate charged and the way interest and other charges are calculated and collected
- interest capitalization is restricted to a maximum of twice a year
- transitional provision (which ended on 31 December, 2002) which provided for a safeguard clause relating to the existing housing loans of middle/lower income-group debtors. More specifically, debtors with existing housing loans up to the amount of CY£60,000, had the choice between a variable interest rate and a fixed interest rate of 9%.

The abolition of the obsolete interest rate ceiling will allow for the full liberalization of the Cypriot financial sector and its adaptation to the acquis. It will promote modern money and capital markets, contribute towards a more flexible and efficient monetary policy implementation and exert a beneficial impact on economic efficiency.

CBC credit to the government According to the CBC Laws of 1963-2000 (thereafter referred to as 'CBCL'), the CBC may grant advances and credit facilities to the government. More specifically, the CBC may:

- grant direct advances, up to a limit of 34% of the estimated budget revenue of the government, for the financial year during which the advance is to be made
- purchase negotiable treasury bills, maturing not later than twelve months from the date of the acquisition by the Bank, up to a limit of 39% of the estimated budget revenue of the government
- buy and sell government and government guaranteed securities, which have been publicly offered for sale, provided that the total amount of such securities owned by the CBC does not exceed a limit of 20% of the total sight liabilities of the CBC (plus a fixed sum of 5.6 millions)
- buy and sell fixed term securities which have been publicly offered for sale by public and private corporations up to a limit of 5% of the total liabilities of the CBC

Since 1994, the government has followed a policy of gradual reduction of the above limits in line with the relevant Treaty provisions, especially Article 101 of the Treaty and Article 21(1) of the Statute of the ECSB, which prohibits the central bank of a member state from giving credit or any overdraft facility to its government or to any other body governed by public law. According to the relevant provision in the new legislation of the CBC,[10] financing of the government by the CBC is prohibited and all existing outstanding claims of the CBC on the public sector (i.e. all claims existing at the date of entry into force of the new law), will be converted into long-term debt under market terms. Even though there has been a gradual reduction of borrowing limits, the effect of such a provision in the legislation means that the public sector will be deprived of a very important source of financing and, consequently, it will have to turn to the private sector.

Prohibition of privileged access of public authorities to financial institutions Neither the government nor any other body governed by public law has privileged access to any financial institution. The obligation of insurance companies to invest at least 20% of their investible funds in government securities, as an approved investment[11] has been abolished as of 1998. Thus, in essence harmonization has been achieved.

Central Bank independence The CBC was set-up in 1963, three years after the establishment of the Republic of Cyprus, as a public corporate body, autonomous from the government and governed by its own law. Its Board of Directors consists of, the Governor, the Deputy-Governor and five Directors who are appointed by the Council of Ministers for a period of five years. According to section 15(1) of the CBCL, the Governor is the chief executive officer of the CBC and carries out the policy of the CBC, with power to act on all matters which are not reserved for the Board of Directors.

Even though in practice the CBC is virtually independent in its decision making, a number of provisions of this law, as well as certain provisions of the Constitution, limit considerably the degree of statutory independence enjoyed by the CBC. In fact, the degree of dependence of the CBC from the executive power is extensive. This dependence is expressed within the powers of the President of the Republic, the Council of Ministers and the Minister of Finance.

The CBCL need substantial amendments primarily in relation to the issue of independence and prohibition of monetary financing of the public sector. The principle of the independence of a national central bank is expressly referred to in Article 107 of the Treaty and Article14(2) of the Statute. More specifically, Article 107 contains a prohibition on attempts to influence the ECB, a national central bank or the members of their decision-making bodies and Article 14(2) provides for security of tenure for such members. The European Monetary Institute (EMI)[12] has established a list of features enhancing central bank independence, namely, features of an institutional, personal and financial nature.

Regarding institutional independence, what is considered incompatible with the Treaty and/or the Statute – and thus requires adaptation – are provisions in the law of a central bank which (a) give rights to third parties (e.g. government and Parliament) to give instructions to their central bank or their decision-making bodies; (b) approve, suspend, annul or defer decisions of their central bank; (c) censor their central bank's decisions on legal grounds; (d) participate in the decision – making bodies of their central bank with a right to vote; (e) be consulted (*ex ante*) on their central bank's decisions.

Regarding personal independence, the law of a national central bank must ensure three things:

- that the Governor is not dismissed for reasons other than those mentioned in Article 14(2) of the Statute (i.e. if he/she no longer fulfils the conditions required for the performance of his/her duties or if he/she has been guilty of serious misconduct)

- that other members of the decision-making bodies of a central bank involved in the performance of ESCB-related tasks have the same security of tenure as governors
- that no conflicts of interest will arise, between the duties of members of the decision-making bodies of a national central bank and other functions, which members of the decision making bodies involved in the performance of ESCB – related tasks may perform and which may jeopardize their personal independence

Finally, financial independence requires that a national central bank should avail itself of the appropriate financial means to fulfil its mandate.

In order to enhance the statutory independence of the CBC, a new law repealing the old one was enacted, taking into account all the above features, so as to comply with the relevant requirements of the Treaty and the Statute and came into force on 5 July 2002. At the same time, and for the same reasons, the relevant articles of the Constitution had to be amended. To this end, the Fourth Amendment of the Constitution Law of 2002 came into force ensuring a fully independent CBC.

The amendments in the Constitution concern mainly the following:

- Amendment of Article 118(3) which provides that the Governor may be a member of the permanent public service and thus shows a degree of dependency on the government;
- Amendment of Article 118 (4) which provides that the President of the Republic has the power to terminate, at any time, the appointment of the Governor – ensuring that it is not the same person who appoints him and terminates his appointment. With the amendment of this Article, the Council of the Supreme Court shall have the exclusive competence to terminate the Governor's appointment on the grounds prescribed in the law of the CBC (Article 153(8) of the Constitution);
- Article 118(5), which stipulates that if the Governor was, immediately before such termination, a member of the permanent public service he shall be given other suitable post in the permanent public service, has been abolished;
- Article 119(4) of the Constitution, which provides that the Governor shall, with regard to the financial policy relating to his office, carry out the decisions of the Council of Ministers in this respect and the provisions of any law and, with regard to the manner of the carrying

out of such policy, he shall consult and be guided by the advice of the Minister of Finance has also been abolished. Again, in this way, institutional independence will be ensured.

The above provisions have been amended so as to avoid any direct influence of the government towards the decision-making bodies. Besides, an independent Central Bank is in a better position to fulfil its mandate with enhanced credibility and effectiveness.

Exchange rate policy:

The Cyprus pound has been unilaterally linked to the Euro as from 1 January 1999 with a fluctuation margin of ±2,25% from its central rate,[13] whereas in the period from June 1992 to December 1998 it was pegged to the ECU at the same central rate and narrow bands. This link was successfully maintained and has served well the objective of a stable currency policy, which cushioned inflationary pressures and enhanced credibility in the efforts of achieving convergence with the EU. Cyprus intention is to participate in the Exchange Rate Mechanism 2 (ERM 2)[14] as from the date of its accession and enter the Eurozone within two years after accession.

Convergence in free movement of capital issues[15]

The Cypriot financial system has been operating for many years under a regime of widespread exchange restrictions in a way isolated from the global financial markets. The movement of capital to or from Cyprus is primarily governed by the Exchange Control Law (Cap199 and Law No.53 of 1972). Under this Law, permission of the Minister of Finance – in his capacity as Financial Secretary – is required for payments by residents to non-residents as well as for the registration of domestic securities in the name of non-residents and some other international transactions. However, it must be clarified, that the powers vested in the Minister of Finance, by virtue of this law, are exercised by the CBC which has been authorized to act on his behalf.

In January 1991, current payments were liberalized through acceptance of the obligations arising out of Article VIII of the IMF Agreement. Since then, capital movements have been gradually liberalized through directives issued by the CBC under the Exchange Control Law. The liberalization measures concerned particularly the fields of direct[16] and portfolio investments (both inward and outward) and a number of personal capital movements, including gifts, inheritances and transfer of emigrants' funds.

The liberalization of capital movements is carried out in accordance with a plan of action submitted to the Commission. The plan is divided into three phases.

The First Phase, which was completed by 31 March 1999, included the following liberalization measures: abolition of restrictions on the use of credit cards for current payments abroad; liberalization of agreements concerning payment of royalties (patents, designs, trade marks and inventions by residents to non-residents); introduction of a more liberal policy on inward and outward direct investments; increase in the limits on non-resident participation in the issued capital of companies listed in the Cyprus Stock Exchange; partial liberalization of investments in foreign stock exchanges by resident investment companies, listed in the Cyprus Stock Exchange, and by resident insurance companies; abolition of restrictions on the transfer by non-residents of the proceeds from the sale of real estate acquired by the payment with foreign exchange; abolition of restrictions on the transfer of funds which were previously imported in Cyprus and converted into local funds by Cypriot repatriates who decide to emigrate again; relaxation of restrictions on the following personal capital movements: gifts and endowments granted by residents to non residents; transfer of local funds inherited by non-residents; transfer of local funds of residents in the event of emigration; maintenance of foreign currency accounts with domestic banks by more categories of residents.

The Second Phase which was completed by the end of year 2000, included the liberalization of medium-term and long term borrowing by residents in foreign currencies; liberalization of direct investments in Cyprus by residents of member states (not including investments in real estate); liberalization of portfolio investments (in capital market securities) in Cyprus by residents of member states; liberalization of direct investments abroad by residents; abolition of block accounts; liberalization of borrowing in local currency by non-residents who are economically active in Cyprus as well as by resident firms which are owned wholly or partly by non-residents and are engaged in local activities.

The Third Phase is to be completed by accession and includes: liberalization of portfolio investments in Cyprus by residents of third countries; liberalization of portfolio investments abroad by residents, initially for institutional investors and subsequently for any other persons;

liberalization of investments in real estate abroad by residents; liberalization of loans granted by residents to non-residents; free maintenance of accounts by residents with foreign financial institutions; removal of restrictions on the physical export of money and any remaining exchange control restrictions.

More specifically, (from 1 January 2000 up to 1 January 2001) direct and portfolio investments in Cyprus, from EU residents, as well as direct investments abroad by residents of Cyprus, have been liberalized. Restrictions on the repatriation of proceeds from real estate sales, by non-residents, have also been lifted. Under the previous regime, part of such proceeds had to be deposited in blocked accounts, and could not immediately be transferred abroad. In fact, transfers abroad from blocked accounts were limited to CY£50,000 per year. As of 1 January 2001 blocked accounts have been abolished and as a result, these funds will be transferable abroad. Cypriots are now allowed to borrow on a medium and long term basis, in foreign currencies, from banks in Cyprus or abroad. In addition, domestic banks are authorized to grant loans and credits in local currency to non-residents to finance their activities in Cyprus.

On 10 July 2003, a new framework law (the Capital Movement Law of 2003) was enacted by the House of Representatives with a provision of entry into force on the date of accession to the EU. In particular, the new law will repeal the Exchange Control Law, with effect upon accession and provide for the complete liberalization of capital movements and payments between residents and EU residents and between residents and residents of third countries, subject to certain safeguard clauses.

On 4 August 2003, the CBC lifted a number of exchange control restrictions on capital movements and payments. It abolished the 50% ceiling on the participation of non-residents in the share capital of domestic banks listed on the Cyprus Stock Exchange. The remaining quantitative limits have been abolished. The CBC also abolished certain procedural requirements for the following capital movements whereby its authorization was needed:

- transfer abroad by non residents of the proceeds of sale of real estate in Cyprus that was not acquired by payments in foreign exchange;
- transfer abroad by non-residents of fee proceeds of sale of securities listed on the Cyprus Stock Exchange;
- prepayments for the imports of goods;
- personal capital movements, gifts and endowments (including

dowries), inheritances and legacies, and transfers of emigrants' funds;
- cash withdrawals abroad through credit of debit cards held by residents.

Moreover, the CBC simplified the procedures applicable for current transactions, by abolishing all remaining requirements for the verification of genuineness by the CBC in the case of certain transactions exceeding indicative amounts.

On 5 August 2003, direct investments abroad by residents were fully liberalized. The remaining exchange control restrictions concerning portofolio investments abroad by residents (other than banks and insurance companies, which are not subject to exchange control restrictions) and investment in real estate abroad by residents are to be abolished by accession to the EU. Very few types of capital transactions are still subject to restrictions but will also be fully liberalized upon accession.

An area which has encountered difficulties in transposing the acquis concerns investments in real estate on national territory by non-residents. Under the Immovable Property Acquisition (Aliens) Law, foreign natural or legal persons and Cypriot companies under foreign control, cannot acquire immovable property in Cyprus, otherwise than by inheritance, except with the approval of the Council of Ministers. Approval may be granted for the acquisition of real estate by a non-resident, for residential, professional, commercial or industrial purposes. Non-residents of Cypriot origin do not need approval of the Council of Ministers. On 5 June 2003, a law amending the Immovable Property Acquisition (Aliens) Law was enacted, with a provision for entry into force upon accession which provides for the abolition of restrictions on investments in real estate in Cyprus, by EU natural or legal persons, except for the acquisition of secondary residences. With respect to the latter, Cyprus has been granted a transitional period of five years. The justification of the request by the Cypriot side for a transitional period lays with the expected market distortion, the implied social effect that a substantial increase in demand and prices might cause, the small size of the island of Cyprus and the additional environment pressures and detrimental effects on the overall quality of life that may arise from the implied construction activity in order to satisfy part of the additional demand.

It must be stressed, that no restrictions will be imposed on EU residents for the acquisition of real estate linked to primary residence and foreign direct investment as well as on the acquisition of real estate by EU resident real estate agents and land developers. Finally, concerning the acquisition of real estate by residents of third countries, Cyprus will maintain its existing legislation.

Analytically, the relevant aquis comprises Treaty provisions (Articles 56-60), and four Directives: Article 56 of the Treaty provides that 'all restrictions on the movement of capital between member states and between member states and third countries shall be prohibited'. Cyprus's commitment to the EU is to abolish completely all restrictions on capital movements by the date of accession, with the exception of the acquisition of secondary residences. Directive 97/5/EC of the EP and the Council of 27 January 1997 on cross-border credit transfers[17] aims to improve and promote cross – border credit transfer services within the Community. Basically, what the Directive does, is to lay down minimum requirements and obligations for institutions executing cross border credit transfers.

Following the enactment of the Banking (Amendment) Law of 2000, which enables the CBC to issue mandatory instructions to banks on matters of banking practice, the CBC implemented the Directive by way of a new CBC directive on cross-border credit transfers issued to banks. The new CBC directive, which is in full conformity with the requirements of the relevant EU Directive, has entered into force on 1 April 2001, save for the provisions governing potential compensation payable by credit institutions, of delays or non-execution of the transfers, which will come into force at a later stage and in any case prior to accession. The harmonization with the EU Directive will have a positive impact in relation to remittances of personal capital movements (e.g. remittances to students in other member states) especially in terms of speed, reliability and cost.

Regarding Council Directive 91/308/EEC of 10 June 1991, on the prevention of the use of the financial system for the purpose of money laundering, Cyprus has a comprehensive anti-money laundering legislation in place, since 1996, through the enactment in that year of the Prevention and Suppression of Money Laundering Activities Law, which fully transposes the Council Directive. The Law applies to all types of businesses, domestic or international and provides for the establishment of a Unit for combating money laundering with investigative powers (MOKAS). A mandatory reporting of suspicious transactions to MOKAS is provided under the law, by all persons who are engaged in financial businesses, including lawyers and accountants, and obliges them to take the appropriate preventive measures (e.g. identification of customers, record keeping books). The Unit is composed of three Counsels of the

Republic from the Attorney General's Office, three police officers and three customs officers. The supervisory authorities are the following: (a) The CBC is the authority for all persons licensed to carry on banking business in or from Cyprus, as well as for international financial services companies operating through Cyprus; (b) The Securities and Exchange Commission, with regard to the Cyprus Stock Exchange; (c) The Superintendent of Co-operate Societies and Co-operative Development for the Co-operative Credit Societies and (d) The Superintendent of Insurance for insurance companies.

It is worth mentioning, that Cyprus has signed and ratified the Vienna Convention Against Illicit Traffic in Narcotics Drugs and Psychotropic Substances, and the Council of Europe Convention on Laundering, Search, Seizure and Confiscation of the Proceeds from Crime.

On the alignment with Directive 2001/97/EC on the prevention of the use of the financial system for the purpose of money laundering, 'the Prevention and Suppression of Money Laundering Activities (Amending) Law of 2003' was enacted by the House of Representatives on 25 July 2003, which provides among other provisions that accountants, auditors, and tax advisors, as well as lawyers, when engaged in the activities specified in the Directive, are required to take the preventive measures against money laundering, stipulated in chapter VIII of the basic law of 1996 (as amended).

Council Directive 98/26 of 11 June 1998, relating to the finality of settlement in payment and securities settlement systems covers payment and securities settlement systems of a domestic as well as of a cross-border nature. It is aimed at reducing systemic risks. It defines when transfer orders related to payments or securities become final and also establishes a legal framework for the cross-border provisions of collateral security. The Directive was transposed in the Cyprus legal system by 'the Finality of Settlement in Payment and Securities Settlement Systems Law of 2003' which will come into force by accession to the EU.

Concluding remarks

Cyprus appears to be in a position to implement the acquis with respect to EMU so that, by the date of accession, Cyprus legislation and practices in this area will be in line with EU requirements.

On the macroeconomic front, during 2002 and 2003 the economy of Cyprus experienced a slowdown, triggered by the unfavourable external environment, and most notably the aftermath of the September 11 events, the revived fear of international terrorism and the Iraqi war. The economic slowdown coupled with the effects of a comprehensive tax reform contributed significantly to a worsening of the fiscal accounts and the public sector deficit widened to 3.6% of the GDP in 2002 and an estimated 5.4% of GDP in 2003. Inflation was also on an uptrend reflecting mainly the effects of the increases in the VAT rate and in other indirect taxes. The government of Cyprus in its pre-accession economic programme of 2003 has included specific measures to lower the fiscal deficit and the public debt to levels below those prescribed in the convergence criteria, by 2006. Inflation is also expected decline to around 2% as from the next year.

Despite the costs and challenges involved, adopting the Euro is expected to bring significant benefits to Cyprus in the medium as well as the long term. The most obvious costs concern issuing new coins and notes and withdrawing the old ones. In addition, there are costs related to the technical adjustments that businesses have to go through. For example, there may be costs for business, especially in retailing, emanating from consumer confusion during the transitional period, stemming from the existence of dual pricing, in both Euro and the national currencies. However, there seems to be widespread agreement that these short-term costs are outweighted by the significant benefits the Euro will bring to the participating countries. In particular, the existence of a single currency has eliminated the exchange rate risk as well as currency conversion costs for transactions within the Eurozone. Moreover, the use of a single currency in the medium term will improve price transparency in the Eurozone, thus boosting competition for the benefit of the consumer. From a macroeconomic point of view, the introduction of the Euro is expected to be associated with economic stability. Likewise, the expected increase in economic stability and activity in the Eurozone countries will have positive spillover effects on its trade partners including Cyprus. Provided that economic activity in the countries of the Eurozone increases demand in these countries (including non-Eurozone countries like Cyprus) will also rise – the so-called 'trade creation' effect. Perhaps the most obvious benefit for Cyprus, from the introduction of the Euro, concerns tourism where simplification of transactions is expected to benefit the industry as a whole.

Regarding the challenges arising from the introduction of the Euro, Cyprus will have to work hard in order to make its economy resilient and adaptable to the changing and competitive international environment.

Cypriot goods or services destined for Eurozone member states will face intensified competition from within the Eurozone and thus a challenge will be given to the Cypriot markets to work towards offering better quality products in more competitive prices. Briefly put, Cyprus will have to progress with privatization and continue to reduce state involvement in the economy while dismantling monopolies, removing trade restraints and developing flexible labour markets.

In relation to the liberalization of capital movements, no particular problems are foreseen as Cyprus enjoys fairly stable macroeconomic conditions and efficient instruments for monetary policy instruments. In addition, banking institutions are financially sound and well capitalized. By lifting all barriers to capital flows the financial system of Cyprus stands to gain by ending its isolation from the global financial markets, in terms of modernization, efficiency and improved competitiveness. Businesses will be able to turn to new sources of funding at competitive terms while the domestic financial market will be enriched with new participants and new sophisticated financial instruments and techniques. Moreover, by opening up its financial sector, Cyprus will be promoted as a regional and international business centre. As liberalization proceeds, Cyprus will gradually enhance financial integration with the EU and this will result in greater convergence with EU financial policies and indicators. Under a liberalized environment, the financial system in Cyprus is expected to strengthen its robustness and become more competitive and efficient.

The EMU and free movement of capital constitute the peak of the development of the unification procedure in the economic evolution of Europe. The process of financial liberalization in Cyprus, which is necessary for adopting the acquis in this field, has prompted structural adjustments that will no doubt enhance the capacity of the Cypriot economy to take advantage of the substantial benefits from participating in the unified European markets and thus help sustain and even strengthen economic growth and welfare over the longer term.

Harmonization with the EU acquis in general, has not been an easy task. Being a completely new process to everybody with no experience on the field of harmonization, demanded a lot of studying both of the acquis and the relevant Cypriot legislation to be amended or abolished in order to conform with that of the EU. On many occasions the Cypriot side, committed itself in amending a law in order to conform with a Directive, whereas, in the end, a new specific law was needed to be drafted or even several pieces of laws affected by the EU Directive had to be amended. Particularly difficult was the amendment of the Constitution, the reason being that the Constitution is considered to be the supreme law[18] of the Republic and only articles that are not considered 'fundamental' may be amended, whether by way of variation, addition or repeal.[19] Such an amendment shall be made by a law passed by a majority vote comprising at least two-thirds of the total number of the members of Parliament, instead of the simple majority voting required for the passing of any other law.

From personal experience, when transposing a Directive into a legal system the best thing to do is to stick to the wording of the Directive, look at any relevant case law on the interpretation of terms that have ambiguous meanings or of a case challenged on the grounds of bad implementation of a Directive. From my point of view the 'copy-out' technique (*direct transposition*) is the safest! Of course, it is advisable to see what the other member states have done to implement a Directive, in other words the specific national measures taken. Looking up a Directive in more than one language is essential as the drafter will often be confronted with different meanings of certain articles of the Directive. Another important aspect is to use any derogations a Directive has to offer.

Finally, from a practical point of view, when drafting for EU accession the best advice for the drafter is to keep a copy of the Constitution of his country nearby to ensure that proposed amendments are not incompatible with it; for if they are even the Constitution will have to be amended.

Harmonization presupposes a lot of hard work and a lot of hours spent in trying to understand the complicated provisions of an often badly drafted Directive. But it is not an impossible task. The best advice I was given some months before signing the Act of Accession of Cyprus to the EU was to complete the work in time and not to worry about mistakes, which could be corrected at a later stage by amending the relevant legislation. The most important thing was to meet the deadlines.

Notes

1. On 1 January 2002 the Euro was introduced in a physical form and on 30 June 2002 it replaced the national currencies of the participating countries.
2. Twelve countries participate in the EMU namely, Austria, Belgium, Finland, Germany, Ireland, Italy, Luxembourg, the Netherlands, Portugal, Spain and Greece.
3. G. Kyriacou and G. Syrichas (1999), 'EMU and the introduction of the euro:

macroeconomic implications for the Cypriot Economy,' *CBC Quarterly Economic Review*, pp. 25-61.

4. The ESCB comprises of the ECB and the National Central Banks (NCBs) of the member states of the EU-(Art 1.2 of the Statute of the ESCB).
5. Art 109K(1) and (3) of the Treaty.
6. Information from the European Commission, *2000 Cyprus Regular Report on Cyprus progress towards accession*, 8 November 2000.
7. Convergence Criteria: (a) inflation rate ≤ 1.5 percentage points above the average of the three lowest-inflation countries; (b) budget deficit ≤ 3% of GDP; (c) government debt ratio ≤ 60% of GDP; (d) long term interest rates ≤ 2 percentage points above the average long term interest rate of the three lowest inflation countries; (e) currency stability: currency must remain within normal ERM2 fluctuation bands for two years.
8. Two standing facilities: (1) A *short-term CBC facility (lombard-type)* was introduced as from the beginning of 1996, the interest rate of which is intended to provide the upper end of money market interest rates. Credit granted to banks under the 'lombard facility' is made available on an overnight basis and government securities are used as a collateral; (2) The CBC has offered to banks an 'overnight deposit facility' for placing their short-term surplus funds at the end of the day. The interest rate on this facility is intended to provide, in normal circumstances, the floor for short-term money market rates.
9. Divergences do not exist any more due to the new laws passed in relation to CBC independence (the Central Bank of Cyprus Law of 2003) and the Law liberalizing interest rates of 1999.
10. The new law on the CBC which repeals the old one was enacted and came into force on 5 July 2002.
11. Article 20 of the Insurance Laws 1984-1990.
12. The EMI was subsequently substituted by the ECB.
13. CY£1=1,7086 euro.
14. ERM2 is an exchange rate mechanism for the 'pre-ins' in EMU.
15. Information from the European Commission Report on Cyprus Progress towards accession (Supplementary Progress since July 2003).
16. Direct investment is defined as the ownership of 10 per cent or more, of the ordinary shares or voting stock of an enterprise, by a foreign investor while, portofolio investment is defined as the ownership of below 10 per cent, of the ordinary shares or voting stock of an enterprise, by a foreign investor. (Based on the OECD Benchmark definition of foreign direct investment).
17. A 'cross-border credit transfer' is defined in the Directive as a transaction carried out on the initiative of a natural or legal person other than a credit or financial institution-called the 'originator'-via an institution in a member state (e.g. a bank), to make available an amount of money, in a beneficiary's

account, at an institution in another member state.

18. Article 179(1) of the Constitution of the Republic of Cyprus.
19. Article 182(3) of the Constitution of the Republic of Cyprus.

8 Freedom of Establishment and Free Movement of Services: An Opportunity to Harmonise and Liberalise the Cyprus Service Sector

ELENA PAPAGEORGIOU AND ELENI KOUZOUPI[1]

Introduction

The Freedom of Establishment and the Free Movement of Services[2] is a complicated and wide-reaching subject area, not least because it touches on a variety of political issues regarding the extent of the national treatment on aliens and covers a wide spectrum of activities, mainly of financial nature, affecting almost all aspects of the economy.

The fact that this particular subject is considered of pivotal importance by the EU is reflected in extensive references to Articles 43 and 49 (former Articles 52 and 59) of the Treaty of European Community (EC). The harmonisation effort relating to this subject has '...acquired a new eminence in the political agenda of the EU and has been the subject of various consultation papers and Commission Communications'[3] which were discussed and welcomed by both the European Parliament and the Council.[4]

Currently many the member states are concentrating their efforts on the liberalisation of the service industry, so as to allow for the right of legal and natural persons to establish themselves in any member state, while only having to register and comply with the home country's regulatory authority. The attention of the EU naturally gravitates to the financial industry, much because of its pervasiveness and of the ease of establishment of financial service companies. The liberalisation process is also, to a large degree, driven by the service industry itself, because of the perceived economies to be realised with leaner regulatory structures and compliance requirements associated with only having to deal with the home country's regulatory authorities. Once again, the financial services industry runs at the forefront of the liberalisation and rationalisation process, with moves such as bringing the various national regulatory authorities – each responsible for the supervision of the banking, insurance, and investment services industries – under one single regulatory body.

Freedom of establishment, covering Articles 43 to 49 EC, requires the removal of restrictions, legal as well as administrative, on the right of individuals and companies to maintain a permanent or settled place of business in a member state. Establishment has been defined as 'the actual pursuit of an economic activity through a fixed establishment in another member state for an indefinite period'.[5] Establishment extends to the establishment through agencies, branches and subsidiary organisations. The right to establishment of self-employed individuals is acutely stressed. The abolition of restrictions provides for freedom to acquire and use land and buildings as well as lifting indirect restrictions, wherever the latter might exist, in the differing treatment of European citizens and locals in obtaining state benefits.

The free movement of services, covered in Articles 49 to 55 EC (former Articles 59-66), requires the removal of restrictions on the provision of services by individuals and companies between member states. In general, the services offered must be provided on payment and include industrial, commercial, manual and professional services.[6] The basis of the provisions relating to both establishment and services, which are usually read in parallel, comprises the principle against discrimination on grounds of nationality, thus promoting market integration.

Apart from Article 43EC on the freedom of establishment and Article 49EC on the free movement of services, the 'acquis communautaire' principally consists of Directives, which fall into three broad categories: those which generally concern the right of establishment and the freedom to provide services in specific fields; Directives which abolish restrictions and extend rights so that the citizens of the member states can have equal treatment; and, finally, Directives which call for the alignment of the legislations, regulations and procedures applied by member states.

The Directives and Treaty articles of the acquis relevant to the subject of freedom of establishment and free movement of services include the following significant unities, which will be presented and analysed separately in this chapter:

Financial services:

- Banking;
- Insurance;
- Investment Services and Securities Markets.

Non-financial services:

- Article 43 EC on the freedom of establishment and Article 49 EC on the freedom to provide services;
- Directive 95/46/EC on the protection of personal data and the free movement of such data;
- Directives on the freedom of establishment and the freedom to provide services for craftsmen, traders and farmers;
- Directive 86/653/EC on self-employed commercial agents;
- Information Society Directive 98/47/EC on the provision of information in the field of technical standards and regulations and of rules and Directive 98/84/EC on the legal protection of services on conditional access.

The right of establishment and the freedom to provide services in many areas of the Cyprus economy is not always regulated by specific legislation relating to each of these fields but by legislation of a more general nature addressing the movement and residence of aliens in Cyprus, as well as the acquisition of immovable property by aliens and foreign exchange control applicable within the framework of government policy regarding the issuing of permits for foreign investments.

It may well be argued that the subject of Freedom of Establishment and Free Movement of Services impinges on a wide spectrum of services, which cover almost all fields of the economy. Therefore, it may also be argued that the pervasiveness of the service industry makes implementation of this subject rather challenging. The task of the Cypriot authorities was made even more cumbersome because by the time of Accession[7] they were obliged to adopt a vast number of Directives, which in contrast to the Regulations by their very nature do not have direct effect.[8] The administrative measures usually aim at creating, introducing, and organising a competent authority to apply the legislation. The legal measures are in the form of primary or subsidiary legislation.

Financial services

Banking sector

The Cyprus banking sector is a dominant player in the local service industry. The banks' power is evident in their dominating presence in all fields of the financial services industry, with the inclusion of the insurance industry (for both general and life insurance products) and the securities and investment services industry. The Cyprus domestic banking system can be broadly divided into three groups of credit institutions:

- commercial banks;
- specialised credit institutions; and
- co-operative credit institutions.

At the apex, is the Central Bank of Cyprus (CBC), the competent authority vested with the power and responsibility for the regulation and supervision of the banking sector.[9] The CBC has always aimed at a high standard of regulation and supervision. The rules and policies applied with respect to banks have, in many ways, outstripped the recommendations of the Balse Committee on banking supervision and the EU Banking Directives. The CBC has its prudential standards under constant review to incorporate new developments and changing circumstances.

Following the application of Cyprus for full EU membership, the CBC has embarked upon a programme of harmonisation of the banking legislation to the acquis communautaire. The most important harmonisation measure instigated so far, in the field of banking, has been the enactment of the Banking Law in June 1997,[10] achieving 'legislative approximation with the EU in the field of banking to a very large extent'.[11]

The Law[12] regulates the banking system in Cyprus and aims to grant protection to depositors. It sets the legal framework within which banking business may be pursued and reflects, to a very large extent, the principles and rules of the EU banking legislation.[13] It should be noted that the legal framework and the methods of supervision apply to domestic banks and offshore banks alike. However, the co-operative credit institutions are not captured by the Banking Law and they are not under the prudential supervision of the CBS (with the exception of the Co-operative Central Bank).

More specifically, the Banking Law defines the term 'banking business' and provides that a banking licence is required for the pursuit of banking business. The Banking Law lays down minimum authorisation requirements and prudential rules, in conformity with the acquis, that must be satisfied so as to permit any entity to operate as a credit institution. The Law also prescribes limits on large credit exposures and non-banking holdings, defines a bank's capital base and requires the maintenance of a solvency ratio. Furthermore, the Law empowers the CBC to exchange information with overseas supervisory authorities, provides for contacts between the CBC and external auditors of supervised banks, and enables the CBC to prescribe the format and content of bank accounts. Moreover, the Law provides for consolidated supervision and provides for the setting up of a Deposit Protection Scheme. The Law also contains extensive enforcement powers and penalties that the CBC may impose on banks that breach its provisions.

The First and Second Banking Directives,[14] the Own Funds[15] and Solvency Ratio Directives,[16] the Large Exposures Directive,[17] the Consolidated Supervision Directive,[18] the Deposit Guarantee Scheme Directive[19] and the Annual Accounts and Consolidated Accounts of Banks Directive[20] are, to a large extent, in conformity with the provisions of the Banking Law. More specifically, the Banking Law covers the First and Second Banking Co-ordination Directives almost in their entirety. Prior approval of the CBC is required for qualified holdings, branches of foreign banks are not required to maintain endowment capital, the CBC has the right to co-operate with foreign supervisory authorities and the principle of 'home country control' is recognised and applied. There are also rules governing holdings in non-bank companies or in companies carrying on business not closely related to banking or which do not consist of business dealing with insurance. The Law also provides for measures and penalties against non-compliance.

The Banking Law – and the Regulations issued by the CBC under this Law – incorporate to a very large extent the provisions of the Solvency Ratio Directive, including the obligation to maintain a solvency ratio at a level not less than 10%, the methodology for its calculation and the requirement for solo and consolidated positions, in the case where a bank is a member of a wider group. The CBC achieves the classification of countries into Zone A and Zone B through the exercise of discretionary power. Under the current methods of classification employed by the CBC, there is some deviation from the EU's classification. The so-called regulations or instructions to commercial banks, issued under the Banking Law (Article 41) and currently in force, do not cover market risk as the risks taken by the banks are small and are well below the threshold laid down by the Directive. Full harmonisation is scheduled to be achieved upon accession.

The definition and computation of the level of own funds is in full conformity with the requirements of the Own Funds Directive.

The Large Exposures Directive is covered by the Banking Law, which prohibits excessive concentration of exposures to any one client or group of connected clients. The various exposures must be measured in relation to the bank's own funds and must not exceed the limits specified, which limits are equal to those specified in the Directive. Specific limitations also apply with regard to the exposures to a bank's director. Monitoring is effected through regular reports and on-site examinations. In addition, the CBC has issued to banks, an instruction concerning the application of the limits on large exposures as stipulated in the Banking Law, including some clarifications on the matter and monitoring procedures,[21] in full compliance with the EU Directive on the Monitoring and Control of Large Exposures of Credit Institutions.[22]

The Consolidated Supervision Directive is fully transposed by the Banking Law, which empowers the CBC to exercise supervision on a consolidated basis, covering the holding company and any of the subsidiaries of a bank. The principle concerning supervision on a consolidated basis is also incorporated in the instructions issued to banks, on the solvency ratio and on large exposures.

Moreover, the Banking Law requires banks to prepare financial statements in accordance with international accounting standards and in addition, it empowers the CBC to issue regulations to banks, as to the content of the public accounts in conformity with the Bank Accounting Directives. Banks are required to submit to the CBC and to publish their balance sheet and profit and loss accounts, the format and the content of which are very much in line with the Bank Accounting Directives. Accounts must be consolidated when the bank is a member of a wider group; branches of banks having their head office outside Cyprus are also required to publish their accounts. An instruction issued to banks at the end of 1999, incorporates in all detail the layout and content of the balance sheet and profit & loss account, as described in the Directives concerning annual accounts and consolidated accounts of banks.

In December 1998, the CBC issued to banks instructions concerning the definition and computation of the level of own funds and the method of computation of the required solvency ratio. These are in conformity with the requirements of the EU Directive on the Annual Accounts and Consolidated Accounts of Banks and other Financial Institutions.[23]

Whilst giving the CBC 'wide-ranging powers'[24] including the power to issue general or specific instructions to banks,[25] the Banking Law explicitly defines the obligations of CBC with respect to the exercise of its discretionary powers, and prescribes that the CBC should take cognisance of international practices and the relevant EU Directives, and that the CBC issues adequately reasoned decisions.

Concerning the application of articles 43 and 49 of the EC Treaty to banking, the authorisation criteria apply similarly to national and non-national applicants, and foreign establishments are accorded national treatment. Following the enactment of the Banking Law, other harmonisation measures have also been instigated. These include the following:

- These mainly consist of the issue of Regulations pursuant to the powers granted to the CBC under section 34(2) of the Banking Law to issue regulations with the approval of the Council of Ministers, on 1 Sepember 2000, for the operation of a Deposit Protection Scheme.[26] The Regulations incorporate all the requirements of the relevant EU Directive.[27] The purpose of the Regulations is to protect private individuals, who deposit money with commercial banks registered in Cyprus, by providing for damages to be paid to them out of the fund if the commercial bank is not in a position to repay the deposit due to its financial position, or a court order has been granted for the winding up of the bank. The minimum capital of the fund has been fixed at CY£2 millions which amount may be increased in the future. The scheme initially covered only deposits in Cyprus pounds. The amount of damages granted to a private depositor could not exceed at any time the equivalent of €20,000 in Cyprus pounds at the time. Regulations concerning the scheme were amended on 25 July 2003 to include deposits in the currencies of the accession states (Public Instrument no. 637 of 2003).
- An amendment of the Banking Law, abolishing article 37 therein, has been effected.[28] As a result, the CBC may no longer be able to exempt offshore banks from the full application of all the provisions of the Banking Law.

The main areas in which Cyprus was not in conformity with respect to the EU Banking Directives were the following:

- The application of the ‘economic need criterion’ in relation to granting a licence for carrying banking business. The Central Bank of Cyprus, in deciding whether to grant a license may take into account the economic need for the services of the applicant. It was thought expedient, as a matter of policy, for the CBC to retain this discretionary power because of the small size of the banking market, which, in its current state, is considered saturated. Nevertheless, it should be noted that this criterion is not enshrined in the Law and this particular discretionary power of the CBC may be eliminated. It is anticipated that the 'economic need criterion' will be abandoned upon harmonisation with the single passport principle by the time of accession.

- The implementation of the Capital Adequacy Directive[29] (CAD). It should be noted that the provisions of this Directive have not been implemented because of the small scale on which banks have hitherto been involved in trading instruments captured by the Directive. Banks in Cyprus have not been engaged, to a significant extent, in activities exposing them to market risk. Their trading book business is small, well below the threshold laid down by the Directive. Therefore, Cyprus is not in breach of its requirements and will implement the Directive upon accession. There are enabling provisions in the Banking Law[30] allowing CBC to take steps for the implementation of CAD as and when the commercial banks' trading business grows to a point where application of CAD will be mandatory.
- The implementation of the Directive on Contractual Netting[31] (amending the Solvency Ratio Directive) and Directive 33/98/EC amending both the Solvency Ratio Directive and CAD. The Commission's 2000 Progress Report on Cyprus,[32] states that 'further alignment is needed in the field of the recognition of contractual netting agreements, consolidated accounts and capital adequacy for market risks'. However, according to the CBC, banks in Cyprus have not always been involved in off-balance sheet items or derivatives, where contractual netting may apply. Thus, while Cyprus has yet to adopt these Directives, it is not at present in breach of their rules. These Directives will be implemented upon accession, as indicated in the harmonogram.[33]

However, relevant amendments to the Banking Law were effected on 25 July 2003 (Law 119(I) of 2003) to include provisions which, among other things, abolished the economic need criterion. The new provisions entered into force upon accession. In addition, with regard the Capital Adequany Directive and the Directive on Contractual Netting, new instructions were issued in 2002 by the CBC to all banks and took effect on 1 January 2003, in full compliance with the abovementioned Directives.

In conclusion, it may be said that Cyprus is at an advanced stage of harmonisation in the field of banking regulation and supervision, with further legislative alignment scheduled for implementation upon accession. In this process, no serious problems are envisaged. By accession, full harmonisation of the banking sector will be in place.

Co-operatives

In addition to commercial banks and specialised credit institutions, the other significant part of the Cyprus banking system is the co-operative sector.[34] The Commission's 2000 Regular Report on Cyprus,[35] states that the financial supervisory structures within the credit co-operative sector are weak and as such they are 'worrisome'. The co-operative credit and saving societies (CCSSs), which account for around 30% of bank deposits, are not subject to the normal banking sector supervision undertaken by the CBC. On top of that, the co-operatives enjoy a number of legal advantages; most notably, exemptions from both stamp duties and required reserve ratios. This may place them at a competitive advantage relative to the commercial banks.

CCSSs are autonomous, voluntary, mutual self-help, non-profit organisations, which focus on meeting the social and economic needs of their members, who are associated together with a common bond. This means that all members are from one stakeholder group (e.g. producers, workers etc), having a common interest, or living in the same geographic area. The CCSSs offer a limited range of banking services basically consisting of the acceptance of deposits and the granting of loans or other credit facilities to their members only (section 37). The emphasis of the co-operative sector's lending activities has traditionally focused on mortgage lending for housing or on small loans for personal purposes.[36]

The first regulatory framework for co-operatives was established in 1914, with the introduction of the Co-operative Societies Law and Rules of 1914. Today, the operation of the CCSSs is governed by the Co-operative Societies Law[37] and Rules of 1987. The Co-operative Societies Law and Rules reflect the internationally accepted co-operative principles.[38] These institutions are not subject to monetary or prudential supervision by the CBC. Instead they are supervised by the Department of the Co-operative Development of the Ministry of Commerce, Industry and Tourism. The Commissioner of the Department is responsible for the overall supervision of the co-operative movement.

An important element of the system is the Co-operative Central Bank (CCB), which was established in 1937. The CCB is subject to the Banking

Law of 1997 and falls under the supervision of both the Department of Co-operative Development and the CBC. Its members are all the CCSSs, for which it acts as their banker and lender of last resort.

There has been a long debate[39] regarding the position of the CCSSs in relevance to the harmonisation process.[40] In the past, the Cyprus position was that the CCSSs were not considered as credit institutions and thus fell outside the scope of the EC Banking Directive (Directive 2000/12/EC). However, following several meetings in Brussels, in October 2000, and in the light of the EC experts consultation study, the question of the possible exclusion of the co-operative credit and saving societies from the scope of the aforementioned EC Banking Directive is no longer under consideration.

A further step to the finalisation of the stand of the Cyprus co-operative has been reached on the 23 February 2001 with the co-operative movement deciding to fully comply with the provisions of the acquis.[41] Cyprus's official revised position on CCSSs provides that, no exemptions will be sought, the EC codified Banking Directive on credit institutions will apply to conforming[42] CCSSs which will be deemed as credit institutions[43] within the ambit of the provisions of the Banking Directive and a transitional period of five years will be sought as from 1 January 2003, so as to give to some of the CCSSs adequate time to fully comply with the requirements of the Banking Directive[44] concerning own funds, solvency ratio and large exposures. During the transitional period, those institutions which will not fulfil all the necessary provisions of the Directive, will not benefit from the 'European passport' for operating in the single market. In the context of the planned periodic review of the progress achieved in the implementation of reforms and the progress of harmonisation, the Department of Co-operative Societies and Co-operative Development will closely monitor and re-assess the overall performance of the CCSSs, in particular the position of the non-conforming institutions. By the end of 2004, the Department will draw up a list of institutions that would become 'permanently affiliated' to a central body, namely the Co-operative Central Bank, whereupon the relevant provisions of the Banking Directive will be invoked, with a view to enabling the CCB and the affiliated institutions as a whole, to satisfy all the regulatory provisions on a consolidated basis.

It may be noted that far from any notion that during the transitional period CCSSs would find themselves in a regulatory vacuum, all CCSSs, while endeavouring to adapt to the new supervisory framework, will continue carrying on their activities in accordance with the provisions of the co-operative legislation and under the watchful eye of the Department of Co-operative Societies and Co-operative Development.

The steps to be taken in the prosed scenario are summarised below:

- Procure amendments to the co-operative legislation so as to make it explicitly clear that the CCSSs are empowered to engage in the business of acceptance of deposits from the public without affecting in any way either their statutory characteristics as co-operative credit institutions or the co-operative principles as enunciated in the present Co-operative Societies Rules and Laws. Thereafter, all CCSSs would be deemed to be 'credit institutions' coming within the ambit of the Banking Directive.
- Implement a series of reforms, including mergers and groupings on a geographical or functional basis, in order for small sized CCSSs to attain 'critical mass' both in terms of membership and market shares, with a view to achieving administrative and operational efficiency.
- Take measures aimed at enabling CCSSs for purposes of the own funds, solvency ratio and the other prudential computations, to make full use of the possibilities in the Banking Directive in respect of certain items such as 'uncalled share capital', 'members' reserve liability' and eligible 'subordinated loans'.
- Review and revise the organizational, procedural and functional structures of the Department of Co-operative Societies and Co-operative Development, with a view to putting in place, the legal, regulatory and supervisory framework envisaged by the relevant provisions of the Banking Directive.
- For the implementation of the reforms the Department of Co-operative Societies and Co-operative Development should be vested with the necessary statutory powers.

The main difficulties to be anticipated by the CCSSs with respect to the prudential measurements of the Banking Directive are associated with these institutions' own funds levels, which, in the wake of the these reforms and actions, could be expected to increase.

Time and effort will by needed to adapt and conform to a system of measurements applicable to both CCSSs and banks. Effective implementation of the reforms presupposes persistent action on several fronts. The Cyprus Co-operative Movement leadership is determined to do its utmost and to guide the CCSSs in the direction of effective harmonisation within set deadlines. The implementation of reforms and the adjustment of positions will obviously be an arduous and time-consuming process.

Against this background, it is hoped that the groundwork will be completed soon, and the co-operative movement will follow the path of harmonisation at a swift pace. To this end, the Co-operative Societies Law was amended on 25 July 2003 (Law 123(I) of 2003) transposing the Banking Directive providing for the full independence of the Commissioner of the Cooperative Societies Supervision and Development Authority as the competent supervisory authority for the CCSSs.

Insurance

The creation of a common market in the insurance sector has always been considered by the EU as one of its priorities. The creation of an internal market in the insurance sector presupposes a market without internal borders within which insurance companies will be able to exercise their activities freely. The is twofold: firstly, to make it possible for all citizens of the EU to have access to the widest possible spectrum of insurance products provided within the EU. Secondly, to safeguard that every insurance company which has a licence to operate in a member-state is enabled to carry out its activities in another member-state, always in accordance with the freedom of establishment and the freedom to provide services. In order to achieve these aims, the EU issued a number of Directives in relation to the main sectors of insurance.

Regarding the Life Insurance sector, the Council adopted the First Life Co-ordination Directive[45] in 1979, which contained the basic rules governing the right of establishment for undertakings operating in the life insurance sector.[46] This was followed by the Second Life Co-ordination Directive,[47] which aimed at completing the framework relating to freedom to provide insurance services throughout the Community.[48]

On 10 November, 1992, the Commission approved the Third Life Co-ordination Directive.[49] According to this Directive, insurance companies established in one member state can operate freely throughout the EU, both in terms of offering their services directly across national borders and subject to the authorisation and control of their country of primary establishment within the Community.

Regarding non-life insurance, the Council adopted the First Non-Life Co-ordination Directive[50] in 1973, which lays the foundation of the right for EEC insurers to establish themselves in another member state, whether as a company, branch or an agency and to offer insurance services in that state (the host state) under the same conditions and with the same rights as nationals of the host country. The details of the application of freedom to provide services by insurance companies of this sector are regulated by the Second Non-Life Co-ordination Directive.[51] Finally, the Council adopted the Third Non-Life Co-ordination Directive[52] under which home state control is required for all insurance service providers.

Regarding motor insurance, the Council adopted the First Motor Insurance Directive[53] on 16 July 1996, which established an international 'Green Card' system which operated as an internationally recognised insurance certificate indicating the countries for which cover is provided and the duration of such cover. The Second Motor Insurance Directive,[54] which was approved in 1984, harmonised both the scope and conditions of compulsory motor insurance cover. Finally, the Council adopted the Third Motor Insurance Directive[55] to resolve many differences which existed between the member states as regards the level and content of compulsory civil liability insurance.

Cyprus legislation regarding the insurance sector consists of the Insurance Companies Law of 1984 and 1990 and the Motor Vehicles (Third Party Insurance) Law of 2000. At present, the Insurance Companies Law of 1984 and 1990 regulates the establishment, operation and supervision of insurance companies in Cyprus and protects the rights and interests of the insured.[56] All the powers of the Law are conferred upon the Superintendent and the Assistant Superintendent, which are civil servants appointed by the Council of Ministers.[57]

This Insurance Companies Law of 1984 and 1990 will be replaced by a new law harmonised to the acquis. The proposed law regulates both life insurance and non-life insurance. It has been prepared by the Ministry of Finance (Insurance Companies Control Service) in collaboration with the Insurance Association of Cyprus and has been sent to the Law Office of the Republic for legal vetting. The law is expected to come into force on 1 July 2001. Provisions of the law regarding the single licence and the home country control principle will come into force upon accession.[58]

The Insurance Companies Law of 1984 and 1990 deviates from the acquis communautaire mainly on a number of areas. Regarding the issue of a single licence by the country of primary establishment of the insurance company within the Community, the Insurance Companies Law of 1984 and 1990 presupposes the issue of a licence to foreign insurance companies to carry out business in the form of a branch or agency.[59] These provisions will be amended so that an insurance company which has a licence to operate in a member state will be able to carry out insurance business in Cyprus (either in the form of a branch or agency) without the issue of an additional licence by the Superintendent of Insurance of the Republic of Cyprus. And, in the same manner, an insurance company whose country of primary establishment is Cyprus, which has been granted a licence to operate from the relevant Cyprus regulatory authorities, will be able to carry out insurance business freely in any member state.

Regarding the supervision system, the Insurance Companies Law of 1984 and 1990 differs partially from that of the EU as at this point in time. With the amendment of the existing legislation, the supervision will be made by the country of primary establishment of the insurance company and not by the Superintendent of Insurance of the Republic of Cyprus. Moreover, the supervision by the Superintendent of Insurance of the Republic of Cyprus will only be restricted to the operation of the insurance companies whose country of primary establishment is Cyprus. This supervision will extend geographically within the borders of the EU so as to cover the activities of the Cypriot insurance companies which carry out insurance business in the EU.

Furthermore, the minimum solvency margin, which the existing Cyprus legislation provides, differs from that provided in the relevant Directives[60] and, therefore, must be adjusted accordingly. The increase of the minimum solvency margin will create financial difficulties to insurance companies which will be obliged to increase their assets withheld so as to cover the solvency limit on a permanent basis.

Prudential provisions concerning minimum capital requirements 'are still quite different from those contained in the acquis'.[61] The Insurance Companies Law of 1984 and 1990 provides as minimum share capital the amount of CY£200,000 for all insurance companies irrespective of the class of business transactions. This provision will be amended so as to increase the minimum share capital to CY£400,000 for the non-life insurance business, to CY£600,000 for the life-insurance business, to CY£1,000,000 for composite activities. A provision will be included in the Law with reference to the interpretation of minimum guarantee fund as the latter is defined in Directive 79/267/EEC.[62]

Regarding the liberalisation of premiums, Cyprus's legislation, at present, defines premiums that insurance companies are obliged to charge in specific sectors. Directives 92/49/EEC[63] and 92/96/EEC[64] provide for the liberalization of premiums. The Ministry of Finance has already submitted an amended bill in the House of Representatives for the liberalisation of premiums.

As the Commission Report had noted '...further alignment is needed as regards accounting rules'.[65] The Insurance Companies Law of 1984 and

1990 covers to some extent the Directive on accounting of insurance companies.[66] At present, no compulsory accounting rules specific to insurance business exist though insurance companies apply International Accounting Standards. The Law will be amended so as to comply with Directive 91/674/EEC on accounting of insurance companies.

Furthermore, according to section 3 of the Insurance Companies Law 1984 and 1998, the Council of Ministers has the authority to exempt a captive insurance company from the provisions of the Insurance Companies Laws 1984-1998, provided that the company complies with any conditions or terms that the appropriate authorities in Cyprus deem it necessary to impose. With the new legislation, this provision will cease being in force since it will constitute preferential treatment in favour of a class of companies, i.e. the captive, a fact which comes into contrast with sections 43 and 49 of the EC Treaty.

Regarding insurance intermediaries, the Cyprus legislation lays down only minimum requirements for the carrying out of insurance business by an agent without though there being a definition of a broker, the process of his registration and recognition of experience acquired in another country. This matter will be completely regulated by the new legislation.

The current legislation concerning the motor insurance, namely The Motor Vehicles (Third Party Insurance) Law,[67] is harmonised with the relevant Directives[68]. More specifically, this Law provides that a 'Green Card' is considered to be a valid certificate recognised by the Cypriot authorities. Furthermore, companies have the obligation to compensate victims of motor accidents irrespective of whether the driver was driving with the consent of the owner of the vehicle and with a valid driving licence, and an insurance certificate issued by a country which is a member of the Multilateral Guarantee Agreement (MGA) is considered to be a certificate of insurance recognised by the Cypriot authorities.

Investment services and securities markets

The issue and trade in securities in Cyprus has, to a large extent, been codified. The various Laws and Regulations which have been enacted, endeavor not only to protect investors but also to harmonise the existing regime with the main EU Directives in the field of securities regulation.[69] The principal pieces of legislation are:

- The Cypriot Securities and Stock Exchange Law
- The Cypriot Securities and Stock Exchange Regulations of 1995, as

amended

- Various Regulations passed under sections 19(3), 60A, and 71 of the Securities and Stock Exchange Law, such as the Mergers and Acquisitions Regulations, of 1997
- The Companies Law.

With respect to the investment services and securities markets,[70] the Securities and Stock Exchange Law and Regulations of 1993 to 2001 established the official Cyprus Stock Exchange (CSE) in April 1993, as a public legal entity through which all stock exchange transactions of listed companies must be executed.[71] The CSE has the responsibility to promote the development of an organised and orderly market in securities and to monitor and supervise trading so as to inhibit fraudulent or unacceptable practices.

The CSE is governed by a seven member Council appointed by the Council of Ministers. The Securities and Stock Exchange Law also provides for the establishment of the Cyprus Securities and Exchange Commission (CSEC). Whilst the CSE is assigned the day-to-day management of the securities market, the CSEC is responsible for supervising the operation of the securities market in accordance with the provisions of the Securities and Stock Exchange Law and Regulations.

Concerning the supervision and enforcement, the Securities and Stock Exchange Laws and Regulations empower the CSE and the Cyprus Securities and Exchange Commission (CSEC), in its capacity as the overall supervisory body, to continuously monitor issuers of securities and brokers. Apart from criminal action against brokers, issuers and investors, the CSE has the power to extend or withdraw licences, as well as to impose disciplinary measures and fines on brokers and issuers.

Furthermore, the Central Depository and Central Securities Register Law[72] and new clearing and trading procedures in the form of the trading rules of the Stock Exchange (Electronic System) Regulations 100 of 1997, were adopted. The coming into effect of the Law will signal the final hours of the share certificate and call into being the 'paperless exchanges'. There has been progress on the harmonisation process, although 'further legislative alignment is needed'.[73] This is due, *inter alia*, to the fact that some of the provisions of the acquis can only be applied upon accession.

Regarding the Directive coordinating the requirements for the drawing up, scrutiny and distribution of the prospectus to be published when Transferable Securities are offered to the Public,[74] and the Directive coordinating the requirements for the drawing up, scrutiny and distribution of the listing particulars to be published for the admission of securities to official stock exchange listing,[75] partial transposition has been effected by the Securities and Stock Exchange Laws and Regulations: '…the prospectus and listing particulars requirements imposed on issuers seeking a listing on the CSE closely follow the principal body of EU law in the field of securities regulation'.[76]

For securities seeking listing or listed on the Stock Exchange in Cyprus, the conditions for listing, the content, scrutiny and publication of prospectuses and listing particulars, and the monitoring of announcements regarding major changes in shareholdings serve disclosure and screening purposes, following mainly the acquis, as the Securities and Stock Exchange Laws and Regulations have been largely modeled on the relevant EU Directives.[77]

Issuers are required to disclose all relevant information on the securities to be listed, their capital and main business activities, their financial position and prospects, their directors and executives, the structure of the shareholding of shareholders and the changes in such holdings. Thus, investors may evaluate in the best possible manner the assets, liabilities and prospects of the issuer and of the rights attaching to the securities to be listed on the CSE. In addition, they must regularly publish yearly and six monthly reports, on the basis of international accounting standards.[78]

The Companies Law also lays down certain prospectus requirements with regard to public issues of securities.[79] They are mainly concerned with invitations to the public to acquire shares or debentures, prohibiting companies from issuing shares without having first filed the appropriate documentation with the Companies Registrar.

Where gaps exist with respects to the acquis, these relate to matters such as the ability of the Cyprus Stock Exchange to exchange information and co-operate with other competent authorities, the mutual acceptability of prospectuses, the treatment of certificates representing shares, Euro-securities, minor offers, certain debt instruments and certain forms and types of companies or institutions, which do not yet exist in Cyprus. There is still the need to permit exceptions for brokers to declare acquisitions.[80]

Furthermore, the Cypriot legislation does not reflect the exclusions contained in the Directive on Prospectuses relating to small offers, UCITS, non-profit organisations, Euro-securities and the possibility of providing for natural recognition of the prospectus. Some of the divergence will be eliminated in July 2001, by amending the Securities and Stock Exchange Laws and the Companies Law (Cap.113, as amended). Full compliance will be achieved upon accession.

However, by the end of 2003, full alignment with the acquis was accomplished. An amending Law and Regulations were approved by the House of Representatives in June 2002, in order to introduce a number of changes to the Securities and Stock Exchange Laws and Regulations bringing them into compliance with the relevant EC directives. The amendments, include, inter alia, the right of citizens and legal entities from EU member states to become members of the Cyprus Stock Exchange, the right of banks to act as brokers, the ability of the Cyprus Stock Exchange to co-operate and exchange information with other competent authorities, and relevant provisions regarding the mutual acceptance of prosectuses. Furthermore, a Law providing for the Requirements for the undertaking of an Invitation to the Public for Investment in Financial Instruments and Other Related Matters (Law 149(I) of 2002) was enacted in July 2002, which extends the requirements for prospectuses and determines what is considered to be private placement. This Law is full in line with the relevant acquis.

With regards to the Directive on Insider Trading,[81] the Law on Possession, Use and Announcement of Privileged Confidential Information was enacted on 15 April 1999,[82] referring to the acquisition, use and disclosure of confidential information. It essentially prohibits insider trading, making the commission of it a criminal offence. This Law is in full compliance with the acquis on insider dealing. The objective of the Law is to secure a free and open market and to discourage share price fluctuations which are not attributable to facts relating to the issuer´s assets, prospects or profits. It thus 'reinforces existing reporting requirements under the Securities and Stock Exchange Law',[83] whereby listed companies are obliged to publish any significant new developments which may affect their share price promptly.

As stated, the Law prohibits insider dealing, which for the purposes of the Law consist of the use of privileged confidential information defined in section 3, acquired under specific circumstances. A person is regarded as having acquired privileged confidential information if such information has been obtained, inter alia, by reason of his position as a member of the managerial board or as a shareholder of the issuer or through his employment, office or profession. The Securities and Exchange Commission of Cyprus sent directions to issuers, in relation to the requirements of the Law, for establishing codes of conduct and internal control on insider dealing by their directors and officers. Issuers were asked to endorse and apply these instructions. Meetings were also held by the Commission to inform the Association of Company Auditors, the Association of Securities Brokers and the Association of Public Companies as to their responsibilities under the new Law.

In relevance to the Directive on the coordination of Laws, Regulations and Administrative provisions relating to Undertakings for Collective Investment in Transferable Securities (UCITS),[84] a harmonized Law on Collective Investment Services and other related matters has been enacted.[85] It aims to regulate issues concerning the structure, organisation, operation and surveillance of Undertakings Collective Investments in Transferable Securities, covering both UCITS and open-ended investment companies, which invest in transferable securities and bank deposits. Its main deviations from the acquis, given the emerging nature of the securities market in Cyprus, relate to some aspects of the investment policies for UCITS laid down in the acquis. It is anticipated that harmonisation will be fully achieved upon accession and the bill became Law on 31 December 2002 (Law 225(I) 2002).

Regarding the Investment Services Directive,[86] which applies to, inter alia, broker members of the SEC who offer investment services, such as execution of orders, underwriting, portfolio, management and investment advice, certain provisions of the aforementioned EU Directive have been already embodied into the Securities and Stock Exchange Legislation such as licensing, supervision, code of conduct and prudential practices. Where gaps exist in the Securities and Stock Exchange Legislation dealing mainly with conditions for licensing, capital adequacy and investor compensation, relevant amendments to the existing legislation will be effected, prior to the end of 2001. The relevant amendments of the Securities and Stock Exchange Law of June 2002, also included amendments to this effect.

As far as 'investment firms' other than broker members of the CSE, a Financial Services Bill has been prepared and will be soon presented before the House of Representatives for approval. It is anticipated that this Bill should be enacted by October 2001. The Bill embodies the provisions of the EU Directive on Investment Services as well as all the relevant provisions of the Investor Compensation[87] and Capital Adequacy[88] Directives. Full alignment with the acquis was achieved by the Investment Services Firms Law of 2002 (Law 148(I) of 2002).

Regarding the Investor Compensation Directive,[89] relating to brokers of the Cyprus Stock Exchange, relevant amendments have been made to the existing Joint Compensation Fund in order to comply with the acquis.[90] The main divergences with the acquis relate to the level of compensation, the clients of the brokers to which it applies, and the automatic triggering of compensation. As far as rules relating to the acceptance of other member states' schemes in part or full substitution of the host country scheme, relevant amendments were included in the Investment Services Firms Law to cover, in addition to the members of the Stock Exchange, other investment Services Firms.

As regards the Capital Adequacy Directive,[91] requirements already exist for broker members of the Cyprus Stock Exchange. However, the levels will be increased, so as to be brought in line with the aforementioned Directive. The relevant amendments were made by the Investments Services Firms Law, providing for implementation of the relevant capital adequacy requirements by the issuance of a relevant Decision by the Securities and Exchange Commission.

In conclusion, and as Neocleous, Georgiades and Zalewski state, 'since the commencement of trading, the regulatory authorities have shown that they are prepared to achieve the objectives of the prevailing securities regime by implementing the relevant laws and regulations in the context of modern business transactions'.[92] One may argue that Cyprus is progressing well with the harmonisation process in the field of securities market. As the last Progress Report[93] on Cyprus indicates, although 'further legislative alignment is needed' there has been shown good progress.

Other services

Article 43EC on the freedom of establishment and Article 49EC on the freedom to provide services

The main legislation of the Republic of Cyprus pertaining to the principles of freedom of establishment (Article 43 EC) and freedom to provide services (Article 49 EC) is the following:

- The Aliens and Immigration Law, Cap. 105;
- The Exchange Control Law, Cap. 199; and
- The Immovable Property Acquisition (Aliens) Law, Cap. 109.

The above legislation contains provisions which restrict, either directly or indirectly, the freedom of establishment and the freedom to provide services, and, therefore, deviates from Article 43 EC and Article 49 EC.

In accordance with the Aliens and Immigration Law, Cap. 105, the necessary requirement for the residence of non-nationals in Cyprus is the possession of a residence permit which is issued by the Immigration Officer. A permit is also required in the case where a non-national wishes to work in Cyprus. Such permits are issued on a case by case basis, using criteria which include, inter alia, the likely impact on the labour market. For a work permit to be issued, a minimum investment is also required. The Aliens and Immigration Law will be amended so as to give individuals the right to enter and reside in Cyprus subject to restrictions based on grounds of public policy, public security and public health.

In accordance with the Exchange Control Law, Cap. 199, a non-resident requires a permit from the CBC to be able to form a company; a permit is also required from the CBC for the issue of company titles (securities, including shares, bonds etc.) to non-residents and for the transfer of titles registered in Cyprus to non-residents.[94]

In accordance with the Immovable Property Acquisition (Aliens) Law, Cap. 109, approval is required from the Council of Ministers in case of a non-resident wishing to acquire immovable property.[95] These rules on ownership of immovable property which discriminate according to nationality are contrary to articles 43EC and 49EC and thus constitute obstacles to the effective exercise of the freedoms guaranteed by the Treaty.[96] In *Commission v. Greece*[97] the Court confirmed that the prohibition concerns not merely rules that relate to the pursuit of the occupation, but also rules relating to matters that assist in access to or excess of the occupation.

Besides the legislation referred to above, it must be stressed that other laws exist[98] which contain restrictions contrary to Articles 43 EC and 49 EC. These laws must also be harmonised.

Cyprus, according to the commitments it has undertaken, must gradually abolish all restrictions and discriminatory provisions which exist in its legislations and practices so that by the time of accession to the EU it should be prepared to adopt and implement Articles 43 EC and 49 EC.

Directive 95/46/EC on the protection of personal data and the free movement of such data[99]

At present there is no relevant legislation concerning the protection of personal data and the movement of such data. The Ministry of Interior has prepared a bill, in conformity with the Directive above, now undergoing legal vetting. This bill is in accordance with the commitments which have been undertaken and is expected to be enacted by 1 July, 2001.

The bill aims to protect the right to privacy with respect to the processing of personal data. More specifically, it lays down the setting up of a competent independent control authority, regulates the transfer of data to third countries with an adequate level of personal data, and specifies rules for the processing of personal data.

Directives on the freedom of establishment and the freedom to provide services for craftsmen, traders and farmers[100]

National legislation[101] contains restrictions to the exercise of the freedom of establishment and the free movement of services by non-Cypriot nationals. The issue of a work permit by the Immigration Officer to non-nationals is a condition for the pursuit of an activity. Permission of the CBC is required for the setting up of companies by non-residents. Restrictions also exist as regards the acquisition of real estate by foreigners and on foreign direct investment.

In addition, the Law on the Registration of Agriculturist of 1987 restricts the provision of services to Cypriot nationals only. Other laws, such as the Mines and Quarries Law of 1953 provide that non-residents and companies whose central office is not in Cyprus should appoint an attorney who must be a Cypriot resident; the Petroleum Law of 1974, provides that the prospecting mining licenses are subject to the approval of the Council of Ministers. The Travel Agents and Tourist Guides Law of 1995 restricts the free provision of services for travel agencies.

These laws will be amended in order to comply fully with the acquis upon accession.

Directive 86/653/EC on self-employed commercial agent[102]

The Regulation of Relations between Commercial Agent and the Principal Law of 1992 transposes 'partially'[103] the above Directive. This Law however, has been amended to fully comply with the acquis in the area of instructions given by the principal, the time limit for the obligation of the principal to notify the agent for the commission due, and the possibility to provide for indemnity or compensation.

Information society Directives[104] *on the provision of information in the field of technical standards and regulations and of rules and Directive 98/84/EC on the legal protection of services on conditional access*[105]

As regards Directive 98/48/EC, at present there is no relevant legislation. However, in accordance with the commitments undertaken by Cyprus, new harmonised legislation must be prepared and come into force when Cyprus joins the EU.

The relevant legislation regarding Directive 98/84/EC is the Private Radio and Television Station Law of 1998 which deviates from the Community Directives in so far as it provides for preferential treatment in relation to Cypriot nationals, leading to discriminatory effects against non-Cypriot nationals. This legislation will accordingly be amended in 2001.

Concluding remarks

Cyprus has always had a European orientation, cultivated through its social, political, cultural, commercial, trade and geographical ties with Europe. Following the official opening of EU accession negotiations on 30 March 1998, Cyprus is seeking to fulfil its ambition to join the EU by 1 January 2003. However, the process of harmonisation of the Cyprus legal order with the *acquis communaiture*, has so far been a healthy one. EU accession has been a powerful incentive for Cyprus to promptly modernise its legal system and regulatory institutions.

With respect to the subject of free movement of establishment and services, the process of adopting established Community Law and practice, though painful at times, has been rewarding so far. Cyprus is primarily relying on the services industry to drive its economy. Any changes in EU legislation regarding the freedom of establishment and free movement of services – legislation which will also have to be adopted and implemented in the Republic of Cyprus – is increasingly becoming of interest to the professionals of the service sector, who aim to adopt practices, which will reinforce the links to EU member states. Cyprus has always been challenged by the relatively small size of its market; the abolition of restrictions pertaining to freedom of establishment and free movement of services will serve as a stepping stone for both Cypriot and European nationals to engage in business transactions of mutual benefit, reaping the profits in the years to come.

The Government of the Republic of Cyprus is keenly following the developments in the EU with respect to the efforts undertaken for the adoption and implementation of the legislation pertaining to the freedom of establishment and free movement of services in the current EU member states. A lot has yet to be done. The opportunity for further change has yet to be undertaken. In this process, quality and precision should not be compromised for. The process is by no means easy. But the European doorway lies ahead of us, and not so far away.

Overall, it may be stated that Cyprus legislation has undergone significant changes in the process of harmonisation. The process of change, from as early as the drafting stage of legislation to the final step of enactment was by no means easy.

Harmonisation meant changes and reforms which in turn gave rise to resistance towards change by some relevant parties. The major blockage to change was due to cultural factors which were always geared towards the traditional practices and approaches. Nevertheless, determination to meet the deadlines and achieve our final goal of accession to the EU, brought about successful implementation of the various reforms and changes driven by the gradual cultural changes towards adopting the acquis.

Notes

1. We would like to thank Evripides Constantinou for his generous support. The views expressed in this Chapter are the personal views of the authors and not those of the institution to which they belong.
2. S. Weatherill and P. Beaumont, *EC Law*, 2nd edition, 1999, p.575-612.
3. E. Avgouleas, 'The harmonisation of Rules of conduct in EU Financial Markets: Economic Analysis, Subsidiarity and Investor Protection', *European Law Journal*, 2000, Vol.6, No.1 p.72.
4. *EU Bulletin* 5-1999, points 1.2.32 and 1.2.35.
5. Case C-221/89, *R v. Secretary of State For Transport, ex p. Factortame* (1991) ECR 1-3905, (1991) 3 CMLR 589, para. 20.
6. For an analysis, see N.G. Green, T.C. Hartley, J.A. Usher, *The Legal Foundation of the Single European Market*, see also P. Craig and G. De Burca, *EU Law, Text, Cases and Materials*, 2nd ed., Oxford, p.727; see also, Weatherill and Beaumont 1999, *op.cit.*, p.671.
7. T.C. Hartley, *The Foundations of European Community Law*, 3rd edition, 1994, p. 210.
8. Article 249EC: 'A directive shall be binding, as to the result to be achieved, upon each Member State to which it is addressed, but shall leave to the national authorities the choice of form and methods.'
9. Domestic and offshore, excluding the co-operative credit institutions.
10. Law 66(I) of 1997, as amended.
11. Central Bank of Cyprus, 'Report on The Harmonisation of the Cyprus Legal and Institutional Framework with the Acquis Communautaire', 22 January 1999, p.7.
12. For an analysis, see S. Laulhe, 'Banking Law' in Andreas Neocleous & Co., *Introduction to Cyprus Law*, Yorkhill Law Publishing, 2000.

13. For a further analysis on the Community Legislation, see Weatherill and Beaumont, *op.cit.*, p.698.
14. Directive 77/780/EEC and 89/646 EEC as amended and codified by Directive 2000/12 EC.
15. Directive 89/299/EEC as amended and codified by Directive 2000/12 EC.
16. Directive 89/647/EEC as amended and codified by Directive 2000/12 EC.
17. Directive 92/121/EEC as amended and codified by Directive 2000/12 EC.
18. Directive 92/30/EEC as amended and codified by Directive 2000/12 EC.
19. Directive 94/19/EC as amended.
20. Directive 786/635/EEC as amended.
21. It should be noted that prior to the issue of this Directive, banks were, for a number of years adhering to guidelines which were in line with the principles of the EU Directive.
22. Directive 92/121/EEC.
23. Directive 86/635/EEC.
24. Neocleous & Co 2000, *op.cit.*, p.685.
25. Section 41(3) of the Banking Law as supplemented by Law 94(1) of 2000.
26. Public Instrument No.66 of 2000.
27. Directive 94/19/EC.
28. Law 74(I) of 1999.
29. Directive 39/6/EEC as amended.
30. Articles 21 and 22.
31. Directive 96/10/EC as amended.
32. European Commission, 2000 Regular Report of the Commission on Cyprus's Progress Towards Accession, 8 November, 2000, p.42.
33. Under Articles 21-22 of the Banking Law, the Central Bank may issue instructions to banks regarding the level of capital requirements as deemed appropriate and in both the above cases determination of the required capital may take into account the provisions of the relevant Directives.
34. For an analysis of the system in Cyprus, see, Neocleous & Co 2000, *op.cit.*, p. 689; comments by Pat McArdle, 'Seminar on Co-operatives' held in Nicosia, Cyprus, 28-29 April 1999.
35. Commission Report 2000, *op.cit.*, p.29.
36. With a view to improving the living standards of their members, their existence is geared towards serving the interests of small communities.
37. Law 22 of 1985 and Law 68 of 1987 as amended.
38. *Report on the Ways and mean of harmonising the Cyprus co-operative movement to European Legislation,* Plunkett Foundation, 14 June 1999.
39. For a detailed analysis, see, P.O. Demetriades, *Interest Rate Liberalisation. A Report to the Cyprus co-operative movement*, January 1998.
40. See 'Ready for new competition', *Financial Times*, 6 April 1998.
41. See 'Evolution of the Co-operative movement and harminisation with the acquis', *Fileleftheros*, 24 February 2001.
42. See 'Evolution of the Co-operative movement and harminisation with the

acquis', *Fileleftheros*, 24 February 2001.

43. 'Co-operative movement Harmonisation later', Phileleftheros Newspaper, February 2001.
44. Including non-conforming institutions as and when they subsequently succeed in satisfying the prescribed requirements.
45. Directive 79/267/EEC,OJL063, 3 March 1979, p.1-18.
46. The First Life Co-ordination Directive deals with the freedom of establishment and the criteria for host state authorisation.
47. Directive 90/619/EEC, OJL330, 29 November 1990 p.50-61.
48. According to this Directive, if an insured voluntarily enters into a policy contract with an insurer not based in his territory, he leaves the supervisory protection of his own member state. On the other hand, those policy holders not within that category will be granted protection by the host state.
49. Directive 92/96/EEC OJ L360, 9 December 1992 p.1-27.
50. Directive 73/239/EEC, OJ228, 16/8/1973 p. 003-0019. According to this Directive, the principle of *home state* control applies to *large risks,* i.e. policies taken out by large undertakings meeting certain minimum turnover, assets and employment criteria. In contrast, *mass risks* (i.e. all risks other than large risks) are under the control of the *host state.*
51. Directive 88/357/EEC, OJ 172, 4/7/1988 p.1-4.
52. Directive 92/49/EEC, OJ228, 11/8/1992 p.1-23.
53. Directive 72/166/EEC, OJL103, 2/5/1972 p.1-4.
54. Directive 84/5/EEC, OJL8,11/1/1984 p.17-20.
55. Directive 90/232/EEC, L 129 19/5/1990, p.33-35.
56. A. Charalambides, *Legal Aspects of Insurance in Cyprus*, Nicosia, 1991, p.9/1.
57. A. Glykis, 'Insurance Law' in Neocleous & Co. 1999, *op.cit.*, p. 721.
58. As a working hypothesis, the Government of the Republic of Cyprus considers that accession to the EU will take place not later than 1 January 2003.
59. Section 5, 7 and 8 of the Insurance Companies Laws 1984-1998.
60. Directives 73/239/EEC and 79/267/EEC.
61. Commission Report 2000, *op.cit.*, p. 43.
62. Directive 79/267/EEC L063, 13/3/1979, p.1-18.
63. Directive 92/49/EEC L228, 11/8/1992, p.1-23.
64. Directive 92/96/EEC L360, 9/12/1992, p.1-27.
65. Commission Report 2000, *op.cit.*, p.43.
66. Directive 91/674/EEC, L374 31/12/1991, p.7-31.
67. Law 96(1) of 2000.
68. Directives 72/166/EEC, 84/5/EEC and 90/232/EEC.
69. See, E. Neocleous, K. Georgiades and M. Zalewski 'Corporate Law in Introduction to Cyprus Law' in Neocleous & Co. 2000, *op.cit.*, p.353.
70. For an analysis on the topic, see *Financial services: implementing the framework for financial markets: Action Plan,* Communication of the

Commission, dated 11 May 1999; see also Weatherill and Beaumont 1999, *op.cit.*, p.702 and J. Wouters, 'EC Harmonisation of National Rules Concerning Securities Offerings, Stock Exchange Listing and Investment Services: An Overview', *European Business Law Review*, 1993, p.199.

71. With some exceptions, for example, movement securities and inheritances.
72. Law 27 (1) of 1996.
73. Commission Report 2000, *op.cit.*, p. 42.
74. Directive 89/298 as amended.
75. Directive 80/390 EEC as amended.
76. Neocleous & Co 2000, *op.cit.*, p.358.
77. See S.57(1) of the Securities and Stock Exchange Law; Securities and Stock Exchange Regulations, leg. 64 and 68.
78. For an analysis on community principles, see E. Avgouleas, 'Market accountability and pre and post trade transparency: the case for the reform of the EU regulatory framework: Part I', *The Company Lawyer*, Vol.19, No.6, 1998, p.162, and E. Avgouleas, 'Market accountability and pre and post trade transparency: the case for the reform of the EU regulatory framework: Part II', *The Company Lawyer*, Vol.19, No.7, 1998, p.202.
79. S. 38-51 and 355-361.
80. For a more detailed analysis on the subject see: D. Tsibanoulis, *Harmonisation of the Financial Services and Capital Movements Sector of Cyprus with the Acquis Communautaire: Learning from the experience and Practice of the E.U. Member States Authorities. The Functioning of Stock Exchanges in the EU: The Securities Regulation: Principles for organisation of Stock Exchanges. The experience and Practice of Greece.* TAIEX CYPRUS WEEK, Nicosia, 23 May 2000.
81. Directive 89/592/EEC.
82. Law 36(I) of 1999.
83. Neocleous & Co. 2000, *op.cit.*, p.360.
84. Directive 85/611 EEC as amended by Directives, 88/220 EEC and 95/26 EC.
85. Law 63(I)2001, 20 April 2001.
86. Directive 93/22/EEC as amended.
87. Directive 97/9/EEC as amended.
88. Directive 93/6/EEC as amended.
89. Directive 97/9 EEC as amended.
90. For example claims to be met without the prior requirement of broker bankruptcy.
91. Directive 93/6 EEC as amended.
92. Neocleous & Co. 2000, *op.cit.*, p.354.
93. Commission Report 2000, *op.cit.*, p.42.
94. Cyprus has adopted a gradual liberalization plan in this field so as by the time of accession all exchange control restrictions on capital movements to be abolished. The policy of Cyprus in respect of the Exchange Control Law, Cap. 199 has been analysed in Chapter 4: *Free movement of capital*.

95. The provisions of the Exchange Control Law, Cap. 199, and the Immovable Property Acquisition (Aliens) Law, Cap. 109, which constitute an obstacle to the free movement of capital and to freedom of establishment and freedom to provide services have been discussed in Chapter 4: *Free movement of capital.*
96. Weatherill and Baumont 1999, *op.cit.*, p.578.
97. Case 305/87 [1989] ECR 1461 [1991] I CMLR 611.
98. Other legislations which contain restrictions contrary to Articles 43EC and 49EC are: The Banking Law of 1997, (b) The Insurance Companies Laws of 1984 and 1990, (c) The Tertiary Education Schools Laws of 1996-97, (d) The Private Schools of Artistic Dance Law of 1997, (e) The Establishment and Operation of Private Employment Agencies Law of 1997.
99. Directive 95/46/EC, OJ L281, 23/11/1995, pp.31-50.
100. Concerning the Directive 63/262/EEC which provides for the freedom of establishment on agricultural holding abandoned or left uncultivated for more than two years, problems may arise due to a great number of absentee landowners, as well as due to restrictions on irrigation water supply and the need for agricultural land to remain uncultivated for more than two years.
101. The Aliens and Immigration Law, Cap 105, The Immovable Property (Aliens) Law, Cap 109. The Exchange Control Law, Cap 199.
102. Directive 86/653/EEC, OJ L382, 31/12/1986, p.0017-0021.
103. Commission 2000, *op.cit.*, p.42.
104. Directive 98/48/EC, OJ L217, 5/08/1998 p.0018-0026.
105. Directive 98/84/EC, OJ L 320,28/11/1998, p.0054-0057.

9 Cypriot Intellectual Property Law: the European Dimension

MARKUS ZALEWSKI

Introduction

Cyprus's strategic location, developed commercial infrastructure and tax incentives are among the factors which have contributed to the island's development as a flourishing commercial and financial centre in the east Mediterranean.Even before independence in 1960 the authorities in Cyprus had realised that international business and multinational corporations were highly reluctant to export certain technologies and know-how to countries that did not adequately protect intellectual and industrial property rights (IP rights or IPRs). In order to encourage trade and inward investment as well as knowledge transfer, the Cypriot legislature has enacted extensive legislation and created the necessary administrative infrastructure to ensure that commerce and industry are offered a high level of legal protection for their intellectual property assets in Cyprus.

Some 20,000 trade marks are currently registered at the office of the Registrar of Trade Marks and every year there are about 3,000 new trade mark applications. Until the end of 2002, 238 national patent applications were filed with the Registrar of Patents under the new patent regime. According to recent estimates about 57% of business software in Cyprus was obtained illegally. It is also estimated that some 40% of music and some 25% of videos sold in Cyprus are pirated. According to recent statistics on copyright enforcement, in 1998 police obtained 8 software piracy convictions from 23 raids on shops suspected of selling illegal copies of licensed software. As far as video piracy is concerned, the 1998 activity report of the Cyprus Federation against Copyright Theft records 18 convictions.

In accordance with the conclusions of the Luxembourg European

Council in December 1997, the fifth enlargement process in the history of the European Union (EU) was formally launched on 30 March 1998. Five and a half years later Cyprus closed the final two chapters of the accession negotiations on 2 and 3 December 2003. The Copenhagen European Council (12 and 13 December 2003) confirmed the overall agreement reached and the results of the negotiations on all 31 chapters of the acquis[1] were incorporated into the Accession Treaty, which was signed in Athens on 16 April 2003. Cyprus ratified the Accession Treaty on 14 July 2003. Following ratification of this treaty by all existing member states, Cyprus together with nine other acceding countries joined the EU on 1 May 2004.

Within the framework of the accession negotiations the intellectual and industrial property acquis was part of the chapter on company law. In its position paper on company law the Cypriot government fully accepted the intellectual and industrial property acquis and declared that it would be able to effectively implement the relevant EU law and practice by its target accession date without any transitional arrangements.[2] For the European Commission the main issues in the chapter on company law were the protection of IPRs for pharmaceutical products after enlargement, the enforcement of IPRs and the extension of the Community trade mark regime to the territory of the new member states.[3]

For the purposes of this chapter we shall first provide a brief overview of intellectual property rights as currently protected in Cyprus. We shall then go on to outline the basic principles of Community intellectual property law and examine in some detail how Community standards affect the four main proprietary intellectual property rights in Cyprus, namely patents, trade marks, designs and copyright. The chapter concludes with an assessment of Cyprus'ss progress towards harmonisation of its intellectual property law and some pointers to likely future developments.

Overview of intellectual property law in Cyprus

The authorities in Cyprus endeavour to adhere strictly to the law so as to ensure the protection of intellectual property rights against infringement. The constant flow of judicial decisions and the increased interest in the subject due to the widespread availability of new technologies has made intellectual property (IP) an increasingly complex and fast developing area of law. Intellectual property can usefully be divided into:

- industrial property, i.e. patents, trade marks, service marks, trade names, industrial designs, designations of origin and geographical indications, plant and seed varieties; and
- copyright and related rights.

Domestic law

Statute and the general principles of common law are the main sources of intellectual property law in Cyprus. Common law principles of particular relevance in intellectual property cases are the torts of passing off and malicious falsehood as well as the breach of confidence action. Statute usually creates proprietary rights which prohibit third parties from using and exploiting a particular intellectual property asset. As the relevant common law principles primarily provide rights of action, these common law rights are supplementary to the statutory formal rights. This sometimes results in overlapping regimes, as for example between trade mark law and the tort of passing off. Turning to the statutory protection of intellectual property, the following statutes form the core of intellectual property legislation applicable in Cyprus:

- the Patents Law, Law No.16(I)/1998, as amended by Laws Nos.21(I)/1999, 153(I)/2000 and 163(I)/2002
- the Trade Marks Law, Chapter 268 of the Laws of Cyprus, as amended by Laws Nos.63/1962, 69/1971, 206/1990 and 176(I)/2000
- the Legal Protection of Industrial Designs and Models Law, Law No.4(I)/2002
- the Partnerships and Trade Names Law, Chapter 116 of the Laws of Cyprus
- the Copyright and Related Rights Law, Law No.59/1976, as amended by Laws Nos.63/1977, 18(I)/1993, 54(I)/1999, 12(I)/2001 and 128(I)/2002
- the Legal Protection of Topographies of Semiconductor Products Law, Law No.5(I)/2002
- the Law for the Protection of the Commercial Exploitation of Cinematographic Films for Public Transmission, Law No.159/1990
- the Trade Description Law, Law No.5/1987, as amended by Laws Nos.201/1987 and 3/1992
- the Registration and Protection of Designations of Origin and Geographical Indications for Agricultural Products and Foodstuffs

Law, Law No.7(I)/2002

- the Legal Protection of New Varieties of Plants Law of 2002
- the Control of the Movements of Goods which Violate Intellectual Property Rights Law, Law No.31(I)/2002

International agreements

Cyprus is a signatory to a number of international agreements. They fall into two main categories, i.e. agreements which (i) lay down minimum harmonised standards of protection or (ii) provide for reciprocal arrangements regarding application or examination procedures for the registration of intellectual property rights.

In an effort to further improve its existing track record of adherence to international agreements to which all member states are party, Cyprus recently ratified the Rome Convention for the Protection of Performers, Producers of Phonograms and Broadcasting Organisations by means of Law No.14(III)/1999 and the Madrid Agreement concerning the International Registration of Marks and its Protocol (see Laws Nos.3(III) and 4(III)/2003).

Moreover, concrete steps are being taken by the Cypriot government to ratify, inter alia, the Lisbon Agreement concerning the Protection of Appellations of Origin and Indications of Source as well as the UPOV Convention for the Protection of New Varieties of Plants.

Community intellectual property law

Sources of law

In terms of sources of intellectual property law at Community level, the following three types of legal rules should be mentioned:

- norms enacted by way of directly applicable regulations;
- Community legislation harmonising national laws relating to copyright, patents, trade marks and other similar or related rights; and
- international treaties which have been ratified by all member states.

Within the 'Directory of Community Legislation in Force', chapter

17.20 gives a complete and current overview of the extent of the Europeanisation of member states' intellectual property laws.[4]

Intellectual property rights and the Treaty establishing the European Community

As mentioned already, and as a general rule, the exercise of an intellectual property right prohibits third parties to use and exploit the underlying intellectual property asset in the relevant territory. Intellectual property rights are therefore essentially negative, restrictive and territorial.[5] This point of principle is reinforced by Article 295 of the Treaty establishing the European Community ('the EC Treaty' or 'the Treaty'), which expressly states that its provisions are in no way to prejudice the rules in member states governing the system of property ownership. Asserting the protection of an IP right within a member state may therefore give rise to problems principally in relation to two areas of Community law, which are the free movement of goods and services provisions (Articles 28-30 and Article 49 of the EC Treaty) and the competition rules as embodied in Articles 81 and 82 of the EC Treaty. As far as the latter are concerned, the European Commission scrutinises in particular agreements between undertakings relating to the use and exploitation of patents and know-how, the delimitation of trade marks, and franchise operations.[6] Thus proprietors or licensees of intellectual property rights may fall foul of Articles 81 and 82 of the EC Treaty, as these rights have the inherent characteristic of restricting competition and conferring exclusive and monopolistic rights in a particular territory.[7] However, in this chapter we will not delve into competition law issues but rather confine ourselves to a brief overview of the rules on free movement in the single market, in so far as they impact on the exercise of intellectual property rights.[8]

Intellectual property rights and the single market

The legal fragmentation resulting from the existence of a separate system of intellectual property law in each member state is capable of creating obstacles to the free movement of goods and services and poses a potential threat to the creation and functioning of the single market.[9] The widely debated problem of 'parallel imports' neatly illustrates the point.[10] 'Parallel imports' concern operations where importers have obtained goods lawfully, directly or indirectly, from licensees in one member state and seek to put them on the market in another member state without the consent of the person owning the relevant IP rights in respect of those goods in both member states. Community law has tackled this problem of market (re-) partitioning from two different angles.

The rules on free movement One approach to counter the (re-) partitioning of the single market consists in the due application of the free movement of goods and services provisions of the EC Treaty (Articles 28-30 and 49). Constrained by the wording of Articles 30 and 295 of the EC Treaty, the European Court of Justice (ECJ) draws a distinction between the *existence*, the *specific subject-matter*[11] or the *essential function* of an intellectual property right and its *exercise*, with the former being unaffected by Community law and the latter being subject to scrutiny under Articles 28, 29 and 49 of the EC Treaty.[12] In order to conceptualise the limitations imposed on the *exercise* of IP rights, the ECJ interprets the free movement provisions as barring holders of IP rights from asserting these rights to prevent the import of goods covered by these rights into a member state in cases where the holder of the rights in question has *consented* to the goods being placed on the market of another member state.[13] This test is also known as the 'doctrine of exhaustion of rights'. Although the aforesaid principles can be stated in relatively simple words, in practice, they have given rise to a fair amount of case law to determine the question whether the rights owner has given *consent*.[14]

Harmonisation of laws[15] The second measure to aid the proper functioning of the single market for goods and services enjoying protection under national systems of intellectual property law consists in the harmonisation of laws.[16] The judiciary has certainly played a role in this area, but overall the ECJ[17] tends to be reluctant to interfere in the scope of protection afforded by IP rights under national law.[18] The policy considerations behind this stance might be the due reward of enterprise and a certain degree of caution not to create any disincentives to innovation.[19] Due to the inherent difficulties in striking a fair balance between stimulating innovation and furthering market integration when applying the general provisions of the EC Treaty (Articles 30 and 295 as opposed to Articles 28-29 and 49) and the seeming unwillingness of the ECJ to harmonise member states' intellectual property laws through its case law, it was left to the European legislature to improve the functioning of the single market in this area. Such legislative initiatives have followed principally two methods of harmonisation of laws,[20] namely: (i) harmonisation of the content of national legislation relating to IP rights mostly through directives; and (ii) creation of unitary systems for the protection of IP rights with Community-wide effect (Community trade marks, plant variety rights, patents, and designs)[21] mainly by means of regulations.

The next part of this chapter deals primarily with legislative initiatives adopted in Cyprus in pursuance of the first method of harmonisation of laws but also makes reference to preparations which are under way to enable Cyprus to give full effect to unitary pan-European IP rights.

Harmonisation of Cyprus's intellectual property law with Community law standards

Patents

Cypriot patents law Until recently the protection of patents in Cyprus was governed by Chapter 266 of the Laws of Cyprus. A new patents law was passed by Parliament (Law No.16(I)/1998) and came into force on 1 April 1998 ('the Patents Law'). The new law departs from the Chapter 266 Law in large measure. Previously only a person who had already been granted a patent in the United Kingdom or his assignee or transferee could file an application for a patent in Cyprus. With the designation of the Department of the Registrar of Companies and Official Receiver of the Ministry of Commerce, Industry and Tourism ('the DRCOR') as the independent authority in Cyprus for the registration of patents, the Patents Law now provides for a direct patent application in Cyprus and renders registration independent of the prior grant of a patent in the United Kingdom. Thus, UK patents and patents granted under the European Patent Convention[22] or the Patent Cooperation Treaty[23] are recognised in Cyprus on registration. The Patents Law requires patents to be published in the *Official Gazette* of the Republic of Cyprus, thereby enabling any person to object to the grant of the patent concerned. Under the new law, a register of patents is maintained to record the name and address of each patentee as well as any other information which the Registrar of Patents considers necessary for identification purposes. Pursuant to section 26 of the Patents Law, rights and privileges of a patent are conferred for a term of twenty years from the date of filing the relevant application.

Table 9.1 Community patents law

Community instrument	*Community reference*	*Cyprus implementation*
Council Regulation (EEC) No. 1768/92 of 18.6.1992 concerning the creation of a supplementary protection certificate for medicinal products, as amended	OJ L182 of 02.07.1992, p.1	Not necessary (directly appli-cable pursuant to Article 249 of the EC Treaty); incorporated in part VIII of the Patents Law, Law No. 16(I)/1998, through Patents (amend-ment) Law No. 21(I)/1999
Regulation (EC) No.1610/96 of the EP and of the Council of 23.7.1996 concerning the creation of a supplementary protection certificate for plant protection products	OJ L198 of 08.08.1996, p.30	Not necessary; incorporated as part VIIIa in the Patents Law through Patents (amendment) Law No.153(I)/2000
Directive 98/44/EC of the EP and of the Council of 6.7.1998 on the legal protection of bio-technological inventions	OJ L213 of 30.07.1998, p.13	Patents (Amendment) Law No.163(I)/2002

Overview of Community legislation in the area of patent In the absence of a unitary Community patent[24] and due to the success of the intergovernmental European Patent Convention, patents law initiatives at Community level have been piecemeal and sector-specific.[25] The following three instruments form the main body of the patents law acquis.[26]

Implementation of Community law requirements[27] Parts VIII and VIIIA of the Patents Law, as amended, give effect to the above-mentioned Community regulations concerning the creation of supple-mentary protection certificates for medicinal and plant protection products ('SPCs'). The certificates constitute *sui generis* intellectual property rights and confer the same rights as the underlying patent. They afford an extension of the patent term for pharmaceutical and plant protection products whose placing on the market is subject to safety testing and controls by government authorities.[28] The length of the period of protection afforded by the certificates is calculated in relation to the period for which protection was lost due to any government approval process up to a maximum of five years. Implementing regulations provide for the procedure under which SPCs are granted in Cyprus.[29] Partly due to the proposed introduction of supplementary protection certificates the pharmaceutical industry in Cyprus, which is heavily dependent on the manufacturing of generic drugs, lobbied vehemently against an early adoption of the new Patents Law.[30] During the negotiations relating to the chapter on company law the EU emphasised the importance it attached to the speedy establishment of an equal level of protection of intellectual property rights for pharmaceutical products within an enlarged Union. The European Commission was, therefore, presumably pleased to note that in the end the Patents Law was adopted very early on in the accession process, especially as under the Chapter 266 Law patent protection had already been available for pharmaceutical products, thus reducing considerably the 'lead time' for SPCs to produce tangible effects in the Cypriot legal order.[31] This stance of the European Commission is reflected in the provisions of the Accession Treaty relating to industrial property rights, according to which holders of patents in the accession countries will be able to obtain SPCs for products for which first market authorisation was obtained prior to the date of accession.[32]

Section 27(3)(i) of the Patents Law provides for an 'exhaustion of rights' clause in relation to patents in cases where a patented product has been put on the market in Cyprus either by the proprietor himself or with his consent. As already discussed, the case law of the ECJ on the 'exhaustion of intellectual property rights' forms part of the acquis, which imposes limits on the monopoly created by exclusive proprietary rights. During the screening of the existing Cypriot intellectual property legislation the European Commission called for exceptions to patent rights protection to be introduced in harmonised legislation to ensure that the exercise by a patentee of rights enjoyed under national legislation does not create obstacles to the free movement of patented goods within the single market. The Cypriot government, for its part, pledged in its position paper on company law to enforce 'the exhaustion of IP rights doctrine'[33] with respect to the boundaries of the EU and the European Economic Area with effect from Cyprus's accession to the Union. In doing so, the Cypriot authorities will have to shift the basic territorial unit for the purpose of IPR protection from the domestic plane to the European single market.

It should finally be noted that in a significant change from the Chapter 266 Law the new Patents Law, under certain conditions, allows compulsory licensing.[34] Section 49A of the Patents Law, which was inserted by the Patents (Amendment) Law No.163(I)/2002, introduces a new regime for compulsory licensing and cross-licensing of bio-technology inventions. This regime deals with the interrelationship between patent protection for biological inventions and plant variety protection.[35] On accession to the EU, it will be necessary to ensure that any compulsory licences granted by the Cyprus Registrar of Patents do not lead to discrimination against businesses from other member states seeking to export to Cyprus.[36] Again, this will involve a shift of the basic territorial unit to the EU as a whole.

The design of semiconductor chips may also be regarded as an intellectual effort akin to an invention. The need for the protection of semiconductor chips, which was felt as most urgent in the mid-eighties, has been strongly influenced by the rapid development of the market in information and new technologies within the Community.[37] The relevant legislation was passed at Community level in 1986 and introduced protection by a *sui generis* right.[38] Accordingly, the Cypriot legislature took the view that the Semiconductor Directive should be implemented by introducing new legislation, which it did in the form of the Legal Protection of Topographies of Semiconductor Products Law No.5(I)/2002. As in most member states semiconductor chip protection in Cyprus requires registration with the relevant Registrar within two years from its first commercial use (see section 4(3) of Law No.5(I)/2002).

Trade marks

Cypriot trade marks law The registration and protection of marks in relation to goods and services is governed by the Trade Marks Law, Chapter 268 of the Laws of Cyprus, as amended by Laws Nos.63/1962, 69/1971, 206/1990, 176(I)/2000 ('the Trade Marks Law'), the trade marks regulations and the general principles of common law.[39] The Cypriot legislature has adopted the international classification of goods, whereby goods and services are categorised into 34 classes for goods and 8 classes for services. For a mark to be registrable and protected it must be distinctive, i.e. it must be capable of distinguishing goods or services of one undertaking from those of other undertakings.[40] The Trade Marks Law provides for a full examination and opposition procedure. Trade marks and service marks are registered in Cyprus for an initial period of seven years and on application may be renewed for periods of fourteen years from the date of expiration of the original registration or the last renewal of registration, as the case may be.

Table 9.2 Community trade marks law

Community instrument	*Community reference*	*Cyprus implementation*
Council Directive 89/104/EEC of 21 December 1988 to approximate member states' laws relating to trademarks, as amended	OJ L40 of 11.02.1989, p.1	Trade Marks Law, Chapter 268 of the Laws of Cyprus, as amended by Law No. 176(I)/2000
Council Regulation (EC) No. 40/94 of 20 December 1993 on the Community trade mark, as amended	OJ L11 of 14.01.1994, p.1	Not necessary (directly applicable pursuant to Article 249 of the Treaty); however, infrastructure improvements in terms of administrative and institutional enforcement capacity required
Commission Regulation (EC) No.2868/95 of 13 December 1995 implementing Council Regulation (EC) No.40/94 on the Community trade mark	OJ L303 of 15.12.1995, p.1	See above
Commission Regulation (EC) No.2869/95 of 13 December 1995 on the fees payable to the Office for Harmonisation in the Internal Market (Trade Marks and Designs)	OJ L303 of 15.12.1995, p.18	See above
Commission Regulation (EC) No.216/96 of 5.2.1996 laying down the rules of procedure of the Board of Appeal of the Office for Harmonisation in the Internal Market (Trade Marks and Designs)	OJ L28 of 06.02.1996, p.11	See above

A registered mark may be assigned, and the assignee may register his title in accordance with the provisions of sections 24-27 of the Trade Marks Law. Section 29 of the Trade Marks Law allows the registration of licensees as registered users of a trade mark. The Trade Marks Law is modelled on the UK's Trade Marks Act 1938. Therefore the principles and case law which have evolved under that act are of considerable persuasive authority in trade mark disputes before Cypriot courts. The latest major influence on the Trade Marks Law stems from the Trade Marks (Amendment) Law 2000,[41] which transposes Council Directive 89/104/EEC into Cypriot law.

Overview of Community legislation in the area of trade marks As far as trade marks are concerned, the Community has followed a two-pronged strategy of approximating national laws by means of a harmonising Directive, whilst at the same time focusing on the establishment of a Community trade mark ('CTM').[42] The CTM is of a unitary nature, which means that the mark is designed to have the same effect throughout the whole of the EU, affording EU-wide protection through the filing of a single application with the Office for Harmonisation in the Internal Market (Trade Marks and Designs) ('OHIM'). The legal instruments resulting from this strategy are listed below.

Council Directive 89/104/EEC, in conformity with the relevant provisions of Council Regulation (EC) No.40/94 on the Community trade mark ('the CTMR'), harmonises the conditions for registering national trade marks and the rights conferred thereby, lays down a common definition of the signs of which a trade mark may consist and lists grounds for refusing a trade mark or declaring it invalid. The CTMR encourages businesses to operate on a European scale by marketing their products throughout the EU under the protection conferred by a single set of rules.[43] The unitary system created under the CTMR is designed to coexist with national trade marks, which permits enterprises to choose between a bundle of national rights or the unitary Community right, depending on which legal structure best supports their business strategy.[44]

Implementation of Community law requirements During the accession negotiations no particular difficulties arose concerning the implementation of the trade marks acquis. However, the Cypriot delegation was concerned about the position of an earlier national trade mark from the time a similar CTM was used on Cyprus's territory. This situation is not covered by the existing provisions of the Trade Marks Law. In such cases of conflict holders of an earlier national trade mark may oppose the use of a later CTM in Cyprus through an action in the Cypriot courts, if appropriate, by means of an application for interim relief. The new Article 142a(5), in conjunction with Articles 106 and 107 of the CTMR, which is due to come into force on 1 May 2004,[45] now expressly provides for this remedy. Some of these potential future conflicts may also be avoided through close cooperation and exchange of information between the Cyprus Registrar of Trade Marks and the OHIM.[46]

Whereas no express provision has been made in the domestic legal order to address the problem of invoking earlier national rights against the extension of a CTM to Cyprus (see above), the Trade Marks Law as amended by Law No.176(I)/2000 deals with the opposite situation in that a conflicting CTM or CTM application is to be taken into account as an 'earlier right', precluding the registration or prejudicing the validity of a younger national trade mark registered in Cyprus.[47] The protection of CTMs filed before the date of accession will automatically be extended to the territory of the acceding countries upon the coming into force of the Treaty of Accession (see the new Article 142a(1) of the CTMR)[48]. From the date of accession automatically extended CTMs constitute earlier rights in the new member states against any trade mark application or registration with a filing or priority date on or after the effective date of accession. It would appear that in the absence of appropriate transitional provisions the existing wording of Law No.176(I)/2000 does not clearly reflect these arrangements.

Section 6(7) of the Trade Marks Law in conjunction with section 26 of Law No.176(I)/2000 gives effect to the Cypriot government's pledge to enforce the exhaustion of rights conferred by a trade mark with effect from Cyprus's accession to the EU.[49] The provisions of section 6(7) are identical to those of Article 7 of Council Directive 89/104/EEC.

Designs

Cypriot design law Until 1994 the legal protection of designs in Cyprus was governed by the United Kingdom Designs (Protection) Law, Chapter 269 of the Laws of Cyprus. For a design to be protected in Cyprus under the Chapter 269 Law it first had to be registered in the United Kingdom. In civil appeal No.7768 *Eureka Limited* v *Unilever plc*[50] the Cypriot Supreme Court held that the United Kingdom Designs (Protection) Law was unconstitutional and therefore unenforceable. Following this judgment, there was no registered design protection in Cyprus until the enactment of the Legal Protection of Industrial Designs and Models Law[51] ('the Design Law') in 2002. However, in Cyprus designs may, subject to the limitation of section 3(3) of the Copyright and Related Rights Law, also benefit from copyright protection if they qualify as artistic or scientific works. Moreover, under copyright law authors of documents or drawings on which a design is based may be protected against three-dimensional reproductions of these two-dimensional works. Depending on the circumstances of the specific case, a proprietor of a design may also rely on trade marks law, the tort of passing off or the law of breach of confidence.

Overview of Community legislation in the area of designs

With respect to designs the Community has taken a similar approach to that which it followed for trade marks. First the Community adopted a directive approximating the main rules governing designs registered in the member states. This was followed by a regulation on a unitary Community design right to obviate the need to apply for registration in different member states according to different national procedures. The procedures at the OHIM for the registration of Community designs are closely aligned with those for registering CTMs. Registration of Community designs started on 1 April 2003. Table 9.3 shows the legal acts which the Community has passed in the area of designs.

Directive 98/71/EC, inter alia, harmonises the definition of a design, the conditions for registering a design and the rights conferred by registration. There is however no requirement under the Directive to harmonise the procedures concerning registration, renewal and invalidation of design rights. The harmonised national design legislation applies without affecting the protection afforded by Community or national legislation related to copyright, unregistered design rights, trade marks, patents and utility models, unfair competition or civil liability.

The Community Designs Regulation 6/2002 ('the CDR') establishes two types of designs, which are directly applicable in each member state, i.e. the registered Community design and the unregistered Community design. Whereas the unregistered Community design is intended to provide short-term protection against copying for industries whose products have short life cycles, the registered Community design affords extensive protection against copying and the independent development of a similar design for up to twenty-five years. The rights conferred by Community designs are enforced by an infringement action in a national Community design court. The unitary regime under the CDR leaves national registered design protection systems, as harmonised by Directive 98/71/EC, unaffected.

Table 9.3 Community design law

Community instrument	*Community reference*	*Cyprus implementation*
Directive 98/71/EC of the EP and of the Council of 13 October 1998 on the legal protection of designs	OJ L 289 of 28.10.1998, p.28	The Legal Protection of In-dustrial Designs and Models Law, Law No.4(I)/2002
Council Regulation (EC) No.6/2002 of 12 December 2001 on Community designs	OJ L 3 of 05.01.2002, p.1	Not necessary (directly applicable pursuant to Article 249 of the EC Treaty); but infrastructure improvements in terms of administrative and institutional enforcement capacity required
Commission Regulation (EC) No.2245/2002 of 21 October 2002 implementing Council Regulation (EC) No. 6/2002 on Community designs	OJ L 341 of 17.12.2002, p.28	See above
Commission Regulation (EC) No.2246/2002 of 16 December 2002 on the fees payable to the Office for Harmonisation in the In-ternal Market (Trade Marks and Designs) in respect of the registration of Community designs	OJ L 341 of 17.12.2002, p.54	See above

Implementation of Community law requirements The Design Law of 2002 fills the lacuna left when the Cypriot Supreme Court struck down the old Chapter 269 Law. It aims to harmonise Cypriot law in line with Directive 98/71/EC on the legal protection of designs. To qualify for protection under the Design Law a design must be new and have an individual character. The registration of a design confers on its holder the exclusive right to use the design and to prevent any third party not having his consent from using it (section 18(1) of the Design Law). According to section 19 of the Design Law, the rights conferred by a design right do not extend to, inter alia, acts done privately, for non-commercial, experimental or academic purposes. Finally, the Design Law reproduces the exclusions from protection with respect to complex products as well as functional features and interconnections laid down by the Directive (see section 4(6) and section 6(2) to (4) of the Design Law). It is interesting to note that although section 20 of the Design Law provides for an exhaustion of rights clause, unlike in the Trade Mark (Amendment) Law No.176(I)/2000 there is no transitional provision concerning its entry into force. Overall Cyprus opted to enact a close copy of Directive 98/71/EC, which was facilitated by the fact that at the time there was no existing registered design protection in Cyprus.

The accession-related measures which the Community has taken to protect the unitary character of the Community design are similar to those agreed for the CTM (see page 174). As from the date of accession existing registered and unregistered Community designs will automatically be extended to Cyprus's territory (see new Article 110a(1) of the CDR[52]). As a consequence of the automatic extension of Community designs, problems of conflict with national rights acquired in Cyprus prior to its accession may arise. In these cases the holder of an earlier national right will be able to prohibit the use of an extended Community design in Cyprus on the basis of the new Article 110a(4) of the CDR.

Copyright and related rights

Cypriot copyright and related rights law The principal piece of legislation regulating copyright and related rights in Cyprus is the Copyright and Related Rights Law, No.59/1976, as amended by Laws Nos.63/1977, 18(I)/1993, 54(I)/1999, 12(I)/2001 and 128(I)/2002 ('the Copyright Law'), together with the regulations made under section 16 thereof.[53] Copyright subsists in: literary works (including computer programmes), musical works, artistic (including photographs) works, scientific works, cinematographic films, sound recordings, broadcasts, databases and publications of previously unpublished works. Copyright protection is acquired immediately upon creation of the work provided it is original and recorded in, written in, or otherwise reduced to, some material form. The first owner of the copyright is the author (i.e. the writer, painter, composer, programmer, etc.) who:

(i) in the case of a motion picture or sound recording, is the person who undertook the arrangements for the making of the film or sound recording.
(ii) in the case a broadcast, is the person who undertook the arrangements for the making of the transmission and
(iii) in the case of a photograph, is the person who owns the material on which the photograph is taken.

There are no registration or notice requirements for copyright works under Cypriot law. Copyright vests in the proprietor an exclusive right of control to:

(i) reproduce the work in any form,
(ii) advertise it,
(iii) sell, rent, distribute, lend and exhibit it in public,
(iv) communicate it to the public, broadcast it, show it in public by way of satellite or cable transmission and
(v) make a translation, adaptation and any other arrangement of it.

By virtue of this exclusive right the copyright owner may stop others from copying or exploiting the protected work without his permission by means of civil and/or criminal law remedies. The protection afforded by the Copyright Law covers natural persons who are either citizens of the Republic of Cyprus or a member state or have their habitual residence in Cyprus and legal persons registered under the laws of Cyprus or a member state (section 4(a) of the Copyright Law). Although normally there is no protection for works whose authors do not fall within the above categories or which are not first published in Cyprus, section 6(1) of the Copyright Law extends the scope of application of the law to works of non-Cypriot or non-EU origin, which are eligible for protection by virtue of international agreements binding the Republic, as for example the Berne Convention[54] and the Universal Copyright Convention.[55]

Table 9.4 EU copyright and related rights law

Community instrument	*Community reference*	*Cyprus implementation*
Council Directive 91/250/ EEC of 14 May 1991 on the legal protection of computer programmes	OJ L122 of 17.05.1991, p.42	Copyright Law, No. 59/1976, as last amended by the Copyright and Related Rights (Amendment) Law No.128(I)/2002
Council Directive 92/100/ EEC of 19 November 1992 on rental right and lending right and on certain rights related to copyright in the field of intellectual property, as amended	OJ L346 of 27.11.1992, p.61	See above
Council Directive 93/83/ EEC of 27 September 1993 on the coordination of certain rules concerning copyright and rights related to copyright applicable to satellite broadcasting and cable retransmission	OJ L248 of 06.10.1993, p.15	See above
Council Directive 93/98/ EEC of 29 October 1993 harmonising the term of protection of copyright and certain related rights, as amended	OJ L 290 of 24.11.1993, p.9	See above
Council Regulation (EC) No. 3295/94 of 22 December 1994 laying down measures to prohibit the release for free circulation, export, re-export or entry for a suspensive procedure of	OJ L 341 of 30.12.1994, p.8	Not necessary (directly applicable pursuant to Article 249 of the Treaty); the Control of the Movements of Goods which Violate Intellectual Property Rights Law, No.31(I)/2002; sections

counterfeit and pirated goods, as amended		13-14A of the Copyright Law, as amended; the Trade Description Law, No. 5/1987, as amended; the Customs and Excise Law, No. 82/1967, as amended; additionally, infrastructure improvements in terms of administrative and institutional enforcement capacity required
Commission Regulation (EC) No.1367/95 of 16 June 1995 laying down provisions for the implementation of Council Regulation (EC) No.3295/94, as amended	OJ L 133 of 17.06.1995, p.2	See above
Directive 96/9/EC of the European Parliament and the Council of 11 March 1996 on the legal protection of databases	OJ L 77 of 27.03.1996, p.20	Copyright Law, No. 59/1976, as last amended by the Copyright and Related Rights (Amendment) Law No.128(I)/2002
Directive 2001/29/EC of the European Parliament and of the Council of 22 May 2001 on the harmonisation of certain aspects of copyright and related rights in the information society	OJ L167 of 22.06.2001, p.10	Outstanding; to be implemented by means of an amendment to the Copyright Law
Directive 2001/84/EC of the European Parliament and of the Council of 27 September 2001 on the resale right for the benefit of the author of an original work of art	OJ L272 of 13.10.2001, p.32	See above

Copyright is transmissible by assignment, testamentary disposition or operation of the law as movable property. The term of protection of literary, musical and artistic works is the life of the author and seventy years after his death. The duration of copyright in films also depends on the life of the author. The copyright in broadcasts is fifty years from when the broadcast was first made. The *sui generis* right in non-original databases expires fifteen years from the time of completion of the database or its publication (for full details see section 5 of the Copyright Law).

EU legislation in the area of copyright and related rights. There has been significant harmonisation of member states' systems of copyright and related rights, which the Community has embarked on with a view to doing away with barriers to trade and adjusting the legal framework to new forms of exploitation created by technological development and innovation. In harmonising copyright in Europe, the Community legislature concentrated on specific aspects where a large degree of disparity or legal uncertainty existed between member states.[56] Because of the fragmented nature of copyright and the sometimes widely varying solutions followed in different member states, it has not been possible to harmonise this area of law by means of a single comprehensive directive. Accordingly, the Community had to resort to adopting a variety of legislative measures, the most important of which are summarised in Table 4.[57] Concerning important international agreements in the area of copyright and related rights, which have been concluded by all member states or the EU, suffice it to say that Cyprus is a signatory of the Berne Convention for the Protection of Literary and Artistic Works (Act of Paris 1971), the Agreement on Trade Related Aspects of Intellectual Property Rights ('the TRIPS Agreement'),[58] the Rome Convention for the Protection of Performers, Producers of Phonograms and Broadcasting Organisations[59] and the World Intellectual Property Organisation (WIPO) Copyright Treaty (Geneva 1996).[60]

Implementation of EU law requirements As can be seen from Table 4 above, Cyprus proceeded to align its copyright legislation with Community law requirements only in July 2002 by the enactment of the Copyright and Related Rights (Amendment) Law. An explanation of this may be found in the Cypriot government's long-held view that the Copyright Law was substantially in conformity with the relevant acquis.[61] Cyprus has therefore primarily concentrated on infrastructure improvements to enhance its administrative capacity to implement the intellectual property acquis. An 'Intellectual Property Rights Management Centre' was established within the DRCOR for the coordination of the existing enforcement bodies,[62] effective market surveillance, follow-up of all pending IPR cases and the promotion of public awareness. In addition, there have been ongoing programmes of (i) staff recruitment and training, (ii) upgrading of facilities (computerisation, on-line IPR registration, IPR case database, etc.) and (iii) cooperation with international bodies (WIPO, OHIM, European Patent Office), involving the intellectual property section of the DRCOR and the Department of Customs and Excise. In an effort to comply with the requirements set by Council Regulation (EC) No.3295/94 and Commission Regulation (EC) No.1367/95 new legislation in the form of the Control of the Movements of Goods which Violate Intellectual Property Rights Law No.31(I)/2002 was introduced. In accordance with this law, a registration system has been put in place, through which owners of IPRs can record their rights with the Department of Customs and Excise. The border control capacity of the Department was also strengthened by the establishment of a special unit dealing with the protection of IPRs and by enhanced cooperation with the DRCOR, e.g. through exchange of information and direct access to IPR registers.

A number of information technology-induced additions to Cypriot copyright law were introduced by the Copyright (Amendment) Law 1993, which treats electronic computer programmes as literary works. The restricted act of 'copying' includes copying by electronic means and recording in any other form. 'Electronic means' refer to means which are actuated by electric, (electro-)magnetic, electrochemical or electro-mechanical energy. The exclusive right also extends to the making of adaptations (including translations), which in the case of computer programmes encompasses the form of the programme in which it is converted out of or into a computer language or a code other than that which is coincidental to the running of the programme.[63] These provisions went some way to approximating Cyprus's Copyright Law with Council Directive 91/250/EEC on the legal protection of computer programmes but fell short of the required detail in relation to, for example, the scope of protection of computer programmes, applicable exceptions to the restricted acts for the purposes of error correction, back-up, testing, interoperability, etc., as well as availability of special protection measures. These issues have now been addressed in sections 7B and 7E of the Copyright Law, which were introduced by Law No.128(I)/2002.

Like the most recent amendments to the Copyright Law, the adoption of EU legislation in the area of databases has been strongly influenced by the rapid development of the market in information and new technologies within the EU.[64] The Database Directive 96/9/EC provides for copyright protection for databases which constitute the author's own intellectual creation as well as for *sui generis* protection for an investment in the obtaining, verification or presentation of a database's contents.[65] As the two-tier database regime established under the Directive is closely related to copyright, the Cypriot legislature decided to incorporate the relevant harmonising provisions in the Copyright Law and not to opt for separate legislation, as it did in the case of topographies of semiconductor products.

Turning to some examples of required amendments to the existing copyright legislation, Cyprus will have to introduce, for the benefit of authors of original works of art, a compulsory resale right (*droit de suite*) to align Cypriot law with Directive 2001/84/EC. This right entitles authors of an original work of art to receive a percentage of the price obtained from any commercial resale of the work. The rights of reproduction, communication to the public and distribution laid down in Directive 2001/29/EC on the harmonisation of certain aspects of copyright and related rights in the information society are already protected under Cypriot law (section 7(1)(a) of the Copyright Law). However, harmonisation in line with the Directive will be required, particularly with respect to the scope of the right of communication to the public, the exceptions and limitations to the rights of reproduction and communication to the public as well as the legal protection of technological measures and rights-management information.

Finally, it should not be forgotten in the present context that copyright and related rights fall within the area of application of the provisions of the EC Treaty. As already discussed, the ECJ has interpreted the provisions of the EC Treaty as affecting the scope and enforceability of national intellectual property laws in circumstances where they are in conflict with Community law.[66] Basic Treaty principles, such as non-discrimination on grounds of nationality between citizens of member states, may therefore be directly effective in the national legal order. Member states' copyright laws, for example, may not exclude authors and performing artists from other member states from rights enjoyed by their nationals.[67] Accordingly, the new wording of section 4(a) of the Copyright Law introduced by Law No.128(I)/2002 now provides for an extension of copyright protection to EU citizens and legal persons registered under the laws of a member state.

We shall now adopt a slightly broader view of the subject matter. In the following we shall briefly analyse the European Commission's stance on Cyprus's progress towards harmonisation of its intellectual property law, as expressed in its regular reports and attempt to give our own assessment of what has been achieved so far.

Cyprus's progress towards harmonisation of intellectual property law

The European Commission's regular progress reports

Already in its first regular report the European Commission expressed the view that as far as the Cypriot economy was concerned Cyprus would be able to meet the challenges posed by the adoption of the acquis.[68] In its 1999 report the Commission clearly stated that Cyprus fully complied with the political and economic criteria for EU accession.[69] According to all Commission reports to date, there is, however, room for improvement with regard to the third Copenhagen criterion, i.e. Cyprus's ability to assume the obligations of membership. We shall therefore examine Cyprus's performance against this criterion in more detail below.

In its 1998 regular report the Commission identified the internal market field, especially the approximation of trade marks and copyright and neighbouring rights legislation as key areas where substantial harmonisation efforts had yet to be undertaken.[70] However, the Commission was pleased to note the introduction of the Patents Law, in which provision for a supplementary protection certificate for pharmaceutical products had been made.[71]

In its 1999 report the Commission commended Cyprus on having had enacted new patent regulations,[72] facilitating the implementation and enforcement of the Patents Law.[73] It also emphasised the progress which had been made with respect to the ongoing computerisation of the register of patents. However, the 1999 report expressed concern over the distinct lack of transposition of directives on rental and lending rights, the term of protection of copyright and related rights, satellite broadcasting and cable retransmission as well as computer programme and database protection.[74] As far as administrative capacity for the implementation of the IP acquis was concerned, the Commission stressed the need to strengthen the existing enforcement bodies and called for the introduction of stricter legislation to curb the entry, release or (re-)export of counterfeit and pirated goods.[75] In this respect the 1999 report welcomed Cyprus's efforts to establish an 'Intellectual Property Rights Management Centre' within the DRCOR.

In its 2000 report the Commission appeared satisfied that Cyprus's alignment with the acquis in the field of industrial and intellectual property rights continued at a steady pace.[76] According to the Commission, Cyprus made good progress, especially as regards trade mark protection and the implementation of the Patents Law.[77] However, in the eyes of the

Commission further legislative and enforcement measures were needed with respect to copyright and neighbouring rights.[78]

In 2001 the Commission established that Cyprus had made further progress in the protection of intellectual and industrial property rights, but that the harmonisation process needed to be accelerated.[79] While in the Commission's opinion the harmonisation of the Patents and Trade Marks Law was far advanced, there was also a significant delay in implementing the copyright acquis.[80] As far as law enforcement capacity was concerned, the Commission called for improved coordination and cooperation among the administrative and judicial bodies involved in enforcement as well as for targeted training so as to enable Cyprus to step up the fight against piracy and counterfeiting.[81]

In its last regular report in 2002 the Commission came to the conclusion that since its first report in 1998 Cyprus had made steady progress in terms of legislative harmonisation with the IP acquis.[82] Cyprus was given full credit for the number of IP-related legal acts which had been passed in 2002.[83] However, the Commission also voiced criticism about outstanding legislative measures to comply with the Information Society and Resale Right Directives.[84] Finally there was a strong reminder that the strengthening of enforcement capacity of IPR legislation and the fight against piracy and counterfeiting continued to be priority issues for Cyprus.[85]

In order to provide further guidance to the acceding states in their efforts to complete their preparations for accession, the Commission produced comprehensive monitoring reports in November 2003. The report on Cyprus's preparations for membership confirms the high level of alignment that Cyprus has reached in most policy areas.[86] In the field of protection of IPRs the Commission highlights the need for further legislative adjustments in respect of copyright and related rights, notably for those required in the digital environment of the information society.[87] As in most previous reports the Commission insists that Cyprus maintain sustained efforts to enhance the coordination and training of enforcement bodies.[88] Overall, the Commission expects Cyprus to be in a position to implement the IP acquis as required by the time of accession.[89]

Assessment of the harmonisation of Cypriot intellectual property law

It is interesting to note that whereas the Commission's earlier regular reports noted a certain slackening of Cyprus's endeavours to align with the intellectual property acquis, the Commission's latest reviews of Cyprus's efforts to assume the responsibilities of EU membership adopt a mainly positive tone. This is, of course, due to the fact that a substantial amount of Community instruments in the field of IPRs was transposed only in 2002. Throughout the accession process it has been the EU's position that the incorporation of the acquis into national legislation was not in itself sufficient, but that the accession countries had to ensure that it was actually applied to EU standards.[90] The Commission has been consistently critical of Cyprus's track record of credible and effective enforcement of the IP acquis. With deadlines for implementation set very close to its target date for accession, it is submitted that Cyprus has weakened its capability to demonstrate effective application of the acquis.

Our examination of the implementation of Community law requirements for patents and trade marks clearly demonstrates that Cyprus has reached a high degree of integration with the existing body of EU law and practice in these areas, which is certainly a creditable achievement. As far as patents and related rights are concerned, this was effected by incorporating the relevant Community regulations on supplementary protection certificates for pharmaceutical and plant protection products in the domestic Patents Law. This eagerness on the part of Cyprus to apply the key parts of the patents acquis may be explained by the fact that the EU stressed during the accession negotiations the great importance it attached to the existence of an equal level of protection of pharmaceutical products within an enlarged Union. This would offer, on a pan-European scale, suitable incentives and rewards for research and development ('R&D') to pharmaceutical manufacturers. Accordingly, the EU strongly encouraged applicant states to apply the relevant Community regulations as early as possible. Upon accession, however, Community regulations will be directly applicable in the domestic legal order of the new member states (Article 249 of the EC Treaty). It is therefore widely held that from a technical point of view it is not satisfactory to insert provisions into national law whose wording is identical to that of the relevant Community regulations and that this legislative technique should be avoided whenever possible.[91] The reasons for this are as follows. First and foremost the transformation of Community regulations into national law may lead to certain changes or adjustments, which may jeopardise their uniform application.[92] A further important reason is that national implementing measures may obscure the Community nature of the relevant provisions to citizens and, particularly, to national courts, which before and after accession have to give proper effect to the 'harmonised' laws incorporating these provisions.[93] In view of these concerns it is therefore desirable that upon accession the Cypriot legislature repeals all legislative measures transforming Community regulations into Cypriot law.

Turning now to copyright and related rights, it would appear that these areas of IP law have been the 'poor relation' of the Cypriot harmonisation programme, with the majority of harmonising legislation passed only in 2002 and implementing measures outstanding for another two directives. Although this may be partly attributed to the fact that initially the Cypriot government considered the existing Copyright Law substantially in conformity with the relevant acquis,[94] it is submitted that a high level of copyright protection was, perhaps, regarded as less of a priority for business development and inward investment purposes than the modernisation of the rules and procedures governing patents and trade marks. Undoubtedly, it is patents and trade mark cases which make up the majority of existing intellectual property work for legal practitioners and government officials in Cyprus. However, if one takes a more long-term view, the failure to regularly update national copyright law in line with requirements determined by technological development and the ensuing new forms of exploitation, may present a serious disincentive for high-technology firms to do business with or from Cyprus.[95] It does therefore not come as a surprise to see that despite a number of competitive advantages (e.g. good infrastructure, a comparable low cost base, favourable immigration rules) 'business incubators', 'research and development centres' and 'science parks' have not yet made much headway in Cyprus, especially when compared to developments in neighbouring countries in the region, such as for example Israel.[96] Although the Cypriot government has adopted a policy of promoting the creation of high-technology businesses on the island,[97] this initiative would seem to be rather late and essentially of a defensive nature. Experience from other European countries shows that such government-led technology and innovation policy is likely to attract mainly migrant foreign high-technology firms, whose output, in most cases, does not 'trickle down' into local industry.[98] Unless this initiative commits substantial resources to the reinforcement of technology-driven industrial activity and innovative capacities of Cypriot small and medium-sized businesses (which form the backbone of commerce and industry in Cyprus) the Cypriot government's getting on the bandwagon of R&D investment is unlikely to translate into long-term positive effects for the local economy.[99]

The EU's latest views on Cyprus's preparedness for membership in large measure centre around the post-Copenhagen accession criterion[100] of capacity to apply and/or enforce EU rules *effectively* through the creation of substantial new institutional and administrative machinery and procedures.[101] The EU itself would seem to offer accession countries little guidance on a model for developing and demonstrating *effective* implementing capacity. The few guidelines available refer, in the main, to the objective or the end result of implementation (e.g. 'creation of special units to enforce border control',[102] 'upgrading of existing infrastructure',[103] 'strengthening of human resource base',[104] 'combating of piracy and counterfeiting',[105] etc.). In order to be *effective*, programmes for the adoption of the acquis should properly address the specific local conditions, needs and impact of implementing measures.[106] Transposing this to the alignment of IPR protection in Cyprus with EU standards, it is submitted that *effective* enforcement capacity is primarily a function of a developed sense of legal responsibility and wrongdoing on the part of citizens, who will be subject to the new rules and procedures. Accordingly, only if there is a shared common understanding that IP rights constitute a valuable form of intangible property worthy of a level of protection equal to that of tangible property can the risk of nominal harmonisation in this area of law be avoided in the long term. It is further argued that apart from the public institutions which are responsible for administering and enforcing IPRs it is incumbent also on the private sector, e.g. retailers, the media and the societies for the collective management of IPRs[107] to assume a more prominent role in fostering such a shared common understanding.

Concluding remarks

As the accession date of 1 May 2004 drew nearer, all acceding countries made special efforts to complete the approximation of their respective legal system, including their existing intellectual property laws, with the acquis *communautaire*. In the case of Cyprus, the Patents Law, as last amended by Law No.163(I)/2002, the Legal Protection of Industrial Designs and Models Law No.4(I)/2002 and the Copyright and Related Rights (Amendment) Law No.128(I)/2002 provide good examples of its ongoing integration into the EU system. Further amendments to the Copyright Law are expected in the very near future to take account of the ever-increasing Community law in this area (Resale Right and Information Society Directives). As regards topographies of semiconductor products, the existing copyright regime was deemed not adaptable enough to accommodate the novel category of protected subject matter created by the relevant Community directive. Hence, the existing body of Cypriot intellectual property law was supplemented by new legislation in the form of the Legal Protection of Topographies of Semiconductor Products Law No.5(I)/2002. In present context one should also not forget that alignment with the acquis is a moving target. Existing proposals on intellectual property enforcement, the patentability of computer-implemented inventions and the Community patent may be enacted into law any time soon, which will necessitate further adjustments to existing legislation and institutional infrastructure.

This chapter is has also attempted to demonstrate that the proper implementation of the body of EU law and practice in the area of IP rights requires accession countries to take into account also basic Treaty principles and the ECJ's case law. Given the enormous amount of secondary Community legislation to be transposed,[108] it is plain to see that these elements of the acquis are likely to be overlooked rather easily during the implementation process.

The assessments of Cyprus's progress towards harmonisation of its intellectual property law given in section 5 above bear out clearly that Cyprus has reached a high degree of integration with the existing body of EU law and practice in this area and that the Cypriot authorities are committed to resolving the outstanding issues in transposing and implementing the IP acquis by the time of accession. However, our discussion has shown that there are serious challenges ahead for intellectual property rights as currently protected in Cyprus, not least due to the speed of technological development and popular attitude.

With previous legislation, in the case of patents and trade marks, dating back to the 1950s and the last major amendment to the Copyright Law having been made only in 2002, the prospect of EU accession has provided a vital catalyst for Cyprus to modernise and update its intellectual property law – a long overdue and arduous process, which without the likely reward of EU membership would not have been set in train and would not have spurred the necessary forces into action.

Notes

1. The body of EU law and practice, also known as the *acquis communautaire*, comprises, inter alia, the treaties upon which the EU is founded, all secondary legislation enacted to date, European Community ('EC' or 'Community') acts, measures adopted in the EU framework, the case law of the ECJ, international agreements concluded by the EU and those concluded by

member states among themselves relating to EU activities, informal administrative practice of the European civil service, as well as political declarations. In other words, it denotes the rights and obligations of the EU system and its institutional framework.

2. Paragraph A.(a) of the Cypriot government's position paper on company law, available at www.cyprus-eu.org.cy/eng/09_position_papers/chapter_05.htm.
3. See European Commission, Directorate-General Enlargement, *Enlargement of the European Union – Guide to the Negotiations Chapter by Chapter*, p.16, available on-line at www.europa.eu.int/comm/enlargement/negotiations/chapters/index.htm.
4. Available at www.europa.eu.int/eur-lex/en/lif/reg/en_register_1720.html.
5. W.R. Cornish, *Intellectual Property*, 3rd ed., Sweet & Maxwell, London, 1996, paras.1-04, 1-29; D.I. Bainbridge, *Intellectual Property Law*, 2nd ed., Pitman Publishing, London, 1994, p.11.
6. For a more detailed account of EC competition law problems arising from the exercise of intellectual property rights, see R. Whish, *Competition Law*, 3rd ed., Butterworths, London, Edinburgh, 1993, ch.19; D.G. Goyder, *EC Competition Law*, 3rd ed., Clarendon Press, Oxford, 1998, ch.13; I. Maher, 'Competition Law and Intellectual Property Rights: Evolving Formalism' in P. Craig and G. de Búrca (eds), *The Evolution of EU Law*, Oxford University Press, Oxford, 1999, pp.597-624.
7. Cyprus has enacted into domestic law mirror versions of the block exemptions issued under Article 81(3) of the EC Treaty, such as for example the Block Exemption (Technology Transfer Agreements) Order of 1997, which is based on Commission Regulation (EEC) 240/96 of 31 January 1996 on the application of Article 85(3) to certain categories of technology transfer agreements, OJ L 31 of 09.02.1996, p.2.
8. It should be noted that the ECJ uses the same basic criteria in relation to challenges to proprietary rights under the Treaty provisions on the free movement of goods and services as in the context of Articles 81 and 82 of the EC Treaty, see P. Craig and G. de Búrca, *EU Law*, 3rd ed., Oxford University Press, Oxford, 2003, p.1108; S. Weatherill and P. Beaumont, *EU Law*, 3rd ed., Penguin Books, London, 1999, p.978; J. Holyoak and P. Torremans, *Intellectual Property Law*, 2nd ed., Butterworths, London, Edinburgh, Dublin, 1998, p.129.
9. This concern was expressed by the ECJ as early as in 1968 in Case 24/67 *Parke Davis & Co.* v *Probel, Reese, Beintema-Interpharm and Centrafarm* [1968] European Court Reports ('ECR') 55, p.71.
10. See D. Wyatt, 'Quantitative Restrictions and Measures Having Equivalent Effect' in *Wyatt and Dashwood's EU Law*, 4th ed., Sweet and Maxwell, London, 2000, p.360; Cornish 1996, *op.cit.*, paras.1-42, 1-51 *et seq.*; Holyoak and Torremans 1998, *op.cit.*, p.111 *et seq.*; N. Cooper, D. Alexander and L. Lane, 'Intellectual Property' in G. Barling and M. Brealey (eds), *Practitioners' Handbook of EC Law*, The Bar Council, London, 1998,

para.19.1.4.

11. From this it follows that IP rights which can be regarded as merely incidental to the relevant property may not be used to partition the market. On this point, see Wyatt 2000, *op.cit.*, p.363.
12. Case 15/74 *Centrafarm BV* v *Sterling Drug Inc.* [1974] ECR 1147, p.1162; Case 16/74 *Centrafarm BV* v *Winthrop BV* [1974] ECR 1183, p.1194; Case 119/75 *Terrapin (Overseas) Limited* v *Terranova Industrie C.A. Kapferer and Co.* [1976] ECR 1039, at para.5.
13. See para.15 of the judgment in Case 15/74 and para.12 of the judgment in Case 16/74.
14. With respect to patents, see e.g. Case 15/74; Case 187/80 *Merck v Stephar* [1981] ECR 2063; Case 19/84 *Pharmon BV v Hoechst AG* [1985] ECR 2281 and Joined Cases C-267 and C-268/95 *Merck & Co. Inc., Merck Sharp & Dohme Limited, Merck Sharp & Dohme International Services BV v Primecrown Limited, Ketan Himathal Mehta, Necessity Supplies Limited*, and *Beecham Group plc v Europharm of Worthing Limited* [1996] ECR I-6285. As regards trade marks, see e.g. Case 16/74 and Case 119/75; Case C-9/93 *IHT Internationale Heiztechnik GmbH v Ideal-Standard GmbH* [1994] ECR I-2789; Case C-355/96 *Silhoutte International Schmied GmbH & Co. KG* v *Hartlauer Handelsgesellschaft mbH* [1998] ECR I-4799. As far as copyright is concerned, see e.g. Case 78/70 *Deutsche Grammophon* v *Metro* [1971] ECR 487; Joined Cases 55 and 57/80 *Musik-Vertrieb Membran GmbH v GEMA* [1981] ECR 147 and Case 341/87 *EMI Electrola GmbH v Patricia Im- und Export GmbH* [1989] ECR 79.
15. No distinction is made between the terms 'harmonisation', 'approximation' and 'co-ordination of laws'.
16. For a comprehensive account of the harmonisation of laws, its functions, methods and present state, see L.W. Gormley (ed.), *P.J.G. Kapteyn and P. VerLoren van Themaat's Introduction to the Law of the European Communities*, 3rd edition, Kluwer Law International, London, 1998, pp.774-801; specifically with respect to the harmonisation of IPRs, see T.C. Vinje, 'Harmonising Intellectual Property Laws in the European Union: Past, Present and Future' [1995] *European Intellectual Property Review*, pp.361-366.
17. Examples of the ECJ upholding IP rights protected under national law can be found, in particular, in Case 144/81 *Keurkoop BV* v *Nancy Kean Gifts BV* [1982] ECR 2853; Case 156/86 *Warner Bros Inc. and Metronome Video* v *Christiansen* [1988] ECR 2605; Case 35/87 *Thetford Corporation* v *Fiamma SpA* [1988] ECR 3585; Case 53/87 *CICRA and Maxicar* v *Régie Nationale des Usines Renault* [1988] ECR 6039; Case 341/87; Case T-69/89 *Radio Telefis Eireann* v *Commission* [1991] ECR II-485 and Case C-9/93.
18. Weatherill and Beaumont 1999, *op.cit.*, pp.994-995; Goyder 1998, *op.cit.*, pp.300-301.
19. Weatherill and Beaumont 1999, *op.cit.*, p.994.

20. European Commission, 'Activities of the European Union – Summaries of Legislation – Intellectual Property: Introduction', *SCADPlus*, available on-line at http://www.europa.eu.int/scadplus/leg/en/s06020.htm; Weatherill and Beaumont 1999, *op.cit.*, p.995; R.E. Annand and H.E. Norman, *Blackstone's Guide to the Community Trademark*, Blackstone Press, London, 1998, p.7.
21. As far as a Community patent is concerned, on 3 March 2003 the Council of Minister reached political agreement on the jurisdictional system, the language regime, the costs, the role of national patent offices and the distribution of fees. The relevant document under discussion is the European Commission proposal for a Council Regulation on the Community patent of 1 August 2000, COM(2000) ,412 final, which has been revised taking into account the common political approach taken by the Council in March 2003. With respect to this proposal, see European Commission, Internal Market Directorate-General, *Single Market News*, Nos.22, 23, 30 and 31.
22. Cyprus signed the European Patent Convention of 1973 in 1997. With effect from 1 April 1998 Cyprus became the nineteenth member of the European Patent Organisation.
23. Cyprus ratified the Patent Cooperation Treaty of 1970 by Law No.27 (III)/1997.
24. See note 21.
25. Weatherill and Beaumont 1999, *op.cit.*, p.996.
26. A new legislative proposal aims to harmonise national patent laws with respect to the patentability of computer-implemented inventions. According to this proposal, inventions whose operation requires the use of a computer programme and which make a 'technical contribution' to the state of the art may be patented. For further details see the European Commission proposal for a directive of the European Parliament and of the Council on the patentability of computer-implemented inventions of 20 February 2002, COM(2002) 92 final. There is also a European Commission proposal for a European Parliament and Council Directive approximating the legal arrangements for the protection of inventions by utility model (COM(1997) 691 final) as amended by the European Commission proposal of 25 June 1999, COM(1999) 309 final, which has stalled in the legislative process.
27. No distinction is made between the terms 'implementation', 'transposition' and 'transformation'.
28. See Holyoak and Torremans 1998, *op.cit.*, p.155; M. Zalewski, 'Cyprus Patents Law, Trade Marks Law and Copyright Law', commentary on section 31 of the Patents Law in D. Campbell (ed.), *World Intellectual Property Rights and Remedies: Laws with Commentary*, Oceana Publications, Dobbs Ferry, New York, release 2001-2, February 2001.
29. Public Instruments Nos.46/1999 and 320/2000, respectively.
30. See C.C. Colota, 'Cyprus to Modernize its Patent Law', *IP Worldwide*, March/April 1998, p.36.
31. European Commission, *2000 Regular Report from the Commission on*

Cyprus's Progress towards Accession ('European Commission 2000'), para.B.3.1, p.47, available on-line at www.europa.eu.int/comm/enlargement/cyprus/index.htm.

32. See Annex II to the Act concerning the Conditions of Accession of the Czech Republic, the Republic of Estonia, the Republic of Cyprus, the Republic of Latvia, the Republic of Lithuania, the Republic of Hungary, the Republic of Malta, the Republic of Poland, the Republic of Slovenia and the Slovak Republic and the Adjustments to the Treaties on which the European Union is Founded ('the Act'), OJ L 236 of 23 September 2003, pp.342-344. The Act is annexed to the Treaty of Accession. Annex II of the Act provides for appropriate amendments to Regulation (EEC) No.1768/92 and Regulation (EC) No.1610/96.
33. Paragraph C.(b) of the Cypriot government's position paper on company law, *op.cit.*
34. See ss.49-56 of the Patents Law. For a detailed account of compulsory licences under the UK Patents Act 1977, see L. Bently and B. Sherman, *Intellectual Property Law*, Oxford University Press, Oxford, 2001 pp.524-530; Cornish 1996, *op.cit.*, para.7-43 *et seq.*
35. Bently and Sherman 2001, *op.cit*, p.529.
36. See Case C-235/89 *Commission* v *Italy* [1992] ECR I-777; Case C-30/90 *Commission v United Kingdom* [1992] ECR I-829; Case C-191/90 *Generics (UK) Limited v Smith Kline & French Laboratories (UK) Limited* [1992] ECR I-5335.
37. See recital 1 of Council Directive 87/54/EEC on the legal protection of topographies of semiconductor products, OJ L 24 of 27.01.1987, p.36.
38. See Directive 87/54/EEC, Art.2.
39. For an overview of trade mark protection in Cyprus, see N. Ktenas and E. Papachristoforou, 'Cyprus' in N.S. Kinsella (gen.ed.), *Trademark Practice & Forms*, Oceana Publications, Dobbs Ferry, New York, release 2003-2, April 2003; K. Chrysostomides & Co., *Trade Marks in Cyprus*, available on-line at http://www.chrysostomides.com.cy/property/; C.C. Colota, 'Trade Marks in Cyprus', *Managing Intellectual Property: Trademark Yearbook 1996*, Euromoney, London, 1996, pp.63-64.
40. See Council Directive 89/104/EEC of 21 December 1988 to approximate the laws of the member states relating to trademarks, Art.2; see also the definition of 'trade mark' in s.2(1) of the Trade Marks Law.
41. Law No.176(I)/2000; with regard to this amendment law, see M. Kannava, 'Cyprus Purports to Bring its Trade Marks Law Up To Date', *European Legal Business*, January/February 2001, pp.58-60.
42. European Commission, SCADPlus, *op.cit.*; Annand and Norman 1998, *op.cit.*, pp.7-8.
43. See recital 1 of the CTMR; European Commission, SCADPlus, *op.cit.*
44. Weatherill and Beaumont 1999, *op.cit.*, p.997.
45. This amendment has been included in Annex II to the Act, OJ L 236 of 23

September 2003, p.342 and will enter into force on the same date as the Treaty of Accession.

46. For further details on the consequences for holders of CTMs due to enlargement see Communication No.05/03 of the President of OHIM of 16.10.2003 concerning enlargement of the EU in 2004, available on-line at http://www.oami.eu.int/en/office/aspects/communications/05-03.htm.
47. See s.14(1) in conjunction with s.14A(1)(a)(iii) of the Trade Marks Law. Generally in relation to this issue, see Office for Harmonization in the Internal Market (Trade Marks and Designs), *National Law Relating to the Community Trade Mark*, OOPEC, Luxembourg, 1999, ch.6.
48. See Annex II to the Act, OJ L 236 of 23.09.2003, p.342.
49. With regard to this commitment applicable to all IPRs. Paragraph C.(b) of the Cypriot government's position paper on company law, *op.cit.*
50. *Eureka Limited* v *Unilever plc* [1994] 1 Cyprus Law Reports 124.
51. Law No.4(I)/2002.
52. This new article of the CDR has been included in Annex II to the Act, OJ L 236 of 23.09.2003, p.344.
53. For an overview of Cypriot copyright law, see T.M. Keane, 'Copyright and Copyright Protection in Cyprus - Part I and II', *Copyright World*, Issue 42, July/August 1994, pp.36-43 and Issue 43, September 1994, pp.31-35; A. Evagelou, 'Intellectual Property Law', *Cyprus Law Tribune*, January-March 1991, pp.142-149.
54. Cyprus ratified the Berne Convention for the Protection of Literary and Artistic Works (Act of Paris 1971) by Law No.86/1979.
55. Law No.151/1990 ratified the Universal Copyright Convention.
56. European Commission, SCADPlus, *op.cit.*
57. With respect to the European Parliament and Council Directive 98/84/EC of 20 November 1998 on the legal protection of services based on, or consisting of, conditional access, OJ L 320 of 28.11.1998, p.54, which is sometimes included in the intellectual property *acquis*, see the chapter on 'Freedom of Establishment and Free Movement of Services'. Current legislative efforts centre on the European Commission proposal for a Directive of the European Parliament and of the Council on measures and procedures to ensure the enforcement of intellectual property rights of 30 January 2003, COM(2003) 46 final, with respect to this proposal, see European Commission, Internal Market Directorate-General, *Single Market News*, No.31, May 2003, p.24.
58. Cyprus ratified the TRIPS Agreement by Law No.16(III)/1995.
59. This convention was ratified by Law No.14(III)/1999.
60. See the WIPO Copyright Treaty Ratifying Law No.23(III)/2002.
61. Para.B.2.(b) of the Cypriot government's position paper on company law, *op.cit.*
62. The institutions responsible for administering and enforcing intellectual property rights in Cyprus are the intellectual property section of the DRCOR,

the Department of Customs and Excise of the Ministry of Finance, the Competition and Consumer Protection Division of the Ministry of Commerce, Industry and Tourism, the Competent Copyright Authority set up under section 15 of the Copyright Law, the Law Office of the Republic, the police and the courts.

63. See s.2(1)(a)(iii) of the Copyright Law.
64. See Directive 96/6/EC of the European Parliament and the Council on the legal protection of databases, Recital 9.
65. See Directive 96/6/EC, Articles 3 and 7.
66. With respect to this point of supremacy of Community law over conflicting national law.
67. Joined Cases C-92 and C-326/92 *Phil Collins* v *Imtrat Handelsgesellschaft mbH* and *Patricia Im- und Export Verwaltungsgesellschaft mbH and Leif Emanuel Kraus* v *EMI Electrola GmbH* [1993] ECR I-5145.
68. European Commission, 'Regular Report 1998 from the Commission on Cyprus's Progress towards Accession' ('European Commission 1998'), *Bulletin of the European Union, Supplement 15/98*, OOPEC, Luxembourg, 1999, para.2.3, p.16.
69. European Commission, 'Composite Paper 1999: Reports on Progress towards Accession by each of the Candidate Countries' ('European Commission 1999a'), *Bulletin of the European Union, Supplement 2/99*, OOPEC, Luxembourg, 2000, paras.III.1 and III.2, at pp.13, 19; generally with respect to EU accession criteria, see M. Zalewski and A. Thoma, 'Accession to the European Union' in D. Campbell (ed.), *Introduction to Cyprus Law*, Yorkhill Law Publishing, Salzburg, 2000, para.25-2 *et seq.*
70. European Commission 1998, *op.cit.*, para.3.1, p.18.
71. Ibid.
72. The Patents (Fees and Rights) Regulations 1999, Public Instrument No.46/1999.
73. European Commission, *1999 Regular Report from the Commission on Cyprus's Progress towards Accession* ('European Commission 1999b'), para.B.3.1, p.24, available on-line at www.europa.eu.int/comm/enlargement/cyprus/index.htm.
74. Ibid.
75. Ibid.
76. European Commission 2000, *op.cit.*, para.B.3.1, pp.46-47.
77. Ibid.
78. Ibid., and in para.D.1, p.97.
79. European Commission, *2001 Regular Report from the Commission on Cyprus's Progress towards Accession* ('European Commission 2001'), para.B.4.1, p.46 and para.B.4.2, p.90, available on-line at www.europa.eu.int/ comm/enlargement/cyprus/index.htm.
80. Ibid, para.B.4.1, p.47.
81. Ibid.

82. European Commission, *2002 Regular Report from the Commission on Cyprus's Progress towards Accession* ('European Commission 2002'), para.B.4.1, p.62, available on-line at www.europa.eu.int/comm/enlargement/cyprus/index.htm.
83. European Commission 2002, *op.cit.* para.B.4.1, p.60.
84. Ibid., p.61.
85. Ibid., p.62.
86. European Commission, *Comprehensive Monitoring Report on Cyprus's Preparations for Membership* ('European Commission 2003'), para.D, p.50, available on-line at www.europa.eu.int/comm/enlargement/cyprus/index.htm.
87. European Commission 2003, *op.cit.*, para.C.2, p.21.
88. Ibid., p.22.
89. Ibid., p.50.
90. European Commission 1999b, *op.cit.*, para.B.3.1, p.24; European Commission 2000, *op.cit.*, para.B.3.1, pp.46-47 and para.D.1, p.97; para.4 of the Annex to Council Decision 2002/84/EC of 28 January 2002 on the principles, priorities, intermediate objectives and conditions contained in the Accession Partnership with Cyprus, OJ L 44 of 14.02.2002, p.15; European Commission 2003, *op.cit.*, para.A, p.3.
91. See T.C. Hartley, *The Foundations of European Community Law*, 2nd ed., Clarendon Press, Oxford, 1988, pp.197-200; D. Chalmers, *European Union Law*, Vol.I, Ashgate Publishing, Aldershot, 1998, pp.156-157; Craig and de Búrca 2003, *op.cit.*, pp.113-114; Gormley 1998, *op.cit.*, pp.324-325. Of course, there are alternative modes of implementation worthy of consideration in the present context, such as for example the incorporation into domestic law of interpretation rules in line with the relevant Community regulation to encourage national courts to read the domestic law in such a way as to conform with the provisions of the regulation, or the introduction of national instruments prescribing the application of the relevant Community legislation before accession.
92. Case 39/72 *Commission* v *Italy* [1973] ECR 101, p.114.
93. Case 34/73 *Variola* v *Amministrazione delle Finanze* [1973] ECR 981; Case 94/77 *Fratelli Zerbone Snc.* v *Amministrazione delle Finanze dello Stato* [1978] ECR 99, p.116; Case 272/84 *Commission* v *Italy* [1985] ECR 1057, p.1074. This case law, of course, relates to implementing measures taken by existing member states. The ECJ may therefore distinguish the case of an accession country, which before accession has transformed EU regulations into its domestic law, from the existing case law on this question, not least because of the Commission's influence on extracting such commitments from accession countries at an early stage of their accession negotiations.
94. See para.B.2.(b) of the Cypriot government's position paper on company law, *op.cit.*
95. For a detailed analysis of the relationship between foreign direct investment in Mediterranean countries and intellectual property rights protection, see M.G. Bosco, 'Integration, Technological Transfer and Intellectual Property

Rights: An Empirical Application to the MENA Countries', paper delivered at the conference *'Policy Modeling for European and Global Issues'*, Brussels, 6 July 2001, paras.2 and 6, at pp.7-9 and 21, available on-line at www.ecomod.net/conferences/ecomod2001/ papers_web/bosco_new.pdf.

96. The first private high-technology 'business incubator' in Cyprus opened in January 2003, see 'New Breeding Ground for Cypriot Innovation', *Cyprus Mail*, 15 January 2003.
97. The Cypriot government adopted its 'New Industrial Policy' in June 1999. This policy includes the promotion of high-technology industries in Cyprus through the establishment of 'business incubators' and the creation of a centre for carrying out applied R&D in high-technology fields. For more information on these incentives and support schemes, see http://www.kypros.org/hightech.
98. See B. Musyck, 'Technology and Innovation Policies in Europe: Lessons for Cyprus?', *The Cyprus Review*, Vol.11, Spring 1999, pp.111, 113.
99. Ibid.
100. The Madrid and Luxembourg European Council meetings in December 1995 and December 1997, respectively, laid down this criterion.
101. European Commission 2002, *op.cit.*, para.B.4.1, at pp.60-62 and para.D, at pp.126-127; para.3 of the Annex to Council Decision 2002/84/EC, *op.cit.*, p.13; European Commission 2003, *op.cit.*, para.A, p.3.
102. European Commission 2000, *op.cit.*, para.D.1, p.97.
103. European Commission 1999b, *op.cit.*, para.B.4.2, p.47; European Commission 2000, *op.cit.*, para.C, p.93 and para.D.1, p.97.
104. European Commission 2000, *op.cit.*, para.C, p.94.
105. European Commission 2001, *op. cit.*, para.B.4.2, p.92; European Commission 2002, *op.cit.*, para.B.4.1, pp.60-62 and para.D, pp.126-127; para.4 of the Annex to Council Decision 2002/84/EC, *op.cit.*, p.15.
106. See P. Nicolaides, 'Enlargement of the EU and Effective Implementation of Community Rules: An Integration-Based Approach', *European Institute of Public Administration, Working Paper No.99/W/04*, EIPA, Maastricht, December 1999, p.2 and p.16. For an institutional approach to building capacity for the *effective* implementation of EU rules, see P. Nicolaides, 'Preparing for Accession to the European Union: How to Establish Capacity for Effective and Credible Application for EU Rules' in M. Cremona (ed.), *The Enlargement of the European Union*, Oxford University Press, Oxford, 2003, pp.43-78.
107. There are a number of societies for the collective management of IPRs in Cyprus, such as the Performing Rights Society, the Cyprus Federation Against Copyright Theft, and the Business Software Alliance.
108. It is estimated that at the time of accession the *acquis communautaire* consisted of some 80,000 pages of the Official Journal of the European Union.

10 Social Policy and Employment

NICOLETTA IOANNOU[1]

Introduction

The EU's social policy is generally seen as an essential aspect of European intergration. Yet, despite the fact that progress in this policy area has been slow, in recent years rapid progress has been achieved making Cyprus's road to accession quite challenging because of the large number of social reforms that would have to be adopted within a limited period of time.

The Commission in its '2002 Regular Report on Cyprus's assessed the Republic's ability to assume the obligations of membership by examining the last of twenty-nine negotiating chapters covering the acquis. The scope of the last report was broadened to cover Cyprus's administrative capacity to apply the acquis under each of the negotiating chapters. The European Council in Madrid underlined the necessity for the candidate countries to adjust their administrative structures in order to create the conditions for their harmonious integration. The Feira European Council emphasised the vital importance of the candidate countries' capacity to implement and enforce the acquis effectively and added that this required significant efforts by the candidates in strengthening their administrative and judicial structures. The Feira European Council also invited the Commission to report on its findings on the matter. As the Commission noted, the 2002 Report provides a 'global assessment of the overall situation for each of the aspects under consideration, setting out for each of them the main steps still to be taken by Cyprus in preparing for accession. Furthermore, ... the 2002 Regular Reports will provide the basis on which the Commission will formulate its recommendation as to which countries are ready to conclude negotiations ...'[2]

As regards social policy and employment, the Commission has commented favourably on the overall assessment of Cyprus's capacity to implement the acquis and the progress achieved since the beginning of negotiations. It noted that substantial progress has been made in this area.

Negotiations on this chapter have been provisionally closed, Cyprus has not requested any transitional arrangements. Cyprus is generally meeting the Commitments it has made in the accession negotiations in this chapter.[3]

The purpose of this chapter is to examine the steps taken by the Cypriot authorities in order to adopt the acquis communautaire in the main areas covered under the field of social policy and employment. These steps do not only involve adoption of binding legal rules but also the strengthening of the existing judicial and administrative structures for enforcement. More specifically the chapter will examine Cyprus's ability to adopt and implement the acquis in the areas of Labour law, Social Dialogue, Health and Safety at Work and Equality of Treatment for men and women.

Approximation in the field of social policy and employment

Labour law

Legislation, case law and collective bargaining regulate terms and conditions of employment in Cyprus. Labour law is a traditional area of law regulated by national legislation, including ratification laws of international agreements since Cyprus has ratified the majority of the ILO conventions.[4] National legislation determines the fundamental rights and provides the basic protection to employees mainly with respect to minimum wage, maximum hours of work, annual leave, rights of workers representatives and termination of employment. Collective bargaining is the main method through which terms and conditions of employment are set by employers associations and trade unions. An Industrial Relations Code[5] sets out the principles and procedures for the settlement of labour disputes and for collective bargaining and labour relations. Industrial relations are, therefore, regulated by domestic law, international instruments ratified by Cyprus and collective agreements between social partners. Legal harmonisation with the acquis in this field has taken into consideration all these prevailing rules.

The problem with collective agreements The choice of the legal instrument through which implementation could be achieved is not always an easy decision since one should be very careful to use methods which produce binding legal rules. In Cyprus, a number of issues covered by EU law form the subject matter of collective agreements. Of course, this problem is not unique since within the EU there are different national approaches to regulate social issues.[6] In some member states the various areas of working conditions are set out by comprehensive legislation. In other member states labour market collective agreements deal with the majority of working conditions and the state participates only when it is asked to do so by the parties. The traditional way of setting out working conditions in Cyprus has been the collective bargaining system.

The social partners suggested that in order to keep the existing industrial relations system in place full alignment with the acquis in areas covered by collective agreements should be achieved by renegotiating those agreements and not by introducing new legislation to that effect. Their basic argument is that although collective agreements are not legally binding, they are enforceable in Courts by individual parties on the basis of contract law and that the great majority of employees are covered by collective agreements.[7]

The Treaty itself and the Directives sometimes give wide discretion as to the means of transposition adopted. However, reliance on non-legally binding measures of transposition conflicts with the binding legal nature of the Directives. In a number of cases the ECJ has ruled that conformity with Community acts can only be achieved through legally binding measures that have a general application.[8] Thus, measures like collective agreements, which are not legally binding, are not considered sufficient instruments for implementing the acquis. Moreover, collective agreements in Cyprus do not cover all the employees but apply only to those employees belonging to trade unions. According to Cyprus's Constitution there is full freedom of association without obligatory memberships or restrictions except with regard to police and defence forces.[9] Thus, it is true that as a result of the high unionisation of workers that exists in Cyprus the vast majority of workers are covered by collective agreements. Still, this method of transposition cannot be regarded as sufficient since a percentage of the employees, though small, are not covered.

The ECJ has stated in a number of cases that sufficient transposition can only be achieved when Community rules are introduced into the national legal order through instruments that are legally binding to all employees and cover all sectors of employment. In the case of *Commission v. Kingdom of Denmark* the ECJ has stated the following:

> It is true that Member States may leave the implementation of the principle of equal pay to representatives of management and labour. That possibility does not, however discharge them from the obligation of ensuring, by appropriate

> legislative and administrative provisions that all workers in the Community are afforded the full protection provided for in the directive. That State guarantee must cover all cases where effective protection is not ensured by other means, for whatever reason, and in particular cases where the workers in question are not union members, or where the sector in question is not covered by a collective agreement.[10]

The social partners were faced with this dilemma, which was actually a one-way option, from the early stages of harmonisation. On the one hand, maintaining the traditional system of setting labour law rules in Cyprus was a common stand for them; on the other hand, harmonisation with the EU acquis was also identified as a priority for the social partners. It was soon realised that a compromise was necessary. All the issues that were regulated at EU level by legally binding acquis would have to be transposed in the national legal order by way of legally binding rules, i.e. legislation, leaving the non-binding issues to be enforced through collective agreements.

Legislative approximation in the field of labour law

Legislative harmonisation in the field of labour law has occurred according to the commitments that Cyprus has undertaken during the screening process and at the position paper submitted. Full compliance was achieved through the introduction of new and the amendment of existing legislation. This was confirmed by the Commission which on a number of occasions commented positively on the progress achieved since the completion of the screening process. The Commission's November 2002 *Regular Report on Cyprus*, for example, states that in the area of Labour law the majority of the acquis has been transposed.[11]

Since the year 2000, important pieces of legislation have been enacted. New laws were introduced on:

- Information of employees in relation to their contract of employment transposing Directive 91/533/EEC
- Safeguarding the rights of employees in cases of transfer of undertakings implementing Directive 98/50/EC
- Protection of employees in cases of collective redundancies implementing Directive 98/59/EC
- Protection of young persons at work implementing Directive 94/33/EC
  Protection of employees in cases of insolvency of the employer

- Protection of employees in cases of insolvency of their employer, implementing Directive 80/987/EC
- Protection of employees with temporary contracts of employment implementing Directive 91/383/EEC, part-time workers (implementing Directive 97/81/EC and fixed term employment (implementing Directive 99/70/EEC)
- Organisation of working time implementing Directive 93/104/EEC
- Protection of Employees in cases of posting of workers, implementing Directive 96/71/EC
- European Works Council implementing Directive 94/45/EC

The drafting of the new laws was certainly not problem-free, especially with reference to the sanctions chosen for each law and the definitions introduced in such legislation. Directives generally leave the form of sanction to the discretion of the member state. Sometimes they do not even prescribe that breach of national law implementing a Directive must be punished by civil or criminal penalties. The choice of such penalty has proven to be a difficult task, more so since the discretion is not completely free. Firstly, the form of national sanction chosen must be effective enough to ensure that the aims of the Directive are achieved. This is even more difficult in cases where the Directive includes judgmental terms such as 'adequate sanctions' or 'sufficient sanctions'. Secondly, there must be no discrimination between the sanctions adopted for measures implementing Directives and sanctions laid down under related national legislation.

The definitions adopted in the various laws implementing Directives proved to be equally problematic in some cases. As regards terminology, following the exact wording of the Directives is the safest way to ensure correct implementation and avoid deviations from the scope of the Directive. This problem arose while drafting the law for the protection of employees in cases of collective redundancies. The social partners at the technical committee suggested the inclusion of the national definition of redundancies, which in their view corresponded with the definition in the Directive. The Law Office did not follow their suggestion since the national definition was not broad enough to cover all types of dismissals, which were regulated under the Directive. In the case of *Commission v. United Kingdom*,[12] the ECJ decided that the national definition of redundancies adopted in the UK narrowed the scope of the Directive. Since the national definition of redundancies in the Termination of Employment Law was similar to the one adopted in the UK it was finally decided that the new law on collective redundancies should adopt the exact wording of the Directive as regarded the definition.

Participation of workers' representatives in decision-making and the safeguarding of their rights are highly protected under EU law. The law ratifying ILO Convention No.135 on workers' representatives recognises rights to members of trade unions and to elected representatives. Provisions for the protection of workers representatives also exist in Trade Union Law, the Public Service Law and the Termination of Employment Law.

The law on the protection of employees with fixed term contracts of employment has proved to be one of the most controversial issues in the field of labour law. Legislation ensures that employees with fixed term contracts are not discriminated against permanent employees and that renewals of fixed term contracts for a period of over thirty months renders the contract of employment contract of indefinite duration. These principles created problems for employment in the public sector where around 2,300 persons are employed on fixed term contracts. In practical terms this means that such contracts could be terminated or not renewed upon expiration without being subjected to the Termination of Employment Law in relation to prior notification or any kind of compensation.

Parliament was reluctant to approve such legislation without knowing the impact on those employees. The main concern being that instead of providing protection this legislation could lead to termination of their employment before the expiration of 30 months. The Ministry of Finance was unable to provide the Parliament with definite answers as to the possibility of such dismissals or to estimate the costs in the event that their contracts became of indefinite duration. Although in the end the legislation was approved in July 2003, following a relevant study presented by the Personnel Department of the government, the impact on employees remains to be seen.

The same legislation identified another problem concerning the definition of 'comparable employee' in the public sector. Who is a 'comparable employee' the permanent civil servant or a small category of employees employed under a 1985 law on a contract, which is since then automatically renewed by the Parliament? Problems in the public sector were also encountered after the enactment of legislation on working time especially in relation to departments working on shifts (such as air traffic controllers or customs services) and the status of employees while being on-call. Thje problem has not been resolved and, in my view, both legislations will soon be tested on those issues before tribunals since the matter is not a merely legalistic one but relates to those employees' rights and benefits.

Enforcement of the acquis Despite the various problems, the overall assessment as to the ability of the social partners and the government to implement new legislation is positive. The competent authority for enforcement of such legislation is in place. However, further strengthening of the departments and the competent Courts is absolutely necessary due to the increasing responsibilities placed upon them by the new legislation. Not surprisingly, practical measures, e.g. recruitment of additional staff and training of the existing stuff, are recognised as immediate priorities in the National Programme for the Adoption of the Acquis (NPAA).

The competent Court for resolving any dispute arising from the application of labour law is the Industrial Disputes Court, which deals with issues of individual labour conflicts and issues concerning claims from the Redundancy Fund. Lodging an application to this Court is an easily accessible procedure and it is widely used by employees. The procedure is much quicker than that before a District Court and the cost of application is not discouraging. Trade Unions play a significant role in the effective application of the legislation through information provided to employees concerning their rights under the legislation and through free legal advice and assistance.

Social dialogue

Collective bargaining in Cyprus is well developed. Articles 21 and 27 of the Constitution, the Trade Union Law as well as ILO Conventions Nos.87, 98 and 154, which were ratified by Cyprus, constitute a comprehensive legal framework for social dialogue. There is a long-standing practice of tripartite dialogue[13] in labour and social fields. The dialogue may take the form of either tripartite consultations, in which government, employers' organisations and trade unions participate, or collective bargaining or other bipartite consultation. All social issues are covered through a network of consultative bodies, the most important being the Labour Advisory Board chaired by the Minister of Labour and Social Insurance himself. The main task of the Board is to advise the Minister on all labour and social policy matters, including all legislative proposals.

The usual method to resolve disagreements is by trying to reach a consensus in this Board. Especially as regards proposed legislation, the aim is to reach a consensus at this level so that all interested parties can agree on the context of the bill submitted to the House of Representatives; otherwise it might be difficult to adopt a bill which is not acceptable by either of the parties. This can be easier understood if one bares in mind that Cyprus has a Presidential system and, therefore, the political party that has the majority in the House of Representatives is not necessarily the same political party that forms the government[14] (what the French refer to as 'cohabitation'). The plenary session of the House of Representatives is not always willing to vote for government bills, which is why consensus in the Labour Advisory Board for the proposed legislation carries significant weight. Still, both trade unions and employers associations are sometimes invited to express their views before the Parliamentary Committee on labour and social affairs when examining a specific bill. This practice is particularly important especially in cases where there are disagreements in the Labour Advisory Board or where the proposed bill is of such important nature that the Parliament considers it necessary to hear the views of the interested parties.

The adoption of harmonising legislation has proven to be a challenge for the well-established procedures existing in this field for two reasons. Firstly, the procedure followed was time consuming and there were difficulties in keeping the deadlines that were agreed with the European Commission. Secondly, the provisions of the acquis bind the parties and, therefore, any agreement between trade unions and employers' associations infringing such provisions could not be followed.

It was well understood that involvement of the social partners in drafting legislation was vitally important and should be encouraged. The aim was to find a procedure by which the social partners would be involved in the stages of drafting and introducing new legislation while ensuring that the minimum requirements of the Directives were followed. Thus, the social partners had a significant role in the cases where the implementation of certain provisions of the acquis is left to the discretion of the member states and in cases of 'minimum requirements' Directives, that is Directives which allow the member states to offer the employees a higher level of protection than the one provided by the Directive.

The competent Ministry in cooperation with the Labour Advisory Board, the Law Office of the Republic and the House of Representatives have established a special procedure to be followed in cases of introducing harmonising legislation. The new agreed procedure begins with the discussion of the relevant EU acquis at the tripartite technical committee of the Labour Advisory Board. At this stage, the implications to Cyprus's labour market are identified and a technical committee for the drafting of the bill is appointed. The competent department of the Ministry in cooperation with the Law Office of the Republic prepares a draft law, which is submitted to the technical committee as a working document. Once the working document is discussed a report expressing the views of each party is prepared. The draft law and the report are then submitted and discussed at the Labour Advisory Board. The social partners are in this way involved from the beginning of the procedure. However, their impact on the proposed draft is limited due to the binding nature of the acquis and the commitments already undertaken towards the Commission.

Bipartite social dialogue although not formalised in Cyprus is important and is developing rapidly. Bipartite conducts between representatives of employers' and workers' organisations are frequent on a wide range of issues concerning labour and social security. In this way, the process of approximation has provided Cyprus with valuable experience and proved that state involvement (as in tripartite consultations) is not always necessary when it comes to social dialogue.

Equality of treatment for men and women

The issue of equality is perhaps one of the most important covered by social policy and is an area of great and rapid developments in Europe. In this part of the chapter I will firstly present the current Cyprus legislation then deal with the requirements of European law and finally examine the extend to which the equality principle is safeguarded in Cyprus through administrative bodies and the competent courts.

The legislative measures introduced aim at combating discrimination and improving the position of women in economic activity and in society in general. The new strategic development plan (1999-2003) emphasises the introduction of the necessary legislative measures, which will ensure compliance with the acquis in this field. Currently, legislation consists of national legislation and international agreements ratified by Cyprus. Equal treatment is introduced by Article 28 of the Constitution, which safeguards the right of all persons to equality before the law, administration and justice and prohibits, *inter alia*, any direct or indirect discrimination on the grounds of sex. This right has formed the subject matter in a number of cases before the Supreme Court and the case law developed in this area is of considerable importance. In its judgments the Supreme Court has often gone beyond the letter of the law giving the principle of equal treatment a very wide interpretation, thus, covering to a large extend the same ground that is covered by EU legislation. Case law has extended the principle of equal treatment to cover, for example, cases of indirect discrimination by giving this term a wide meaning similar to the one given in EU law.[15]

However, the safeguards of the Constitution were not regarded sufficient to meet the requirements of the acquis and new legislation to cover this field had to be enacted. A new law transposing Directive 76/207/EEC on the equal treatment of men and women in employment and vocational training and Directive 97/80/EC on the burden of proof was enacted in December 2002. This new law also covers issues of positive action, gender-based advertising and sexual harassment. It applies to all sectors of the economy and will prohibit discrimination on the grounds of sex to all working conditions including selection criteria, access to all jobs or posts and to all levels of occupational hierarchy.

The issue of positive action raises difficulties. The relevant provisions in the legislation, in the light of a decision of the Supreme Court of Cyprus, run the risk of being found by the Court to be unconstitutional. In the case of *The Republic v. Eleni Constantinou*[16] the Supreme Court held that provisions in the legislation allowing for positive measures in the cases of disabled persons – and persons who suffered because of the war – is contrary to the provisions on equality introduced by Article 28 of the Constitution. It should be noted that one of the judges of the Supreme Court delivered a dissenting judgement based on the view that positive action for these groups promotes equality in practice. However, the approach of the majority resulted to the annulment of the legislation because it clashed with the Constitution. In practical terms this indicates that a similar decision might be given in the case of positive actions for gender issues. Of course, positive actions are provided by both, Directive 76/207/EEC and the Treaty itself. Thus, even if such an approach is followed by the Cypriot Courts, EU law will still prevail. Amending the Constitution so that it specifically provides for the introduction of positive measures for certain groups, is also a possibility. This approach was followed by three other member states (Greece, Austria and Finland). However, amending the Constitution is a political decision and at the moment the government seems unwilling to proceed. However, in my view, accession to the EU renders such an amendment necessary.

Full harmonisation with this Directive will occur only when Cyprus renounces ILO Convention No.45 on underground work for women, which according to the ECJ violates the principle of equal treatment. According to the ILO rules Convention No.45 can only be renounced after 30 May

2007. This brought some concern to the negotiating team of Cyprus since the date of accession is the year 2004. From a practical point of view it meant that Cyprus would have to negotiate this issue as a request for derogation from the acquis. However, neither a derogation nor a transitional period was in fact asked. Because Cyprus would have simply been unable to comply with such a requirement because of other international obligations it confirmed that it would denounce the convention on the first possible occasion. The issue has no practical implications either since there are no underground work activities such as mines or quarries in Cyprus. At the technical consultations held for this chapter, the EU was finally satisfied that this request was not actually a request for derogation.

The legislation regarding the protection of pregnant workers and workers who have recently given birth complies with many provisions of the relevant acquis (Directive 92/85/EC), such as those concerning entitlement and minimum period of maternity leave and the protection of dismissal. Harmonisation for full compliance was achieved through regulations and consequential amendments to existing legislation, which were enacted in 2003.[17]

As regards equality in social security issues and self-employment, legislation in force complies to a considerable extend with the relevant acquis (Directives 79/7EEC, 86/ 613/EEC and 86/378/EEC). The social insurance legislation covers all employees and self employed persons, with limited exceptions, and does not contain discriminatory provisions between men and women regarding the payment of contributions, the conditions for benefit purposes, the calculation of benefits and the pensionable age. Social insurance legislation was also amended to eliminate certain discriminatory provisions on the basis of sex, such as the payment of the marriage allowance only to women, the payment of grants for dependants only to males and the non-coverage by the social insurance scheme of women in the agricultural sector.

Equal Pay legislation was also repealed.[18] Previous legislation safeguarded the right of equal pay for work which is of 'like' or 'substantially like' nature. In other words, the scope of the law was more limited than the scope of Directive 75/117/EEC since it didn't cover work of equal value. Given the free system of collective bargaining this principle was promoted through collective bargaining according to the ILO Convention No.100 of 1951 on Equal Remuneration, ratified by Cyprus in 1987. However, in order to ensure full harmonisation, legislation was amended to cover work of equal value. New Regulations complying with the new legislation have been introduced in order to enable better enforcement of the law. These Regulations define the powers of the inspectors as well as the composition and terms of reference of the technical committee, which will assist the Industrial Dispute Court in determining work of equal value and the criteria that will be applied for comparison purposes.

In June 2002, the Law on Parental Leave was enacted implementing Directive 96/34/EC. The Directive leaves discretion to the Member States as to the total duration of parental leave (provided it is at least 3 months), the period of notification necessary and the terms and conditions of access and the detailed rules for applying parental leave. This discretion gave rise to discussions at the technical committee of the Labour Advisory Board. The main disagreement related to whether the period of parental leave should be paid or unpaid. Following the example of the majority of member states, the legislation enacted in Cyprus provides for an 'unpaid period', a factor which in my view discourages employees to apply for parental leave. This is evident by the fact that the competent authority has yet to receive an application for parental leave, even though the law came into force on 1 January 2003.

Administrative capacity to implement the acquis on equality

The institutional and administrative infrastructure implementing the acquis in the field of equal treatment is the responsibility of several Ministries. The Ministry of Justice and Public Order is the competent authority to promote the issue of equality. In 1989 the National Machinery for Women's Rights was established under this Ministry in order to advise the Council of Ministers of the Republic on issues related to equality, to help with the implementation of national policy, to establish educational programmes and to support women's organisations. NGO's dealing with issues of equality are currently represented in the National Machinery for Women's Rights. At the beginning of the negotiations, commenting on Cyprus's slow progress in this area the Commission representative commented that the 'Machinery needs oiling'. Indeed, although the establishment of this body constitutes a positive attempt to promote equality issues there is still work to be done so that it can play a significant role in the promotion of equality and positively influence policymaking. In my view, the main problem is that the machinery is not completely free from politics since the majority of the NGO's represented are the women's organisations of the political parties.

The Ombudsman is one of the most important independent authorities on monitoring and enforcement mechanisms for equality legislation dealing with the non-judicial control of the administration. It was established in 1991 and is empowered, *inter alia*, to investigate and report on actions of the administration that constitute a violation of fundamental rights and liberties. The Ombudsman submits an annual report to the President of the Republic concerning the execution of his duties and this report can include recommendations and remarks. The Ombudsman can take action either upon complaint or *ex proprio motu*. Although the Ombudsman has helped significantly in promoting the principle of equality it cannot be regarded as the main body through which this principle could be effectively promoted, for two reasons. Firstly, the Ombudsman can only investigate actions of the public sector and local administration but not the private sector, where most violations take place. Secondly, as the reports issued for each case investigated do not bind the authorities but provide only guidance there is no guarantee that they will be pursued.

It is obvious that administrative structures need to be reinforced in order to be able to apply effectively the acquis in this field. Practical measures to guarantee the enforcement of the equality principle can only be achieved though the establishment of an equality committee. This committee should deal with issues related to equality, should have the powers to investigate and report on specific cases – including complaints for the private sector – and its decisions should be binding; it should also provide information to individuals as regards their rights. Although it is not the usual practice for NGO's to participate in such committees, it might be useful to investigate such a possibility since participation will give them the chance to be more actively involved in the promotion of equality.

The experience of other member states in enforcing equality legislation is very important in the building up of similar structures in Cyprus. Most member states have 'equality committees' or 'equality directors' with wide powers in enforcing legislation. A model that could be followed in Cyprus is that of the Republic of Ireland – which is a common law jurisdiction and a small administration so there are similarities in the two systems. In Ireland, the main body of enforcing equality legislation is the 'Equality Director', employing trained equality officers with powers to investigate complaints and act as mediators if the parties wish so. The investigation takes the form of a hearing and the officers have quasi-judicial powers. Their decisions, mostly imposition of fines, are binding and enforceable unless they are reversed on appeal to the Labour Court.

Court protection

The right to redress – possible remedies in domestic Courts

Under Article 146 of the Constitution every person may file a recourse to the Supreme Court against decisions, acts or omissions of any person, institution or authority exercising executive or administrative power which is contrary to the provisions of the Constitution or any law, or is made in excess or abuse of powers vested in such authority. Only persons having legitimate interest can actually file recourses to the Supreme Court. The Supreme Court has the power to either annul or uphold the decision of the administration but has no jurisdiction for the award of damages or any other remedy. The Supreme Court is in fact an administrative court checking the legality of the administrative decision and cannot examine the merits of a case. A successful applicant has the right to claim damages under Article 146(6) of the Constitution, by filing an action to the District Court. The power of the District Court to grant remedy under this Article is not simply confined to compensation but extends to every remedy a Civil Court has power to grant.

The Supreme Court is the competent Court for issues concerning employment in the public or semi-public sector. However, unequal treatment in the private sector does not fall within the jurisdiction of the Supreme Court. In fact, there are no remedies for unequal treatment in terms of employment as regards the private sector apart from the breach of the principle of equal pay and the termination of employment due to unequal treatment.

Under section 3 of the Termination of Employment Law[19] a person can claim damages assessed under the first annex of the Law in case of termination of employment on the ground of unequal treatment. Under section 30 of the Law the Industrial Disputes Court has exclusive jurisdiction to deal with any dispute arising from the application of the Law. Under the Protection of Maternity Law[20] the termination of employment during the period of pregnancy is an illegal termination and damages can be claimed. Where infringement of the principle of equal pay leads to termination of employment by resignation such termination is considered to be a constructive dismissal and the employee can claim damages under the first annex of the Termination of Employment Law. Upon application of an employee the Industrial Disputes Court can also issue an order calling for the termination of the violation of the principle of equal pay and award damages to the aggrieved party. New harmonised legislation on Equal Pay and Equal Treatment in Employment,[21] provides that damages can be claimed at Industrial Disputes Court as well as District Courts.

Protection under EU law – the requirement of effective judicial control and effective remedy

The ECJ has dealt in a number of cases with the principle of effective judicial control laid down in Article 6 of Directive 76/207 and has interpreted it in the light of the general principle of judicial protection. In *Johnston v. The Chief Constable of Royal Ulster Constabulary*[22] the ECJ stated that all persons have the right to effective judicial control and the right to obtain an effective remedy in a competent court against measures they consider to be contrary to the principle of equal treatment. Member states must take measures to guarantee real and effective judicial protection and ensure that such measures have a real and deterrent effect on the employer.[23]

In the cases of Emmott,[24] Cotter[25] and Marshall II[26] the ECJ stressed the importance of ensuring the effectiveness of the equality principle by requiring the provision of adequate national remedies. In all three cases the ECJ ruled that particular national rules, both procedural and substantive, must be set aside where they have the effect of depriving an aggrieved person of an effective remedy. An effective remedy for the cases of violation of the sex discrimination legislation can only be achieved if the victim is fully reinstated or alternatively financial compensation covering damages and loss is sustained. Such compensation must amount to more than purely nominal compensation.[27]

The application of the principle of equality in Cypriot Courts

Effective judicial control and adequate remedy is a general principle of EU law and has been interpreted expressly by the ECJ. National rules must follow the interpretation of ECJ and all national rules must be seen in the light of this general principle. It is therefore obvious that certain legal rules applicable in Cyprus, both procedural and substantive, must be modified in order to guarantee the protection that EU law aims to offer.

The procedure before the Supreme Court when dealing with cases of equality creates some problems in the application of EU law mainly as a result of the status of this Court. The Supreme Court is an administrative Court that merely examines the legality of a particular decision and does not go into the substance of a particular case by examining its merits. The argument here is that the individuals involved are deprived of effective judicial control at least as it was interpreted in a number of cases before the ECJ. In the Johnston case,[28] the ECJ stressed the importance of judicial control, which can only be effective if the court checks both the legality of the decision of the administration and the merits of each particular case.

Under Article 146(6) of the Constitution the award of damages to a successful applicant forms the subject matter of a separate action before another court namely the District Court. The procedure before the District Court satisfies the requirements of EU law for adequate remedies at the national level since the District Court can award financial damages with no ceiling limitation including the award of interest. Apart from compensation, the District Court can also issue any other decision including orders and injunctions for the removal of the illegality, which in practice reinstate the victim of the violation. However, because such cases deal with employment in the public and semi public sector, it is not possible for the Court to decide on the appointment or promotion of the applicant since this would mean interference with the work of the administration.

Reversal of the burden of proof in cases of unequal treatment is a basic principle of EU law, derived both by case law[29] and legislation.[30] In procedures before District Courts in Cyprus reversal of the burden of proof was not applicable and thus the need for amendment was identified. As mentioned above, the competent court for all disputes arising in contracts of employment in the private sector is the Industrial Disputes Court. Reversal of burden of proof is a principle applicable in the proceedings before this Court and the evidence rules applicable are not as strict as in District Courts. However, there were certain procedural rules, which prevented the individual from enjoying the effective judicial control and the adequate remedy that is guaranteed under EU law.

Firstly, under the Termination of Employment Law, an individual can file a claim in the Industrial Disputes Court only if he or she has been employed for continuously at least for six months. Individuals employed for a shorter period can apply to the District Court but costs are higher for such procedures and the procedural rules – as already mentioned – are not as favourable as in the Industrial Disputes Court. Thus, it can be argued that this limit set by law deprives some individuals from the kind of sufficient judicial protection that every member state has to offer.

Secondly, the Termination of Employment Law provides for a fixed ceiling on damages, which must not exceed two years' salaries. The ECJ has dealt with this issue in the Marshall II case.[31] The ECJ ruled that fixing a ceiling on damages could not be regarded as proper implementation of the remedial provision of the equal treatment Directive since such a ceiling limits the amount of compensation to a sum that was not adequate to compensate for damages incurred as a result of sex discrimination. An individual claiming higher compensation than the one fixed in the Law can apply to the District Court but for the reasons explained above, this might not be regarded as sufficient to satisfy the requirements of EU law.

Most of the problems described above have been dealt with through the introduction of the new harmonised legislation on equality.[32] Under new legislation, reversal of the burden of proof applies to all procedures related to equality before District Courts or Industrial Dispute Courts. The procedural problems of time-limit and ceiling in damages do not apply any more when the Industrial Dispute Court deals with cases of equality. Under the new law the Court is able to give unlimited damages, including interest. Under the new legislation the Industrial Dispute Court, can also issue orders for reappointment, appointment or promotion of the applicant. However, this order cannot be issued by the District Court when deciding a case under Article 146(6) of the Constitution and, therefore, the problem in that case still remains.

Health and safety at work

The formulation of policy, as well as the introduction of legislation and other measures in the field of health and safety at work, is effected through cooperation with the social partners. The Declaration of National Policy on Occupational Safety and Health, which was signed by the social partners and the government of Cyprus in May 1995, constitutes the fundamental code guiding governmental action in this area and establishes a framework of obligations and rights for employers and workers. The main legislation in force is the Safety and Health at Work Law 89(I)/96, which goes some way towards satisfying the requirements of the EU Framework Directive on health and safety and some aspects of the specific Directives.

Legislative harmonisation in this field was achieved by a number of Regulations issued under the 1989 law implementing provisions of the specific Directives (e.g. Regulations on the biological agents at work. Regulations on the use by workers of personal protective equipment, Regulations on health and safety signs etc.). The competent authority for enforcement of the health and safety legislation is the Labour Inspection Department, which employees inspectors with technical expertise in all areas covered and was recently upgraded in order to exercise the increasing responsibilities emanating from the transposition of the acquis.

The introduction of new measures to improve the health and safety of the workers was a relatively easy task as employers recognised at an early stage that such measures were necessary and beneficial to both themselves and their employees. Indeed, health and safety issues were a subject for consultation and discussion at various consultative tripartite bodies and the Declaration on national policy was partly agreed through such procedure. By signing the Declaration the social partners have agreed to implement the necessary measures for achieving its priority goals – among which is the harmonisation with the EU acquis.

However, disagreements at the level of technical committees occurred as regards the 'phasing in' provisions existing in some of the health and safety Directives. These provisions give the member states a certain period of 'grace' by which the existing enterprises (workplaces, work equipment, fishing vessels, mineral extracting sites etc.) have to comply with the acquis – especially where the measures introduced will put heavy financial burden on the employer. The problem is that the same period of 'grace' cannot be given to acceding countries if it exceeds the date of accession. Thus, Cyprus had only the period leading to accession to comply with the minimum requirements listed in the Directive. The same period also applies to existing enterprises. This was received negatively by the employers, who saw it as unfavourable treatment against enterprises in the acceding countries.

Given the fact that most enterprises in Cyprus are small or medium size, the financial burden on them could be very heavy. Still, it is difficult to see a way out of this problem since the EU expects the accession countries to adopt such Directives without making use of the 'phasing in' provisions and treats any request to the contrary as a request for derogation. The negotiating team of Cyprus decided not to ask for derogation in this field, hoping that the issue will somehow be resolved domestically. In fact, this is an area where action by the government, in the form of technical and financial support, seems to be absolutely necessary if small and medium enterprises are to survive and compete.

New acquis

The Commission's 2002 Progress Report states: 'No progress can be reported with regard to the transposition of the Community Acquis in the field of anti-discrimination'. The Report also notes that 'legislation transposing EC anti-discrimination Directives based on Article 13 of the EC Treaty will have to be introduced and implemented.'[33] In my view, the above comments were at the time unfair for two reasons: Firstly, both anti-discrimination Directives[34] come under the new acquis, since they were issued in 2000. Cyprus undertook the obligation to implement such Directives by accession. Secondly, the member states themselves had not yet implemented the Directives at that time, since the dates for implementation were July and December 2003. It was, therefore, unfair to criticise Cyprus for not achieving any progress by that time since Cyprus had not bridged any commitment and because in this way a heavier burden was placed on Cyprus that the member states themselves. Interestingly, by May 2004 (date of accession) full compliance with both directives was achieved.

A law implementing the anti-discrimination Directive in relation to employment (Directive 2000/78/EC as well as the employment aspects of Directive 2000/43/EC) was introduced in Spring 2004. The law deals with discrimination on grounds of religion or belief, age, sexual orientation, race or ethnic origin. Discrimination in employment on grounds of disability was dealt with through an amendment to the law on the Protection of Persons with Disabilities so as to achieve full harmonisation. Finally, a third law dealing with protection of persons irrespective of race or ethnic origin in fields other than employment was enacted at the same time. The law covers areas such as education, social benefits, housing, medical treatment, provision of goods and services.

The need for political decisions was identified in the area of anti-discrimination. These decisions included the establishment of a new independent body to deal with complains on discrimination, the issuing of positive actions as mentioned above[35] and the role of NGO's dealing with these issues. At the moment, the independent body to deal with anti-discrimination issues is the ombudsman. Following a decision of the Council of Ministers the law was amended in order to give the ombudsman authority to deal with these issues in the public as well as in the private sector.

Concluding remarks

It was well understood from the beginning of the negotiations that Cyprus's ability to apply the acquis in all the negotiating chapters had to be evidenced if the application for membership was to be successful. In fact, in some respects, the ability of accession states to apply the acquis through the transposition of EU law into national law appeared to be a significant benchmark indicating their suitability for accession.

In this chapter I have extensively discussed the capacity of Cyprus to adopt and implement the acquis in the field of social policy. In this field, preparation for membership proceeded in full speed through the reforms, which took place right up to accession. By the time of accession Cyprus was in a position to undertake the duties and responsibilities of a member state but also to provide for its citizens all rights enjoyed by citizens in other member states. However, social policy in Europe is far from comprehensive and therefore meeting the minimum standards of EU social rights might not be enough for any member state. As a new member state Cyprus, should not only enjoy the benefits of EU social rights but also try to contribute towards their imporovement. The way forward requires both vision and political decisions for achieving this end.

Notes

1. This chapter represents the personal views of the author.
2. Commission of the EU '2002 Regular Report on Cyprus', October 2002, p.9.
3. Ibid, p.82.
4. Cyprus is a Member to the ILO since 1960, but certain commitments were taken prior to that from the time when Cyprus used to be a British colony. After independence such commitments were reconfirmed. Cyprus has until today ratified 52 ILO conventions.
5. Industrial Relations Code is a non legally binding agreement at national level between employers and workers organisations.
6. See EC Commission, 'Comparative Study on Rules Governing Working Conditions in the Member States', SEC (89) 1137 30 June 1989.
7. Around 70% of the employees belong to trade unions and thus are covered by collective agreements.
8. Case C 433/93 *Commission v. Germany,* (1996) ECR 1 p.2311, Case 312/86 *Commission v. France*, (1988) ECR, p.315.
9. Article 21 of the Constitution.
10. Case 143/83, (1985) ECR, p.427.
11. Commission of the EU '2002 Regular Report on Cyprus', October 2002 p.81
12. Case 382/92 *Commission v. UK*, (1994) ECR, p.2479.
13. Dialogue between government, employment and trade unions.
14. Article 39 of the Constitution provides that the president is directly elected.
15. Cases *The Republic v Alexia Christoforou and others*, (1986) 3 CLR, p.1523.
16. Appeal no.3385, 26 September 2002.

17. The Maternity Protection Law and Social Insurance Law and implementing regulations.
18. The Equal Remuneration for men and women for work of equal value Law 177(I)/2002.
19. Law 24/67 as amended.
20. Law 100(i)/97.
21. Laws 177(i)/2002 and 205(i)/2002.
22. Case 222/84 *Marguerita Johnston v. The Chief Constable of Royal Ulster Constabulary*, [1986] ECR I, p.1663.
23. See also Case 14/83 Sabine *Von Colson* and *Elisabeth Kamman* v. *Land de Nordrhein-Westfalen*, [1986] ECR, p.1891.
24. Case 208/90 *Emmott v Minister of Social Welfare*, (1991) ECR I, p.4269.
25. Case 377/89 *Cotter and Mc Dermott v Minister of Social Welfare and Attorney General*, (1991) ECR I, p.4387.
26. Case 271/91 *Marshall v South West Hampshire Area Health Authority*, (1993) ECR I, p.4367.
27. Case *Von Colson* 1984, *op.cit.*, p.23.
28. Case Johnston 1986, op.cit., p.23.
29. See case 109/88 *Danfoss* (1989) ECR, p.3220, Case 180/95 *Draehampaehl v Urania Immobilien Service*, (1997) ECR I, p.2195.
30. Directive 97/80/EC.
31. Marshall 1993, *op.cit.* 26.
32. Laws 177(i)/2002 and 205(i)/2002.
33. Commission of the EU '2002 Regular Report on Cyprus', October 2002, pp.80-82.
34. Directives 2000/78/EC and Directive 2000/43/EC.
35. Ibid., p.11.

11 The Preparation of Cyprus for Justice and Home Affairs: Nomos and Politics on the Troubled Waters of the Mediterranean

MICHALIS KAMPERIS[1]

Introduction

Among the various fields of EU politics and policies, Justice and Home Affairs (JHA) stands out as the one posing the most fascinating and controversial legal, political and institutional issues. Since its genesis, the Third Pillar has evolved in a fragile equilibrium between Community competence and intergovernmental cooperation, subsidiarity and sovereignty and, after the Treaty of Amsterdam, harmonisation and differentiation or flexibility.

Meanwhile enlargement, the most recent episode in the process of European integration, poses new challenges. Cyprus, as one of the countries which acceded to the EU on 1 May 2004, undertook a significant effort to transpose, implement and enforce the acquis in Justice and Home Affairs. However, the adoption and implementation of the JHA acquis goes far beyond the legal and institutional reforms needed. The *de facto* division of the island following the Turkish military invasion in 1974 and Cyprus's geographical position making it a target country for illegal immigration,[2] raise crucial political issues and challenges.

The aim of this chapter is twofold. Firstly, it seeks to focus on the legislative process and the administrative steps taken by the Cypriot authorities to harmonise laws and practices with the JHA acquis; secondly, it aims to examine the political implications of the *sui generis* status of Cyprus in view of its membership and participation in the area of freedom, security and justice. After a brief discussion dealing with the ongoing evolution of the Third Pillar from Maastricht to Amsterdam and Nice the third section analyses the multidimensional legal and political issues raised during the accession negotiations of Cyprus with the EU in the field of JHA. The next two sections examine Cyprus's measures to align its legislation and reinforce its administration in respect of the JHA acquis. Section 6 turns to the debate on the settlement of the 'Cyprus problem' and discusses the significant role that JHA could play for the reunification of the Cypriot polity.

A constantly evolving area of freedom, security and justice

The concept of a Third Pillar covering significant issues, such as asylum, immigration, police and judicial cooperation, was introduced at EU level by the Treaty of Maastricht. The entry into force of this Treaty was a new step towards the metamorphosis of the European Community from an economic to a more political oriented 'union among the peoples of Europe'. It was nevertheless evident, on the threshold of the new Millennium, that the ambiguous structure of the Third Pillar, which was based on member state cooperation, could not cope with the changes. The instruments available were inappropriate and the problem was aggravated by the cumbersome decision-making process[3] and the lack of democratic and judicial supervision. The increasing use of modern methods in organised crime and the imminent approach of enlargement, with all of its consequences, led the citizens and governments of Europe to demand an efficient institutional driving mechanism.

The Amsterdam Treaty of 1997 satisfied this demand to some degree. It introduced the concept of an 'area of freedom, security and justice'[4] for all the citizens of Europe. European integration is no longer confined to the economic concept of a market, but extends to all aspects of life in European society.[5] Significant innovations were introduced: (a) transfer of powers from the intergovernmental Third Pillar to a new Title IIIA of the Treaty encapsulating provisions on visa, asylum, immigration, and judicial cooperation in civil matters; (b) the integration of the Schengen agreement into the EU legal order; and (c) a clear list of all the Union's objectives in the field of JHA and a new system of co-ordination between the institutions and the member states, aiming to achieve these goals within the next five years.

In 2000, the Intergovernmental Conference for the Treaty of Nice took the staff, ran a few meters and passed it to the Convention on the Future for

Europe. It proclaimed the Charter of Human Rights of the European Union and extended co-decision to three areas in the field of JHA to which it decided to apply qualified-majority voting. This affected Art. 65 (judicial cooperation in civil matters), Art. 62 and Art. 63 (visas, asylum and immigration). With Declaration no.5 annexed to the Treaty of Nice the member states expressed their agreement to apply the co-decision procedure starting from May 2004 for those provisions on freedom of movement of third-country nationals and for measures on illegal immigration.

One must, however, always bear in mind that EU and politics are not a fixed set of values; rather they are part of an ongoing process towards the establishment of priority activities and objectives. At this moment, the Draft Treaty establishing a Constitution for Europe is under discussion. As Europe enters a new era, the concept of an area of freedom, security and justice evolves in order to face the new challenges related to enlargement. At the same time, the candidate countries undertook the Herculean task of comprehending, transposing and enforcing the complex acquis in the field of JHA. Cyprus, on the south-eastern frontier of Europe, is one of these countries.

The *sui generis* case of Cyprus and the area of freedom, security and justice: legal and political implications

Until recently, the group of accession countries was expressed arithmetically as the 10+3 group. The +3 candidates were Cyprus, Malta and Turkey and the '+' symbol was used in order to distinguish them from the rest of the applicants, which were all Central and Eastern European countries. Geographic location, however, was not the only difference between Cyprus and the other candidates or even the member states. In this Section, I shall first examine the effect of the unique political, legal and institutional features of Cyprus under the prism of its harmonisation effort in the field of justice and home affairs.

Soon after the beginning of the screening exercise of the acquis in the field of the Third Pillar, three sensitive issues emerged:

a) Despite the fact that the Republic of Cyprus has, since its independence, been a presidential democracy based on the respect of human rights, the rule of law, and the separation of the three powers of the state, there was initially some concern regarding its ability to implement effectively the third pillar acquis. This concern stemmed from the fact that the Cypriot legal system, traditionally based on the English common law built up over the years by judicial decisions, is currently a *melange* of civil and common law. As a consequence, basic substantive legislation such as the Criminal Code and the Law of Contract incorporates the basic principles of English Law in codified form. However, this common law skeleton is also accompanied by civil continental administrative and family law, making Cyprus a *sui generis* case.

There was clearly a question as to whether this unique combination of legal philosophies would create obstacles for the proper transposition and implementation of the complicated acquis. In the event, the fears proved ill-founded. One could even say that the experience which those involved in the harmonisation process had of both civil and common law elements of the Cypriot legal system enabled Cyprus to cope better with the difficulties resulting from the complex nature of the JHA acquis. After all, this acquis is the result of demands, conflicts and compromises between member states with different legal traditions. This, coupled with the strong political commitment of the Cypriot authorities, turned a potential problem into an advantage.

b) Another source of concern was the *de facto* division of the island due to the Turkish military invasion in 1974. As a result of this, the government of the Republic of Cyprus has been prevented from exercising full control of the northern part of the island, which is still occupied by the Turkish army. This situation raised two issues. First, there was concern that the route through the northern occupied areas would be a gateway for illegal activities, such as drug trafficking and illegal immigration. Secondly, the occupation meant that the Turkish Cypriots could not benefit from the policies and the objectives of the area of freedom, security and justice in contrast with the spirit of the Luxembourg and Copenhagen European Council conclusions.

In its effort to deal with the *de facto* situation, the Cyprus government enhanced the controls along the cease-fire line in order to better monitor and prevent criminal elements from infiltrating the government-controlled area. In addition, the government declared the ports of entry situated in the occupied area closed and established close cooperation with the United Nations and the authorities of the British Sovereign Base Areas.

There were substantial, but fruitless, efforts by high level authorities of the Republic to involve Turkish Cypriot representatives in the accession negotiations. The reason for this failure has been the persistent refusal of the leadership of the Turkish Cypriot community to acknowledge the benefits that the accession of Cyprus to the EU would bring for both Cypriot communities.

c) The geographical position of Cyprus, an island in the east Mediterranean basin, has two dimensions. In the general context of EU enlargement, Cyprus has great geostrategic importance, since it will become a portal for the expansion of the Union to the Mediterranean and the Middle East. However, in the specific context of JHA, this geographical position makes Cyprus a potential transit area for illegal migration. The Commission and certain member states have expressed concern that, Cyprus might become an attractive destination for illegal immigrants and drug traffickers. The Cypriot government shared the Commission's view that a reinforcement of border controls and the adoption of clear legal instruments would be needed to cope with this influx of migration. The legislative and infrastructure measures taken by Cyprus in this field will be examined in the next Section of this chapter.

This special attention attached to immigration and asylum issues is not surprising. Immigration has been placed at the top of the enlargement agenda because it impacts not only upon security and control but also on highly sensitive political issues such as free movement of persons, minority rights and anti-discrimination laws.[6] At the same time, the absence of a coherent EU immigration policy[7] has led to confusion and scepticism among the candidate countries despite the different nature of the problems envisaged by them. Cyprus has come to realise that being part of the external border of the EU has serious political and economic repercussions.

So far, I have briefly examined some specific issues that arose during the first stages of the negotiations between Cyprus and the EU in the JHA field. However, there were a plethora of problems shared by all the then candidate countries and had their roots in the distinctive nature of JHA. As noted earlier, JHA is a rapidly changing area of EU policy, and an ongoing process that was drastically altered by the Treaty of Amsterdam. Although Amsterdam and Nice introduced instruments and mechanisms to reinforce the effectiveness of JHA, the horizon is still cloudy for the ten new member states. The new member states did not have the opportunity to influence the evolution of the acquis, and were simply required to adopt an extremely complex system, consisting of instruments of an uncertain legal status arranged into two pillars. The Schengen acquis is a clear example: the legal complexity of the system is exacerbated by the British and Irish opt-outs, the inclusion of non-EU states and the fact that Denmark is a signatory to Schengen but opposes the communitarisation of those areas falling at present under the Third Pillar.[8]

For various reasons, and despite their good intentions, Community institutions were unable to guide and assist the candidates effectively.

Although the Commission's power of initiative has significantly increased since Amsterdam, the Directorate-General for Justice and Home Affairs of the European Commission is still building up its internal resources and competences in order to be able to tackle the challenges in this field. Moreover, the new member states – especially Cyprus – did not receive adequate financial support for the overwhelming costs of purchasing and installing the high-tech equipment and the infrastructure needed for the implementation of the JHA acquis.

How did Cyprus and the other candidates tackle these problems? The keyword is cooperation. From the early stages of the negotiations, Cypriot authorities realised that bilateral and multilateral cooperation among the European states would be the only way to produce the results desired. A network of consultation and exchange of information and expertise developed between the then candidate countries, the member states, and the EU institutions. JHA-Experts' meetings took place very often in Brussels and the capitals of the candidate countries while twinning programs were in progress.The EU was determined to assist the efforts of the candidate countries through the provision of expertise and training.

Other forms of cooperation existed within the framework of third pillar Programs such as Falcone, Oisin or Grotius (now renamed AGIS). These programs were addressed to judges, prosecutors, police or customs officers and other professionals called to enforce the legislation adopted during the pre-accession period. Finally, Cyprus pursued its direct and regular involvement in the EU working groups, as a significant step for the enhancement of the existing cooperation on technical and practical aspects of the acquis.

Transposition and implementation of the JHA acquis: changes in the law are not enough

In November 2001, Cyprus managed to close provisionally Chapter 24 of the enlargement negotiations, dealing with Justice and Home Affairs. Cyprus adopted various important legislative and administrative measures for full alignment with the acquis and, in general, the timetable for fulfilling the commitments was respected.

As noted earlier, Cyprus, along with all the other candidates, was requested from the beginning of the negotiations to incorporate in its legislation the polymorphous set of legal and political instruments comprising the JHA acquis. This acquis covers, *inter alia*, control of external borders, immigration and asylum, the fight against organised crime, drug trafficking and terrorism and police and judicial cooperation.

It is not the purpose of this chapter to ask whether Cyprus ought to implement the acquis because this was not up for negotiation. It is, nevertheless, plain that the negotiations passed directly to the 'how' and 'when' without dealing with the '*if*'. Candidates simply had to accept and implement the acquis.[9] Of course, it could be argued in pragmatic terms that if a state wishes to enter the EU it should be obliged to accept the terms of its laws, however difficult this might be – *dura lex, sed lex.* Arguing that the accession negotiations had a 'democratic deficit' opens a debate that has little practical importance. However, the implementation of Community acts is not only a matter of enacting national legislation. The candidate must be capable of applying and implementing these national rules and regulations in an effective manner.[10]

> The EU is now saying it is not sufficient to transpose Community Law. The candidates must show that they have the institutions, the people and the budgets to apply the acquis with the same degree of rigor and commitment as the existing Member States.[11]

This mentality applies to the whole spectrum of Community acts but more so to the JHA acquis, which relates to the enforcement of sensitive political issues. Both the Commission and the member states repeatedly examined the independence and efficiency of Cyprus's judiciary, the organisation and professional ethics of the police and the existence of authorities that ensure personal data protection. Most of the time, putting Cyprus under the microscope in this manner revealed nothing untoward. The Commission, acting as a co-ordinator, gave particular emphasis to the in-depth training of officials and to the establishment of national contact points. In this context, it is prudent to elaborate on the legislative changes introduced by Cyprus and focus on the establishment of adequate administrative mechanisms for the implementation of this legal framework.

Visa policy – external borders

A sensitive issue on visa policy arose because Cyprus did not require a visa for countries that are on the EU's 'grey list'[12] of third countries whose nationals must be in possession of visas to enter EU territory. In alignment with the EU visa obligations, Cyprus proceeded with the introduction of visa obligations for nationals of Russia, Yugoslavia, six countries of the

Gulf and Zimbabwe. These arrangements were accompanied by the upgrading of a number of embassies and consulates in order to react effectively to the increased workload for the issuing of visas. Consular and local staff was recruited and the necessary logistical apparatus and security equipment was installed. The practice of issuing visas at the borders was terminated. Despite this effort significant work remains to be done; Cyprus has to establish new diplomatic missions and align its legislation with the Common Consular Instructions.

External border protection is all about effective checks at border crossing points. Cyprus adopted a program of acquiring the necessary equipment, e.g. new fast patrol boats, helicopters and coastal radar surveillance systems. In addition, the two law enforcement agencies, police and customs, became fully computerised using latest technology intelligence and information system.

Asylum and migration

In January 2000, Cyprus enacted a new Asylum Law, which is compatible with both the EU acquis on asylum and the Dublin Convention.[13] The enactment of this law was applauded by the EU, which stressed the need for effective implementation. By virtue of the new Asylum Law, a Refugee Authority was established on 1 January 2002. By the end of March 2003, case-workers responsible for interviewing and preparing a recommendation on a claim for refugee status submitted 172 recommendations to the Refugee Authority. On February 2002, the Law was amended in order to introduce an independent review of decisions on asylum claims. Implementing Regulations were also adopted incorporating the principle of the non-refoulement and the proper processing of asylum claims.

The Aliens and Immigration law regulates migration in Cyprus. In view of the particular concern expressed by the EU in this field,[14] legislative amendments were enacted concerning family reunification, marriages of convenience, the standard travel document and the responsibility of carrier companies to ensure that all passengers transported are in possession of the appropriate travel documents. A number of legal instruments still have to be adopted to align the legislation with the acquis on the uniform format of the residence permit. Cyprus should focus its attention on the conclusion of the negotiations of readmission agreements with other member states and the countries of origin of illegal immigrants. Illegal employment of third country nationals without a work permit must be combated.

Police cooperation, organised crime,money laundering and corruption

The framework for police cooperation is provided in Title VI of the EU Treaty. The Union has already legislated and acted in various ways in order to prevent crime, terrorism, trafficking in persons and offences against children, corruption and fraud.[15]

Despite the fact that the crime rate is relatively low in Cyprus, the law enforcement agencies have to be constantly on guard in their effort to monitor and suppress the illegal activities of local and international criminal groups. National legislation is, to a large extent, compatible with the EU acquis, although there is a need for some legislative changes to be introduced. A significant step forward is the enactment of a Police Law amendment, which will facilitate the collection of necessary evidence by focussing on the improvement of investigation procedures. Legislation enacted in January 2000 contains measures against child pornography and the sexual exploitation and trafficking of human beings. New legislation is in place regulating the protection of witnesses and the lawful interception of telecommunications.

The Cyprus Police has set up an intensive training program, which focuses, *inter alia*, on 'white collar' and 'high-tech' crime. Police officers participated in various projects organised under European programs, such as Grotius, Oisin and Falcone. Furthermore, Title VI provides for operational cooperation between police forces, customs authorities and other competent authorities of the member states, both directly and through the European Police Office. Cyprus also prepared for its accession to Europol and the Europol Convention[16] has been already ratified.

Money laundering is a sensitive issue repeatedly raised by EU officials during the negotiations. Cyprus, a successful financial services centre, was alleged to be a channel for financial crime such as money laundering. In order to counter such fears, Cyprus ratified the relevant international conventions and enacted a law for the prevention and suppression of money laundering activities. The most important development at the level of enforcement was the establishment of a 'Unit for Combating Money Laundering' (MOKAS), which has investigative powers and has achieved material results, including freezing orders and convictions for money laundering offences. The House of Representatives has recently approved 11 new posts aiming to strengthen the staff capacity of MOKAS.

Corruption in Cyprus is a criminal offence under the Criminal Code, the Prevention of Corruption Law and the Customs and Excise Law. Public expenditure and control is within the sphere of competence of the Auditor-

General, who by virtue of the Constitution is an independent Officer of the Republic. Responsibility for the investigation of corruption cases lies with the members of a special team of expert police officers at the Criminal Investigation Department. The Council of Europe 'Criminal Law Convention on Corruption' entered into force in July 2002. Cyprus has signed and ratified the OECD Convention on combating bribery of foreign public officials in international business transactions as well as the Civil Convention on Corruption of the Council of Europe. Cyprus has also joined the Group of States against Corruption (GRECO) of the Council of Europe, which will monitor the implementation of various instruments in this area by conducting evaluations concerning the measures taken against corruption in each member state.

Data protection

The effective protection of personal data occupies a significant place in the context of securing and promoting human rights. The increasing use of computerised networks containing confidential data on European citizens means that an appropriate legislative and administrative framework that prohibits unauthorised access to personal information is needed.

EU officials had urged Cyprus to accelerate the adoption of legislation on personal data protection. Towards that direction, Cyprus ratified the Council of Europe Convention for the protection of individuals with regard to automatic processing of personal data. National data protection legislation was enacted in November 2001. According to the provisions of this law, the Office of the Commissioner for Data Protection was established and started performing its duties in May 2002. The Commissioner has powers to issue directions for the uniform application of the law, report any breach of the provisions of the law and impose administrative sanctions such as fines or revocation of licences.

Drugs and terrorism

The fight against drugs is one of the priority areas in the field of JHA.[17] The EU has underlined that the implementation of the acquis on drugs requires a national strategy supported by adequate legislative and organisational measures. Cyprus enacted legislation for the establishment of the Antidrug Council and Fund, which is responsible for the preparation and implementation of a National Drugs Strategy and the co-ordination of public and private initiatives in the field of drug demand and drug supply reduction.The fourteen members of the Antidrug Council were appointed by the Council of Ministers in February 2001 and the Council started having regular meetings. The Special Drug Law Enforcement Unit of the Police has intensified its cooperation with international organisations and the competent authorities of European states for the collection, analysis and exchange of relevant information. Legislation for the establishment of the National Focal Point connected to the European Monitoring Centre for Drugs and Drug Addiction was enacted on July 2002.

Cyprus has signed and ratified the International Convention against Terrorist Bombings and the Convention for the Suppression of the Financing of Terrorism. In the Ratification law of the latter, a provision was included for the creation of a section for the Suppression of the Financing of Terrorism within the Unit for Combating Money Laundering.

Judicial cooperation and human rights

A priority objective for the achievement of an area of freedom, security and justice is to guarantee European citizens equal access to justice and promote cooperation between the competent ministries and judicial authorities of European states. The acquis in the field of judicial cooperation to a large extent consists of international conventions that Cyprus has already ratified. The aim in the field of judicial cooperation in civil matters is to improve and simplify cooperation in the taking of evidence and the recognition and enforcement in civil and commercial cases. In 2000, Cyprus ratified the Convention on Civil Procedure[18] and the Convention on International Access to Justice.[19] Legislation has also been adopted in order to comply with the provisions of the Rome Convention.[20] It must be noted that the law applicable in Cyprus concerning Private International Law is the common law. Cyprus has also started the negotiations for accession to the Convention on Jurisdiction in Civil and Commercial Matters.[21] The Convention on Jurisdiction, Recognition and Enforcement in Matrimonial Matters[22] has been ratified.

Regarding judicial cooperation in criminal matters one of the main objectives is to facilitate extradition between states and to accelerate cooperation between the judicial authorities in relation to criminal proceedings. Cyprus ratified the European Convention on Mutual Assistance in Criminal Matters[23] and the European Convention on the Transfer of Proceedings in Criminal Matters.[24] Judicial cooperation is further promoted by the conclusion of bilateral agreements with countries, which are not parties to the relevant multilateral conventions. Legislation for the statutory introduction of legal aid was enacted in July 2002. However, amendments to the existing legislation will be introduced for full implementation of the acquis concerning driving disqualification.[25]

The authorities and the society of Cyprus are very sensitive in the issue of the protection of human rights, since thousands of Greek and Turkish Cypriots are victims of continuing violations of their human rights emanating from the illegal Turkish military invasion and occupation. Thus, Cyprus has ratified all the international legal instruments in the field of human rights. Recently, Cyprus ratified Protocol 6 (abolition of the death penalty) and Protocol 7 to the European Convention on Human Rights as well as the revised European Social Charter. Civil, economic and cultural rights are respected. The judiciary supervises the legality of state acts, while independent authorities, such as the Office of the Law Commissioner and a number of NGOs monitor the protection and the free exercise of these rights.

The incorporation of the 'inflexible' Schengen acquis by Cyprus

The agreements of 1985 and 1990 signed in Schengen by the governments of five member states intended to facilitate the free movement of persons by abolishing the checks at the common borders of the participating states and by enforcing external borders of the Schengen area. A major aim was to achieve the free movement of persons without endangering security and order. Thus, common rules for visas and asylum rights were accompanied by measures for the fight against terrorism and organised crime and legal cooperation was strengthened through a faster extradition system. At the time Schengen was considered as an important vehicle for the achievement of the four EC Treaty freedoms.

However, it was soon evident that the existing framework could not keep up with the intended goals. Thus, member states decided to incorporate the Schengen acquis into the EU framework with the Treaty of Amsterdam. The new Schengen Protocol to the EU and EC Treaty permits the 13 participating member states to transfer the relevant decisions and provisions into the First (Title IV) and the Third (Title VI) Pillar. The Council, which replaced the Executive Committee of Schengen, shall take, by unanimous vote, the necessary measures for the identification and implementation of the Schengen acquis. Denmark is bound by the existing acquis but not as part of Community law. Ireland and the United Kingdom are not bound by the acquis but may at any time request to take part in some or all of its provisions.

Thus, Schengen was proclaimed as the banner of close cooperation arrangements made possible by the Treaty of Amsterdam and, for some scholars, the essential factor for forging flexibility[26] within the legal order of the Union. The 'Amsterdamisation' of the Schengen acquis marked the transition from the old fashioned flexibility of international agreements between member states, to the new flexibility within the EU framework. In a general context, the latter appears to facilitate enlargement, since it tends to become a core principle that favours the formation of a heterogeneous European polity of 25 or even 28 states.[27]

Nevertheless, from the new member states' perspective the whole flexibility debate on Schengen belongs to the sphere of academic theory. Member states are adamant that no derogations or opt-outs and opt-ins similar to the Danish or British, would be given to the candidate states. Article 8 of the 'Protocol on the integrating the Schengen acquis into the framework of the European Union' explicitly states the following:

> For the purposes of the negotiations for the admission of new Member States into the European Union, the Schengen acquis and further measures taken by the institutions within its scope shall be regarded as an acquis which must be accepted in full by all States candidates for admission.

This Article is essentially addressed to candidates and draws a clear distinction between the 'inflexible' Schengen and the other, flexible forms of closer cooperation provided in the Treaty.[28] Some member states supported the idea of long transitional periods before the right of free movement of persons from the new Eastern and Central European entrants is implemented. Consequently, candidates faced the reality of the accession negotiations: adopt the complex 'imposed' acquis, and cope with the extremely heavy costs of its proper implementation. Based on that assumption, I will now examine the implementation of the Schengen acquis by Cyprus.

The backbone of Schengen is the Schengen Information System (SIS), which is a central on-line network allowing police stations and consular agents from Schengen States to access data on specific individuals, vehicles and lost or stolen objects. Cyprus is in the process of acquiring the equipment and technical specifications necessary for the establishment and development of its national network (N-SIS) and its on-line system for issuing visas. A project for the establishment of the N-SIS, financed by the Cyprus government and the EU, was successfully completed.

Some measures have been taken to ensure the effectiveness of the law enforcement agencies (reorganisation of all police units dealing with external border control, the Police and the Customs administration signed in August 2001 a Memorandum of Understanding). Moreover, infrastructure changes will be effected at the legal points of entry to the Republic for the purpose of ensuring compliance with the Schengen measures, such as the separation of people travelling within the Schengen area from those arriving from countries outside this area. Concerning judicial cooperation, a simplified and faster extradition procedure will be effected upon the ratification of the relevant EU Conventions on Extradition Procedures.[29]

Some reflections on the reunification of the Cypriot polity: a bi-zonal bi-communal federation of freedom, security and justice

The history of the European polity is one of constant development from the homogeneous market-oriented EEC of the 1950s to the heterogeneous politico-socio-economic Union of the new millennium. As the EU has become an entity whose membership has increased from 6 to 15 and now numbers 25, the process of European integration has shifted from the path of uniformity and harmonisation to the path of flexibility and differentiation. A fertile scholarly debate has developed over the promises and pitfalls of this model of integration, or rather 'disintegration'.[30]

The most representative example of this controversial approach is the partial Communitarisation of the Third Pillar, which has left the achievement of the area of freedom, security and justice partly within EU competence and partly to intergovernmental cooperation. Although it can be argued that differentiation could result in fragmentation and legal and institutional complexity one must also accept the view that JHA can act as a catalyst for shaping the notion and the reality of European citizenship. The creation of an area within which the peoples of Europe are secure and able to move freely and enjoy their fundamental rights is a major step towards the establishment of a stronger notion of European citizenship, which is a crucial element for the formation of the European polity.

Could the implementation of the JHA acquis have similar effects in the context of a unified Cypriot polity? I have already discussed the concern expressed by certain member states regarding the incapacity of the Cypriot government, because of the Turkish invasion and occupation, to implement the JHA acquis over the whole island.[31] In November 2002, the

UN Secretary-General conveyed to the two sides a detailed plan for a comprehensive settlement of the Cyprus problem. Following intense consultations, the negotiations ended in The Hague, where Mr Annan announced on 11 March, the collapse of the effort to conduct separate simultaneous referenda, which would lead to a solution. The reason was the denial of Mr Denktash, the leader of the Turkish Cypriot Community, to put the plan to referendum, due to his fundamental objections. In the meantime, the European Council at Copenhagen decided, on 13 December 2002, that Cyprus together with nine other candidate countries would accede to the European Union on 1 May 2004, without any preconditions.

According to the government of Cyprus, a federal polity would be a viable solution. Such a federation would be bi-communal as regards its constitutional aspects and bi-zonal as regards the territorial perspective. A revised version of the Anan Plan was finally put to a referendum on the 26 of April 2004 in the two communities of the island. Despite the negative vote of the Greek Cypriots, all sides support the view that efforts should continue for a just and viable settlement of the Cyprus problem.

A polity is not only a constitution providing for a political and legal order. It also has effects on the citizens – the demos, that is willing to live under common democratic rule and enjoy its fundamental freedoms in spite of divergence of cultures, religions and languages. In contrast to the absent European demos,[32] a Cypriot demos exists which is willing to coexist under a single sovereign state. This is proven by the crowds of Greek and Turkish Cypriots who cross along ever day the cease-fire line after the partial lifting of restrictions on free movement by the occupation regime on 22 April 2003. The President of the Republic of Cyprus stated that 'Greek and Turkish Cypriots have shown that they desire to and can live together in a reunited country'.

This is where the importance of the adoption and implementation of the JHA acquis arises. In Section 4, I elaborated on the legislation adopted by Cyprus in the fields of asylum, external borders, security, organised crime and human rights. This legislative and infrastructure framework will substantially contribute to the removal of the uncertainty and suspicion accumulated over decades of conflicts and human rights violations. A strong Cypriot citizenship within the context of a European polity shall offer to the Greek Cypriots and the Turkish Cypriots the guarantees they both require and can be the foundation for the reunification of Cyprus.

Concluding remarks

When Cyprus applied for EU membership, it undertook the long and difficult task of harmonising its laws and practices with the acquis *communautaire* in the area of Justice and Home Affairs. In this chapter, I have discussed the extensive reforms currently introduced at legislative and administrative level for the transposition of the JHA acquis. Legislation is being enacted, the public service and the judiciary are strengthened, and new independent authorities are created for the effective implementation and enforcement of the acquis.

However, the JHA acquis has implications for both: legislation (*Nomos*) and politics. Various issues have been raised concerning the *de facto* division of the island and the geographical position of Cyprus. With these issues in mind, the critical question is whether Cyprus can cope with its future role both as a member of the EU and as the external border of a Union of freedom, security and justice. Cyprus has taken all the necessary measures to ensure that these issues will not affect its capacity to implement the JHA acquis.

At the moment, Cyprus is striving to cope with two challenges; resolve its political problem and succeed as a future member state of the EU. Though parallel, these two processes are interlinked; the new state structure, which is proposed as a solution must allow Cyprus to face up to its responsibilities and duties as an EU member state and to ensure that Greek and Turkish Cypriot citizens will enjoy their rights as European citizens in an area of freedom, security and justice.

Notes

1. I would like to thank Rea Apostolidou, Spyros Ierotheou and John Clark for their stimulating comments. The views expressed in this Chapter are the personal views of the author and not those of the institution to which he belongs.
2. European Commission, 2002 Regular Report of the Commission on Cyprus's Progress Towards Accession, 9 October 2002, p.104.
3. European Commission, 'Report on the Functioning of the Treaty on European Union', *Europe Documents*, 1995, p.5 and p.8. The language of the European Parliament is even harsher. According to it, the third pillar results in a 'complex, almost schizophrenic, structure'. European Parliament, Committee on Civil Liberties and Internal Affairs, Opinion on the functioning of the Treaty on European Union, PE 210.525.

4. For an interesting analysis of the term'area' see J. Shaw, 'Constitutional Settlements and the Citizen After the Treaty of Amsterdam' in K. Neunreither and A. Wiener (eds.), *Beyond Amsterdam: Institutional Dynamics and Prospects for Democracy in the EU,* Oxford University Press, Oxford, 1998.
5. K. Lenaerts, P. Van Nuffel and R. Bray (ed.), *Constitutional Law of the European Union* ,Sweet and Maxwell, London, 1999, p.82.
6. Report of the Reflection Group, chaired by Professor G. Amato, on 'the Long-Term Implications of the EU Enlargement: The Nature of the New Border', p.54.
7. A. Favell, 'The Europeanisation of Immigration Politics', *European Integration Online Papers*, Vol. 2, N. 10, 1998.
8. Report of the Reflection Group, *op.cit.*, p.55.
9. On the 'inflexibility' of the Schengen acquis see *infra*, Section 5.
10. P. Nicolaides, 'Enlargement of the EU and Effective Implementation of Community Rules: an Integration-Based Approach', Working Paper 99/W/04, *European Institute of Public Administration*, Maastricht, 1999.
11. Statement of Mr. Francois Lamoureux, who was at that time Deputy Director-General in DG1A in charge of relations with the candidates, published in T*he European Dialogue: Politics and Current Affairs*, Issue 3, May-June 1998.
12. See Council Regulation (EC) 574/1999 of 12 March 1999 determining 'the third countries whose nationals must be in possession of visas when crossing the external borders of the Member States', OJ 1999, L 72/3, replacing Reg. 2317/95, annulled by the ECJ in case C-392/95, *Parliament v. Council*, [1997] ECR I-3213.
13. See the 'Convention determining the State responsibility for examining applications for asylum lodged in one of the Member States of the European Communities' (Dublin Convention), OJ 1997 C254/1.
14. P.J. Kuijper, 'Some legal problems associated with the communitarization of policy on visas, asylum and immigration under the Amsterdam Treaty and incorporation of the Schengen acquis', *Common Market Law Review*, Vol. 37, 2000, p.361.
15. There is a wide range of legal instruments in this field such as the Council Resolution of 19 June 1997 on preventing and restraining football hooliganism, [1997] OJ C193/1, the Joint Action 97/154/JHA of 24 February 1997 concerning action to combat trafficking in human beings and sexual exploitation of children, [1997]OJ 163/2 and many others.
16. Convention of 26 July 1995 on the 'establishment of a European Police Office', [1995] OJ C316/61. However, Europol took up its activities on July I, 1999 with the entry into force of the Protocol on privileges and immunities and the agreements on privileges and immunities for liaison officers.
17. See Joint Action 96/750/JHA of 17 December 1996 concerning the approximation of the laws and practices of the member states of the European Union to combat drug addiction and to prevent and combat illegal drug trafficking [1996] OJ L342/6.

18. Convention of 1 March 1954 on 'Civil Procedure'.
19. Convention of 25 October 1980, on 'International Access to Justice'.
20. Convention of 19 June 1980 on the 'Law applicable to Contractual Obligations', [1980] OJ L 266.
21. Convention of 16 September 1988 on 'Jurisdiction and enforcement of Judgements in Civil and Commercial Matters' (Lugano Convention), [1988] OJ L319.
22. Convention of 28 May 1998, drawn up on the basis of the former Art. K3 of the EU Treaty, on 'Jurisdiction and the Recognition and Enforcement of Judgements in Matrimonial Matters' (Second Brussels Convention),[1998] OJ C221/2.
23. European Convention of 20 April 1959, on 'Mutual Assistance in Criminal Matters'.
24. European Convention of 15 May 1972, on the 'Transfer of Proceedings in Criminal Matters'.
25. Convention of 17 June 1998, drawn up on the basis of the former Art. K.3 of the EU Treaty, on 'Driving Disqualifications', [1998] OJ C216/2.
26. A. Wiener, 'Forging Flexibility – The British 'No' to Schengen', *Arena Working Papers*, WP00/1inhttp://www.arena.uio.no/news/publications/publ_wp.htm#Order%20Form.
27. G. De Burca and J. Scott, Introduction in G. De Burca and J. Scott (eds), *Constitutional Change in the EU – From Uniformity to Flexibility*', Hart Publishing, Oxford-Portland Oregon, 2000, p.4.
28. C. D. Ehlermann, 'Differentiation, Flexibility, Closer Cooperation : The New Provisions of the Amsterdam Treaty', Working Papers, RSC Publication, in http:// www.iue.it/RSC/WP.
29. Convention of March 10, 1995, adopted on the basis of the former Art. K.3 of the EU Treaty, on simplified extradition procedure between the member statess of the European Union [1995] OJ C78/2 and Convention of 27 September 1996, relating to extradition between the member statess of the European Union [1996] OJ C313/12.
30. G. De Burca and J. Scott, 2000, *op.cit.*, pp.1-2.
31. See *supra*, Section 3.
32. J. Weiler, 'European Citizenship – Identity and Differentity', in M. La Torre (ed), *European Citizenship An Institutional* Challenge, Kluwer Law International, The Hague, 1998, pp.7-9 and B. Kohler-Koch, 'A Constitution for Europe?', *Arbeits-papiere – Mannheimer Zentrum fur Europaische Sozialforschung*, No.8, 1999.

12 Cyprus in the EU: A Small State Perspective

RODERICK PACE

Introduction

The accession of Cyprus in the EU has been analysed from many angles with a considerable amount of emphasis being placed on the likely effect of Cypriot accession on a solution of the Cyprus Problem. In this chapter the analysis shall focus on a number of other issues related to the Cypriot membership. The analytical approach in this chapter is based on a 'small state' perspective that seeks to establish whether small states have certain peculiar needs and how these can be met by EU membership. Therefore this chapter focuses on the position of small states in the EU and explores some potential avenues available to Cyprus as an EU member state.

When Cyprus joined the EU, on 1 May 2004, it did so in the company of nine other new member states, eight of which can be classified as small states. The EU is still in 'enlargement mode', meaning that eventually it could consist of at least 28 or more member states. The main characteristic of the EU both as it is and as it will be in the future if it grows further, is its heterogeneity in terms of the levels of economic development, political and legal systems, religions, languages, defence and foreign policy orientation. It is already a Union composed mainly of small states with a population of around 10 millions or less.[1] In this Union, Cyprus is only just above Luxembourg and Malta in terms of population, but equal to Luxembourg in all respects within the EU's institutions. Six of the 25 member states, namely Malta, Luxembourg, Cyprus, Slovenia, Estonia and Latvia can be defined as micro-states since each has a population of less than 2.5 millions while five namely Denmark, Ireland, Lithuania, Slovakia and Finland with populations ranging from little over 3.4 millions to 5 millions can be defined as very small states. Following these two bands there is the 'upper' group of small countries numbering seven in all, with populations ranging from just over 8 millions to around 11 millions and comprising Austria, Sweden, Hungary, Greece, Czech Republic, Belgium and Portugal.

This classification of small states by the population criterion alone shows that even among the class of small states there are marked differences.

The successful conclusion and ratification of the Nice Treaty cleared an important hurdle to enlargement, despite the criticism that was aimed at it because of its failures. The member states have concluded negotiations on a new European Constitution. The more difficult task of securing its ratification has begun.

From a Cypriot perspective, EU membership means that Cyprus has acquired unprecedented influence in the EU itself and, as shall shortly be argued, also in international affairs in general when compared to its non-member status. The same can be said of all new member states, especially those which together with Cyprus can be classified as micro-states.[2] As an EU member state and in accordance with the Nice Treaty, Cyprus will participate fully in the Council (where its weight in qualified majority voting has been fixed at 4 votes), it has the right to nominate a Commissioner, it has 6 seats in the EP, in the ESC and the Committee of the Regions. Cyprus has the right to nominate a Judge to the ECJ and another one to the CFI. Cyprus also appoints one member to the Court of Auditors. On the basis of the principle of 'digressive proportionality' and in common with all small member states Cyprus enjoys a slightly disproportionately bigger weight in the institutions than the larger member states. Indeed, the outcome of the Nice Treaty seems to be in line with the results that Cyprus had previously vaguely alluded to in the ideas it submitted to the Intergovernmental Conference 2000.[3] That said, however, it is deceptively easy to equate Cypriot influence in the EU with its weight in the institutions and thus ignore the broader implications of membership. Much more relevance may lie in the fact that as a member state, Cyprus will be involved in the legislative process from its initial stages and that Cypriot officials will participate in the complex administrative process usually referred to as 'comitology'. Moreover, the Cypriot parliament will also become more directly involved in the EU legislative process and will have to enhance its abilities to scrutinise and influence it. The main drawback in all this, and one which Cyprus shares with all small states, is the shortage of trained human resources to make its participation in the institutions as effective as it would want to. Participation in the institutions means that Cypriot policy stances will have to be taken seriously by fellow member states and that third countries will also begin to attach new importance to this island state precisely because of its position as a member of one of the world's largest markets and increasingly unified global political actor.

As a member state Cyprus has not reached the end of its adjustment to the 'acquis communautaire'. This process, which began in around 1998 in preparation for the start of the membership negotiations and subsequently continued during the negotiations themselves, is not a process which will stop primarily because the acquis is evolving continuously. In addition Cyprus still has some adjustments to make gradually in line with the Act of Accession and above all one major important appointment to keep – which is that of joining the EU's Economic and Monetary Union (EMU) and eventually adopting the Euro at the appropriate time. This requires Cyprus to focus on the macroeconomic fundamentals and the so called 'Maastricht Convergence Criteria' (in so far as they continue in their present form) in order to achieve this aim. By no measure does the latter task promise to be easy or straight forward as was amply demonstrated in 2002 when the Cypriot rate of inflation increased slightly while the current account and the fiscal deficit deteriorated.[4] In addition it has still to grapple with the Cyprus' 'political problem' since the Annan Plan was rejected by the Greek Cypriots in a referendum, in April 2004. On the brighter side the Cypriot economy has shown in the past a resilience of its own and a capability of adjusting, often in the most seemingly unfavourable conditions.[5] Far from being an end in itself membership imposes adjustment burdens but also opens up new opportunities, which Cyprus can exploit to its benefit. This chapter will analyse some of the implications of EU membership for Cyprus from a small state perspective keeping in mind the following:

1. The special characteristics of Cyprus as a small island state on the periphery of the European Union and how the challenges posed by these characteristics can be addressed by EU membership;
2. The possible effect of EU membership on Cyprus's 'international position' and on the Cyprus Problem.

Small, peripheral, insular and divided

Cyprus is a small state (population 865,300 including the Turks/Turkish Cypriots living in the northern occupied part), on Europe's periphery facing the turbulent region of the Middle East, an island with all the setbacks of insularity, but a strategic location. It is an island which is ethnically and forcefully divided with its capital Nicosia, the last divided capital of Europe. Together with Iceland and Malta it completes the team of Europe's only island micro-states. EU membership stands to reverse most of the island's disadvantages:

- it can help Cyprus overcome its peripheral location by linking it to the heart of European politics;
- it allows Cyprus unrestricted access for its goods and services in the EU market thus enabling it to overcome the disadvantages of its restricted domestic market;
- it increases its political importance in international affairs and in the Middle Eastern region helping it to play a more important role in that sub-region;
- it enhances Cyprus's ability to play a pivotal role, possibly also to develop itself further into a regional economic hub in the Eastern Mediterranean; and
- finally EU membership may help bring to an end the forceful division of the island.

Broader market access or modernisation?

Small states such as Cyprus with a small domestic market require access to large markets in order to sustain meaningful productive sectors of goods and services that can take advantage of economies of scale. Due to the lack of sufficient avenues to mobilise capital at home, and often the lack of know-how, economic growth is usually augmented by inflows of direct foreign investment (FDI). One of the main attractions to FDI is precisely free access to larger markets enjoyed by such small states and the availability of a trained labour force often in combination with some tax incentives.

This pattern of economic development exhibited by most successful small states also leads to more openness, to an increased dependence on the external environment and an increased vulnerability to the vicissitudes of the international economy particularly those resulting from the increased volatility of world financial markets and other international developments. The processes of globalisation and increased interdependence[6] and the impact of the progressive liberalisation and gradual integration of world markets as a result of the World Trade Organisation (WTO) and the communications revolution, has led to the further integration of all states in the world economy, not least among them the small states. Yet, at the same time, globalisation has increased competition in world markets, has led to a marked power-shift towards transnational corporations and a further loss of policy autonomy by most states especially small states. In concert with others, mostly by joining regional groupings, small states can try to overcome the more negative effects of globalisation just described and to recover the powers lost by co-operating with other states.

In the face of these developments small countries have discovered that they have not been spared the need of adjusting to the new realities and challenges with what may be described as 'draconian' measures when compared to their individual small scale. These measures shook many of the old fundamentals and ushered in a new set of priorities in small states as well, which included privatisation, liberalisation of capital, goods and financial markets, liberalisation of telecommunications, standardisation, fiscal reform, social security and pension reform (welfare) and public sector reform. These reforms were accompanied by growing public pressure in favour of environmental and consumer protection – and more recently data protection – which led to the establishment of independent or semi-independent regulatory agencies to oversee the newly liberalised sectors in order to ensure fair play and the protection of the rights of consumers. In addition these demands have taxed the small states' limited reservoir (not of course measured on a per capita basis but in raw terms) of trained human resources and their administrative capabilities.

EU membership or as close a relationship to it as possible, offer small states a good vehicle for overcoming the main hurdles on the road to modernisation and above all of integration in the world economy in the least cumbersome manner. The acquis becomes the tried and tested 'off the shelf' available product, which – with some adjustments and modifications to take account of their smallness – shows them what has to be done to meet the various challenges they face saving them costly experimentation. EU membership offers small states improved access to Europe's internal market and opens the door to the markets of all the other countries linked to the EU by an association agreement or other form of preferential trading arrangement. In other words, it improves their access to the global market. This also makes them more open to imports with possible negative balance of trade effects. On the positive side openness helps small states keep inflationary pressures down and broadens consumer choice. Openness to imports also introduces more competition in the domestic market and helps to increase dynamic efficiencies with positive long term effects on export competitiveness in key sectors.

Indeed, a small state's integration in a larger regional group often develops in various phases in response to the transformations occurring on the domestic front and the broader changes in the state's international environment. A glance at Cyprus's relations with the EU demonstrates this quite adequately as Cyprus progressed through the main three stages:

Stage 1 In 1962 the EEC concluded an association agreement with Cyprus in the wake of the UK's membership application in order to help Cyprus preserve its main export markets. The main issue here was to secure an important life line for Cyprus still in its initial years of independence, grappling with the challenge of state-building and the consolidation of its independence.

Stage 2 The 1973 Association agreement was also intended to maintain market access in the wake of the UK's EC membership but it was also intended to lead to the further diversification of Cypriot exports. This aim was temporarily thwarted by the 1974 invasion and division of the island but it was further strengthened by the EC-Cyprus customs union agreement of 1988.

Stage 3 The main economic motivations behind the 1990 Cypriot membership application as stated in an official 1995 Cypriot Government publication were: eventual inclusion in the internal market characterised by the 'four freedoms', a secure climate, monetary stability, transfers from the Community budget to help Cypriot development, co-operation in technology transfer, research and development and training, in short modernisation.[7]

Thus, the evolution of Cyprus's relations with the EU demonstrates a fundamental transformation in the underlying basis of the relationship that also reflects the manner in which the EU itself has changed over time and the changing Cypriot priorities as Cyprus adapted to world changes. Initially, the emphasis lay on market access provided by the EC market. But as Cyprus moved up the development ladder the emphasis changed from mere market access to achieving the 'quality leap' that could be summarised under the concept of modernisation and integration in the global economy. From this perspective the opportunities provided by EU membership, if well and properly exploited, can better equip Cyprus to deal with the challenges of globalisation.

In its Regular Report on Cyprus's Progress Towards Accession of

November 2000,[8] the Commission stated, that the Cypriot economy was capable of meeting the competitive pressure and market forces within the Union. This broad positive appraisal of the Cypriot economy continues to hold as was clearly indicated in the last Commission Report on Cyprus published in November 2003.[9] However, growth slowed down in the last two years so that while real GDP growth averaged 4.6% per year for the years 1998-2001, in 2002 and 2003 this dropped to 2% per year.[10] The Commission's 2003 Report blames this decline on 'great geopolitical and economic uncertainty' which hit Cypriot exports and the tourist sector.[11] The former Minister of Finance, Markos Kyprianou summarised these uncertainties very succinctly: '...(stagnant) output in the main European trading partners and the threat of international terrorism compounding the negative effects on the exports of tourism services...'[12] The Cypriot authorities tried to ease the impact by adopting a more expansionary fiscal stance but coming at a time when cyclically-determined tax revenues were subdued while the costs of adopting the acquis were mounting, it forced Cyprus to slip from the Maastricht convergence criteria set for the achievement of European Monetary Union.

Structural reform in Cyprus has continued and this may have also contributed to the current difficulties. The recent decline in manufacturing and in the tourist sector underline the need to further diversify the economy towards new growth sectors. To accomplish this task, the Government has targeted telecoms, IT and business services and education. However, the Annual Economic Indicators published by the Central Bank in 2004 show that unemployment remains comparatively low at 3.5%. The danger is that expansion in the new growth sectors may lead to labour shortages. This problem could be addressed by 'importing labour', which would not be difficult now that Cyprus has joined the EU. Better still the 2003 Report advices Cyprus to enhance the flexibility of its labour force or to mobilise the potential labour force through education and training.

In the short-term these changes will undoubtedly result in adjustment costs for Cyprus. This is sometimes wrongly equated with EU membership when in fact other exogenous and endogenous factors often require the same sort of adjustment independently of membership. The fate of the Cypriot International Business and shipping sector illustrates the case.[13] Between 1976 and 1999 cumulatively a total of 41,752 'off-shore' business companies were set up in Cyprus of which around half are still active.[14] Latest estimates put the number of permits for the establishment of international business companies at around 57,000 and the number of expatriates and locals employed in the sector at 3,300 and 2,900 respectively.

Similarly, by 1999, cumulatively 12,187 permits had been issued to shipping companies to establish themselves in Cyprus. By 2002 there were 2,153 vessels totalling 24,860,060 GRT and making the Cypriot shipping register the sixth largest in the world. In addition a total of 30 foreign banks operate from Cyprus. In 1999, the country's total foreign exchange earnings in the sector (shipping and international business) amounted to CY£243.1 millions or 4.9% of GDP rising to CY£350 millions in 2003 or 5.3% of GDP. Pressure has been mounted on Cyprus, as has been on other off-shore havens, to end the special tax treatment of these 'off-shore' companies and to apply the OECD's guidelines against harmful tax competition. The Commission had stressed prior to membership that 'In the field of direct taxation the special regime for offshore companies needs to be addressed.'[15] It is for this reason that during the negotiations the chapter on taxation was one of those which took the longest to close. International Business Companies are taxed at only 4.25% of their profits and are totally exempted from corporation and income tax. There are also special advantageous tax treatment of expatriate employees and beneficial owners. At the same time Cyprus has had to enact and enforce stringent anti-money laundering legislation.[16] In the case of shipping the EU put pressure on Cyprus to increase ship safety and inspections in line with similar measures adopted at EU level.[17]

The International Business sector is an essential one for Cyprus helping the island diversify from overly relying on tourism. In the run up to membership Cyprus had to introduce more stringent supervisory legislation and laws to combat money laundering. But so far, though it is perhaps early to pronounce judgement on its fate, the sector seems to have held well and if the official figures are anything to go by, it has also expanded marginally. However, what is important to note in this case is that even outside the EU membership context, international pressure would have constrained Cyprus to tighten the laws governing this sector while adopting international norms help it strengthen its reputation in the world of international business.

The external dimension of Cyprus's membership: the Mediterranean region

As has already been stated in this chapter, *ceteris paribus* the accession of Cyprus in the EU stands to enhance the importance of Cyprus in external relations especially in the Mediterranean and help maintain the EU's interest in the region. The entry of Cyprus and Malta in the EU must be seen against the backdrop of the shift that has occurred in the EU's centre of gravity towards the countries of central and eastern Europe, resulting from the accession of 8 new states from that part of the Continent. This shift will become more accentuated in the future following the planned enlargement(s).

It must be noted that from its very beginning the EC/EU attached great importance to the maintenance of peace, stability and good neighbourly relations in the Mediterranean region. And for good reason too: many of the member states have a long Mediterranean coast line (France, Greece, Italy and Spain) as well as long-standing historic ties with the countries of the Mediterranean region. The Mediterranean region was the only one where from the very beginning the Community practiced an external policy, which in turn helped legitimise the EEC as a credible international actor. Today, the region is an important outlet for EU exports, not least for its northern member states.[18] Moreover, the Mediterranean region has developed into a strategically important conduit for the supply of a substantial part of the EU's oil and petroleum needs as well as a major world maritime highway for the transport of goods and oil.[19] Environmental degradation has a direct bearing on all states of region, not least among them the key member states.[20] A serious maritime disaster in this comparatively narrow sea[21] could have immediate negative economic effects on all states, especially those that have been expanding their income and employment from tourism. At the same time the expansion of the tourist sector is also increasing the environmental pressures in the region.[22] Sluggish economic growth combined with rapid demographic growth in some of the key southern countries, increases migratory pressures on Europe especially illegal emigration. In sum, negative developments in the Mediterranean region do not only affect the states of the region themselves, but they can also spillover onto the EU itself, sometimes with a knock on effect as well.

A serious military threat to Europe from the southern shore states of the Mediterranean region is most unlikely although the proliferation of weapons of mass destruction needs to be monitored closely. The decision by Libya, announced in December 2003, that it was dismantling its WMD programme was not only important as an initial step in bringing that country out of international isolation but it also strengthened hopes that more could be achieved on this front in the region. The southern Mediterranean countries probably attach more importance to the internal rather than the external threats to their security, while among the latter they mostly fear those coming from fellow southern neighbours rather than from

Europe.[23] To be honest, they are also suspicious of NATO's initiatives in the Mediterranean region.[24] In 1994 the Alliance started the 'Mediterranean Dialogue' with a number of countries of the region to begin to allay these fears and strengthen mutual understanding.[25] Since then the dialogue has matured further but it has not achieved spectacular results. NATO has also started revising its southern flank strategy and a RAND Corporation study commissioned by the Italian Ministry of Defence laid emphasis on the 'soft' security threats as being the main ones threatening the region's stability. This prognosis remained valid until the events of 11 September and the terrorist bombings in Casablanca, Istanbul and Madrid. Soft security threats emanate mainly from the instability that may accompany political upheaval and socio-economic pressures in the southern littoral countries.[26] North African states are critical of Europe's lack of engagement in the security problems of the region, a failure they perceive as one of the causes of the regional arms race.[27] Since 11 September 2001, a paradigm shift has also occurred in the region's security discourse with greater emphasis being placed on international terrorism. This shift was further reinforced by the terrorist attacks in Casablanca, Istanbul and Madrid. Many feared that the terrorist threat would be employed by the governments of the region to halt or reverse the small but important advances made on the human-rights democracy front. However international pressure did not relent at all on this issue. Two Arab Human Development Reports published by the UNDP in 2002 and 2003, a European Commission Communication on 'Reinvigorating EU Actions on Human Rights and Democratisation with Mediterranean Partners' (21 May 2004) and the support, even if somewhat mixed, given to political reform by leaders of the Arab League meeting in Tunis in May 2004 all underlined the resistance to abandoning political reforms in the southern shore countries. Arab governments and their Islamic fundamentalist opposition often find themselves in agreement when describing the West's insistence on political reform as a form of interference in their internal affairs.

Over the years the EC/EU has responded to the challenges it faces in the region by a series of polices, beginning with the Global Mediterranean Policy of the early 1970s and culminating in the Euro-Mediterranean Partnership, the so-called Barcelona Process, which began in 1995. In all these policies the EU sought to enhance stability in the region by acting as a civilian power. The EU's policies towards the region have periodically been criticised as being inadequate. A series of new EU foreign policy initiatives which started in 2003 have complicated matters further. In view of the forthcoming enlargement, the EU proposed a new 'Neighbourhood

Policy' which was followed in June 2004 by a proposal for a 'Strategic Partnership with the Mediterranean and Middle East'.[28] It is not clear how these initiatives will interface with one another and with the Euro-Mediterranean Partnership though it has often been claimed by the EU that these initiatives are all mutually enforcing and not mutually exclusive.

The main aim of the majority of these policies is undoubtedly the Union's own interests, though as a result of the criticism made by the southern Mediterranean shore countries the EU is becoming more sensitive to the idea of gradually engaging the southern shore countries in a true partnership. In the meantime, a broad assessment of the effects of these polices on the Mediterranean Basin countries reveals that indeed they have been instrumental at least in preserving the traditional trade outlets and market access for the southern littoral states and with laying the foundations for newer forms of co-operation across the region. The EC's preferential trading arrangements which have been in operation since the 1970s have also led to increases in the volume of trade between the EU and its partners. It is improbable that the region would have fared better without these agreements. The positive effects of the underlying cob-web of relations and networks that have been established as a result of these policies are already being felt and could possibly intensify in the future, if the Euro-Mediterranean Partnership is more successful. In September of 2000, the European Commission published new proposals on how the Mediterranean Partnership could be strengthened in the future.[29] These proposals formed the basis of discussions during the fourth ministerial meeting of the Euro-Mediterranean Partnership held in Marseilles on 15-16 November 2000.[30] Accordingly, the Euro-Mediterranean Partnership is still viewed by all the member states participating in it as the main instrument for enhancing stability in the region and the ministers encouraged the EU to take a more visible role in fostering dialogue, trust and confidence in the Middle East. This commitment to the Barcelona process was re-iterated at subsequent Foreign Ministers' meetings held in Valencia (2002), Naples (2003) and the Dublin mid-term Foreign Ministers' conference held in May 2004. The situation in the Middle continues to dictate the pace in the Euro-Mediterranean Partnership.

On the economic front the aim of achieving the Euro-Mediterranean free trade area by 2010 is still the main target. This has been helped by the conclusion of nearly all the bilateral free trade accords between the EU and the Mediterranean countries except with Syria which is in an advanced stage[31] and the launching of the Agadir Initiative involving Jordan, Egypt, Morocco and Tunisia in a south-south free trade area.[32] A common system of rules of origin will eventually become operational after which the free movement of services and the removal of residual non-tariff barriers to trade could gain increased saliency. The major problem which has still to be resolved is the region's inability to attract sufficient flows of direct foreign investment (FDI). This is intimately linked to security perceptions about the region in the countries of origin and of course the lack of democracy, good governance and transparency as well as the absence of adequate laws regulating economic and business activities in the recipient states. However, the situation is not static either, but is improving across the region albeit at an uneven pace.

Following the EU's enlargement the main question bedevilling the minds of many in the southern littoral states is whether the Mediterranean Region will eventually be sidelined by a shift in the EU's internal and external priorities. On the internal front the main concern is the completion of the ratification process of the new European Constitution and the gradual assimilation of the new member states. In the external domain the main fear among the Mediterranean countries is that now that the centre of gravity of the EU has shifted eastwards, the Mediterranean region may be given less importance in the Union's priorities.

Enlargement has changed the nature of the Euro-Mediterranean Partnership from 15 EU member states plus 12 Mediterranean states to 25 plus 10 if Libya is also counted among the latter. The accession of the Mediterranean applicants Cyprus and Malta has further extended the EU's borders southwards in a very sensitive and turbulent region. In the EU itself the Mediterranean group presently composed of five member states, namely Spain and Portugal (even if the latter has only an Atlantic coastline), France, Italy and Greece will increase to seven. This does not entirely redress the geographic balance of the EU, which has clearly shifted eastwards. Hence, the EU will continue to maintain its interest in the Mediterranean region only if it perceives serious threats to its own security and stability emanating from it and if it can see that it has important gains to make by maintaining its focus and engagement in the region.

A possible role for Cyprus

As two peripheral island states on the southernmost frontiers of the EU, Cyprus and Malta are both well positioned to be able to transmit the challenges and sensitivities of the region to the heart of the EU decision-making process. This is helped by the fact that small states tend to focus more on their immediate environment than on the broader, global field. The down side of this is that they have to convince the larger member states that their concerns present real challenges to the whole of the EU. In some cases this is not difficult to achieve. For example the aftermath of 11 September 2001, the deteriorating situation in the Middle East and the invasion of Iraq in 2003, led to a marked downturn in air travel and the tourist industry. The effect on Cyprus and Malta was enormous given their dependence on the tourist service sector. The same can be said of the disruption and instability in the world oil markets instigated by the events in Iraq, the Middle East and the Arab Peninsula. In other words, whether it is terrorism, oil, tourism, or illegal immigration serious uncontrolled upheavals in the Mediterranean region tend to spill over onto the EU itself. The main difficulty for Cyprus is the ability to foresee situations developing into crisis or conflict situations. Small states do not have sufficient information-gatherings means to foresee this happening and are more likely to react to situations which have developed and to situations which are still in the pre-crisis or pre-conflict stage.

In as much as Cyprus does not become overly engrossed with its own national question and the peaceful reunification of the island at the expense of a deeper participation in the EU's external policies, the framework of the Euro-Mediterranean Partnership offers unique opportunities for influencing policies towards the regional environment in which it has to survive. In the past, unable to influence events because of its smallness and limited resources Cyprus could only be the consumer of policies not their maker. As an EU member state it can participate in policy making at the highest levels. It can also employ the EU's Mediterranean policies towards achieving its own foreign policy goals. This will inevitably involve the Europeanisation of its national approaches towards the region. However, by working from within the EU's policies it can become more effective and achieve better results. Indeed, in addressing the 'natural' shortfall in its resources a small state like Cyprus can exploit is the bigger resources, regional and global contacts at the disposal of the EU to its advantage.

In addition, the status of Cyprus and Malta in the Euro-Mediterranean Partnership stands to be enhanced in other ways as a result of their EU membership. The EU exercises and has agenda-setting powers in the Partnership. Most policy initiatives begin with the Commission and are approved by the Council before they are transmitted to the Committee for the Barcelona Process and the Partners' governments. The EU also provides the bulk of the finance for the MEDA programmes, comprising both the multilateral and the bilateral initiatives and supporting networks.

As a member state, Cyprus participates fully in the decision-making process of the EU and is in a position to influence policies in the design phase, giving it sufficient leeway to influence the shape of policies from their initial stages. This advantage is bound not to go unnoticed by the non-EU member states of the Euro-Mediterranean Partnership. Thus, it is likely that they will ascribe more relevance and importance to it than they did in the past.

One major drawback for Cyprus is that as a member state, it has to focus on a broader range of issues and policies whose direct relevance to the Mediterranean region might be minimal. Given that participation in the EU decision-making process places important constraints on a small state's comparatively more limited human resources Cyprus may at times lose its focus on the Mediterranean region. In addition this focus also depends on the importance that Cypriot political elites are willing to give it. However, it is important to keep in mind that broadly speaking, while the larger EU Mediterranean states, have multiple foreign policy interests and a divided attention (e.g. their priorities concern the Balkans, Central and Eastern Europe, the trans-Atlantic relationship, the Middle East and Far East) the main concerns of Cyprus are more focused on its immediate environment. This difference in perspective results primarily from Cyprus's smallness, vulnerability and insularity which cause it to focus more on issues of immediate relevance to it, which are in turn intimately connected with the situation in the Mediterranean region where it is situated.[33]

Indeed the stability of the Mediterranean region has a higher premium for Cyprus and Malta, and a relatively higher risk factor than for most other states mostly because the two island states are in the Mediterranean region and will be probably the first to be affected by any backwash of a crisis or conflict eve when they are not directly involved in them . In order to illustrate the point better, the negative effects of the Gulf War are most instructive. In times of regional or international crisis small states' openness coupled with their vulnerability, which is rooted in economic specialisation (e.g. tourism), are much more threatening to their overall stability and social cohesion than is the case for large and more diversified economies. Thus, a serious political disturbance in the Mediterranean region and its environs or a maritime ecological disaster could affect negatively the economic well-being of Cyprus and Malta, where tourism contributes to more than a fifth of their respective Gross Domestic Product. Indeed, the evidence suggests that at the outbreak of the Gulf War in 1990 travel and trade in and across the region was negatively affected and both Cyprus and Malta claimed to have sustained losses.[34] The closure of the

Suez Canal following the 1967 'Six day war' is another example. This had a negative impact on Malta's key ship repair sector. The events of 11 September and the war in Iraq hit many of the world's airlines but they had a stronger effect on Cyprus and Malta by dampening their growth rates and exasperating their balance of payments.

It is also true, and paradoxically so, that some problems in the Mediterranean region could also lead to windfall profits, though this is not the general rule. One such 'windfall' occurred as a result of the war in the Balkans in 1999 by diverting some of the tourism that normally goes to that region to Cyprus.[35] Broadly speaking, while every Mediterranean Basin country reaps economic dividends from peace and stability, small and economically 'open' countries such as Cyprus and Malta stand to gain most from stability and risk losing most in the event of turmoil. Lastly, it can be shown from historic experience that the independence of small and weak states tends to be most at risk in times of conflict.[36] Thus while for most member states, the Mediterranean region may be 'another policy issue' with which they have to deal for a small country like Cyprus, an island in the midst of the region, the issue of Mediterranean stability is objectively the most important matter to which its survival is most intimately linked.

Concluding remarks: possible ways forward

As has been argued above, the independence and identity of small states tends to be more at risk in an anarchical international or regional states system, especially in times of war, rather than in a 'rule-based' one. It is in the interest of Cyprus to strengthen regional stability and the Euro-Mediterranean Partnership serves this purpose very well. The Partnership can be compared to a rule-based international regime that suits Cyprus's interests in the Mediterranean region. The Partnership:

- facilitates the achievement of more open trade, eventually a Euro-Mediterranean free trade area
- strengthens the links of interdependence among the region's states and enhances regional stability
- potentially offers Cyprus a freer access to the markets of the Arab states
- provides a political forum for the discussion of some of the key

regional economic and political issues

- could facilitate confidence-building measures though no spectacular progress has been registered in this domain
- multiplies the horizontal and vertical links of co-operation across the region and keeps both sides of the Mediterranean Basin positively engaged in search of common solutions
- promotes a cultural dialogue which is also relevant to Cyprus's own internal situation but which is more important to the stability of the Mediterranean region
- serves as a means of consultation in times of political crisis in the region

In the final analysis it is a factor of stability for which there is no alternative substitute in sight. Hence it appears to be in Cyprus's interest not only to participate in it in order gain international influence and to be in a better position to attain its national aims through it, but also to strengthen its effectiveness. An ineffective EU Mediterranean Policy can theoretically be treated with indifference by most member states. An island state like Cyprus in the midst of the region simply cannot do the same.

What remains to be analysed are the possible policy avenues open to Cyprus as a member state. The optimal approach begins with recognising the sources of Cyprus's international influence in addition to its EU membership. Beginning first with its Commonwealth connections, together with two other member states, namely the UK and Malta, Cyprus has long standing relations with the countries linked to the EU by the Cotenou (former Lomé) Convention, apart from links with Canada, Australia, New Zealand and India to mention a few others. Cyprus is also a long-standing member of the Council of Europe, the Organisation for Security and Co-operation in Europe (OSCE) and a founder of the Non-Aligned Movement (NAM). The importance of the NAM has declined in the post-cold war setting, but the contacts and working relationships developed by Cyprus over the years may become useful now that it has joined the EU particularly since the states of the southern Mediterranean littoral are members of the NAM.

As a small country Cyprus still lacks enough means, diplomatic resources and critical mass to take a leading role in major problems and challenges (e.g. the Middle East or a crisis such as the Algerian one) which the EU faces in the Mediterranean region. However, Cyprus's role could become important in mobilising EU action. On the CSCE experience,

Cyprus could perhaps play the role of a messenger, an intermediary, a 'mellower', an initiator of third solutions, the provider of a constructive push in times of stalemate and a provider of good offices both in the EU and in the Euro-Mediterranean Partnership.[37] Cyprus can also become more effective by initiating policy initiatives that receive the support of the member states and of the Euro-Mediterranean Partnership. This task is not beyond the means of a small country as is illustrated by the many successful small country initiatives in the history of diplomacy. What they certainly require for success is a more sustained focus on the issues as well as investment in crucial resources required to establish them.

In such tasks, a small state can transform its small size into an asset rather than a handicap. It is recognised that due to its small size, Cyprus does not have the means to project power, it does not present a 'security dilemma' to its neighbours, except in a limited form for Turkey in the context of the Cyprus Problem, it does not have the means to pursue broader territorial or hegemonic ambitions. Furthermore, Cyprus shares a common history of colonialism with most of its southern neighbours, as a colony not a coloniser. Like them it has had a bitter-sweet experience of state-building and the post-colonial era. These credentials enable Cyprus to play the role of a trusted political 'broker' in the region. Cyprus has already had the opportunity of playing this role of a 'broker' during the Conference on Security and Co-operation in Europe (CSCE) together with the other members of the group of European Neutral and Non-Aligned countries (N + N).

A lot will also depend on the role which Cyprus will play in the EU's Common Foreign and Security Policy (CFSP) and the new European Policy on Defence. Cyprus claims that it is ready to take on the CFSP acquis. Its participation in the Petersberg tasks, which are consonant with the preferred policies of neutral and non-aligned states, is not expected to raise serious difficulties. Cypriot participation in the CFSP and the European Defence Policy will, however, enhance the island's credibility within the EU.

The last important aspect that has to be analysed concerns the advantages that Cyprus derives from EU membership and the free trade agreements that the EU has with the Mediterranean countries. Although the free trade agreements between the southern Mediterranean states themselves still lag behind, and the process of ratification of the bilateral accords is still taking place, nevertheless, the Euro-Mediterranean Partnership appears to be achieving its main goal of a free trade area by 2010. These agreements provide Cyprus freer access to the Arab markets and possibly open up new export opportunities, particularly in the Middle East region with which Cyprus already enjoys strong trade links. In 1999 more than 17% of the value of Cypriot exports (domestic exports and re-exports) went to a number of neighbouring Arab countries and Israel.[38]

In conclusion it must be stated that for lack of resources, as a consequence of smallness, small states have to economise on those that are available to them and to optimise their employment. For a small state, the most expensive path to achieving its foreign policy goal is to pretend that it can work alone, that it can do everything 'in house' and nationally. EU membership provides small states with ready made policies, supported by adequate resources and with a critical mass that makes them globally and regionally effective and thus idea for small states to work from within them. A sea change has therefore occurred for Cyprus as an EU member state from one where it worked in relative isolation and self-reliance in a role of a consumer of foreign policy initiatives usually started by others to one where it forms part of a Union of states with growing importance on the world stage, where it could also join in policy making.

Notes

1. Out of the 25 member states, seven member states, namely Germany, France, Italy, the UK, Spain, Poland and the Netherlands have a population size that is clearly above the approximation to ten millions mark.
2. Although the definition of a micro-state defined in population terms varies across the board, with 1.5 millions or less being the preferred cut-off point in many British Commonwealth publications, in the case of the EU this label can be applied without much controversy to Malta, Luxembourg, Cyprus, Latvia, Estonia and Slovenia.
3. *IGC 2000: Contribution from the Government of Cyprus*, CONFER/VAR 3951/00, Brussels, 24 February 2000.
4. 2003 Regular Report on progress towards Accession published by the Commission.
5. For example, the GDP per capita of Cyprus measured in Purchasing Power Standards in 2003 is just 17% below the EU-25 average. This puts Cyprus at the head of the pack of the EU's new member states and also ahead of Greece and Portugal which joined the EU in 1981 and 1986 respectively. See *Eurostat* News Release, STAT/04/73, 3 June 2004.
6. The terms interdependence and globalisation are being employed in the same manner as that of R.O Keohane and J. Nye in *Power and Interdependence*, Longman, 2001, 3rd edition, pp.229-230.

7. Republic of Cyprus, *Cyprus: The Way to Full EU Membership*, 3rd edition, Press and Information Office, 1995, p.10.
8. European Commission, *2000 Regular Report from the Commission on Cyprus's Progress Towards Accession*, Brussels, 8 November 2000.
9. European Commission, *Comprehensive Monitoring Report on Cyprus's Preparations for Membership*, November 2003.
10. Annual Economic Indicators, Central Bank of Cyprus, June 2004
11. Comprehensive Monitoring Report 2003, p.5.
12. Hon Markos Kyprianou, speech at the Joint Annual Discussion, World Bank, September 23-24, 2003, IMF Press Release, No 38.
13. The information in this section comes from data collected, courtesy of the Central Bank of Cyprus during a visit to the island in November 2000.
14. The November 2000 Regular Report by the Commission on Cyprus's Progress towards Accession (p.59) it is claimed that there are 42,000 registered offshore companies in Cyprus. But this figure is disputed by a Central Bank of Cyprus official who claims that only around half of these companies are actually active.
15. Ibid., *Commission Regular Report on Cyprus's Progress towards Accession*, November 2000, p.59.
16. *The Prevention and Suppression of Money Laundering Activities Law* of 1996.
17. Ibid., European Commission, *Commission Regular Report on Cyprus's Progress towards Accession*, November 2000, p.55.
18. In 1999, exports by the EU 15 to the Mediterranean Basin countries amounted to €87.8 billions (11.6%) of total extra-EU exports of the EU, while imports amounted to €63 billions (8.2%) of all extra-EU imports. In 1999, the main EU exporters to the Mediterranean Basin countries were Germany 22%, France 20% and Italy 18%. Source: Eurostatistics, *Data for Short-Term Economic Analysis.* Theme 1, General Statistics, (Monthly), European Commission.
19. It is estimated that 30% of total merchant shipping in the world and 20% of oil shipping cross the Mediterranean each year. See, '*State and Pressures of the Marine Coastal Mediterranean Environment*', European Environment Agency and UNEP, Office for Official Publications of the European Communities, 1999, pp.66-70.
20. See for example the *Dobris Assessment* on the Mediterranean: D. Stanners and P. Bordeau (eds.) '*Europe's Environment: The Dobris Assessment*', European Environment Agency, Copenhagen, 1995, pp.116-121
21. On average there are 60 maritime accidents per annum in the Mediterranean region, with about 15 involving ships causing oil and chemical spills. [ibid., *op.cit.*, UNEP and EEA 1999, page 66]. According to the second assessment of Europe's Environment, carried out by the European Environmental Agency, there are about 40 oil related sites in the Mediterranean region (pipeline terminals, refineries, off-shore platforms etc) and an estimated 0.55

and 0.15 billion tonnes of crude oil and petroleum products respectively are loaded and unloaded every year. See '*Europe's Environment: The Second Assessment*', European Environment Agency, Office for Official Publications of the European Communities, 1998, page 220.

22. For a discussion of the environmental effects of tourism on the region see ibid., pp.49-52.
23. F. Faria and A. Vasconcelos, 'Security in Northern Africa: Ambiguity and Reality', *Chaillot Papers*, No.25, September 1996, p.4.
24. Ibid., p.11.
25. The six non-NATO Mediterranean partners are Egypt, Israel, Jordan, Mauritania, Morocco and Tunisia.
26. N. De Santis, 'The Future of Nato's Mediterranean Initiative', *NATO Review*, 1, spring 1998, pp.32-35.
27. G. Joffe, 'Southern Attitudes Towards an Integrated Mediterranean Region', *Mediterranean Politics*, Vol.2, No.1, summer 1997, p.18.
28. *EU Strategic Partnership with the Mediterranean and the Middle East - Final Report*, published in Euromed Report, No.78, 23 June 2004, European Commission.
29. '*Reinvigorating the Barcelona Process*', COM(00) 497 final, Brussels, 6 September 2000.
30. Press Release, Press 439, No.13434/00, Council of the EU, Brussels 16 November 2000.
31. These bilateral Association Agreements have been concluded with all countries and are at various stages of ratification. The Agreement with Syria has been concluded at a technical level and awaits signature and ratification. With Libya there is no agreement as this country was a late comer to the process and for the moment it still has observer status.
32. The EU is supporting this free trade area initiative which is an important step forward in the achievement of a Euro-Mediterranean Free Trade Area by 2010 and as such it falls within the aims of the Barcelona Process. External Relations Commissioner, Chris Patten attended the signing of the agreement which took place in Agadir on 25 February 2004. Patten stated: 'This agreement brings us closer to our joint objective of a Mediterranean Free Trade Area by 2010' The Agadir Initiative is open to all other Arab countries who wish to join it.
33. The argument used here with respect to the European states can be used with equal force to the 'multiple' foreign policy interests of the Arab states of the region: e.g. Arab politics, African politics etc.
34. The Central Bank of Cyprus had this to say: 'Economic activity during the first quarter of 1991 suffered a severe blow from the eruption of the Gulf war...Tourism and related activities, which are highly vulnerable under conditions of political and military turmoil, experienced substantial losses arising from a greatly reduced tourist inflow. The setback...was enhanced by an expansion of the trade deficit... [resulting] from reduced foreign demand

for manufactured goods , particularly in the Arab countries and the Middle East…', *The Bulletin*, Central Bank of Cyprus, June 1991, No.111, p.1. This is what the Maltese government had to say about the Gulf crisis: 'One of the main factors behind this development (slow down in foreign demand) is the slowdown observed in the export of services, particularly tourism, associated with the adverse repercussions of the Gulf crisis on the economy during the first part of the year.' *The Economic Survey January-September 1991*, Ministry of Economic Affairs Malta, p.23

35. Cyprus, IMF Staff Country Report No.00/123, September 2000, p.6.
36. Morgenthau puts it quite eloquently: 'At the end of the thirty Years' War, for instance, the German Empire was composed of 900 sovereign states which the Treaty of Westphalia in 1648 reduced to 355. The Napoleonic interventions…eliminated more than 200 of the German sovereign states. When the Germanic confederation was founded in 1815, only 36 sovereign states were left to join it. The unification of Italy, in 1859, eliminated seven sovereign states, the unification of Germany in 1871, twenty-four…' H.J. Morgenthau, *Politics Among Nations*, 6th edition, Alfred A. Knopf, 1985, pp. 360-362.
37. This is the role that the N+N group played in the CSCE according to A. Bebler in 'The NN Group in the New European Security Architecture', *The International Spectator*, IAI, Rome, Volume XXVII, No 1, January-March, 1992, p.72.
38. According to figures published in *The Quarterly Economic Review*, Central Bank of Cyprus, June 2000, p.80. The Arab countries referred to here are Lebanon, Syria, Egypt, Saudi Arabia, Kuwait and Iraq.

13 Beyond Transposition of the Acquis: Can Cyprus Maintain the Momentum?

CONSTANTIN STEFANOU

Introduction

Throughout this book we have been looking at the quantitative task of transposing the acquis communautaire into national law. Between the start of the substantive negotiations in November 1998 and the closing of all the chapters at the end of 2003, a period of just over five years, around 800 harmonisation bills and regulations went through parliament (House of Representatives) most of which were unopposed.[1] In other words Cyprus managed an average of around 145 harmonisation bills per year or, to put it in a more dramatic perspective, one harmonisation bill every 1.7 working days. For a small state like Cyprus with a comparatively small public administration this was a monumental task. However, as the Commission makes clear in its five Regular Reports on Cyprus's Progress Towards Accession transposition of the acquis is only part of the harmonisation process. Full harmonisation is a qualitative rather than quantitative process that implies ability to implement and enforce the transposed acquis. Moreover, as a new member state Cyprus will have to go through a period of adjustment where it will learn how to 'be' a full member.

Back in 1998, looking at the Europeanisation of small member states Hanf and Soetendorp referred to three kinds of adaptations that small member states had to go through as a measure of the Europeanisation of their public policy: 'governmental', 'political' and 'strategic'.[2] The logic of that argument was that lack of public policy Europeanisation prevented small member states from reaping the full benefits of EU membership and pursuing effectively their national interests within the EU. In other words, the argument was that small member states need governmental, political, and strategic adaptation in order to be effective members. But what does being an effective member mean? As Nicolaides noted: 'The integrity of the EU system depends on the ability and willingness of each member state to participate in common decision-making and then comply with the common rules'.[3] Taking a pragmatic overall view of recent accession candidates Nicolaides defined 'effective membership' in terms of:[4]

- Ability to influence those rules so that they match as closely as possible a member's own national interests;
- Enforcing the rules rigorously;
- Using all opportunities provided by the single market; and
- Maximising absorption of EU funds.

It is interesting that three of the tests concern benefits to the member state itself and one refers to its relationship with other member states ('enforcing rules rigorously'). The meaning of these four tests of effective membership is twofold. Firstly, that unless the test related to rules enforcement can be demonstrably passed harmonisation has not been achieved and the member state is not a 'loyal' EU member state yet. Secondly, that a member state that fails the other three tests is failing in its efforts to use its EU membership to its advantage.

Having looked at Cyprus's efforts for accession two obvious questions immediately come to mind. Firstly, can Cyprus be an 'effective member'? Secondly, and perhaps more importantly, in an EU of 25 does it matter anyway? This chapter attempts to examine Cyprus's attempts to be an effective member and assess whether the first few years of membership will be traumatic or problem-free.

The 'political problem' again

One can hardly read an article or a reference on Cyprus which does not mention the 'political problem', referring of course to the division of the island. Cyprus's political problem has been sufficiently described and analysed elsewhere and I do not intend to repeat it here.[5] Throughout Cyprus's EU candidacy the 'political problem' gave rise to all sorts of speculations about a possible rejection of Cyprus's application by some member states, despite the clear message given by the Luxembourg European Council in 1997 and the Commission's Regular Reports that a solution to the political problem was not a precondition for membership. However, while the lack of a political solution to the problem was obviously not an impediment to EU membership could the persistence of the problem, especially after the rejection of the Annan Plan in April 2004, have an effect on Cyprus's effort for effective membership?

The comments made by EU officials[6] in the aftermath of the rejection of the Annan Plan might have indicated that Cyprus will not receive a nice welcome to the European family. Cyprus will certainly be isolated on issues related to aid to the Turkish Cypriots or trade with the North. However, in terms of the EU's daily business it is unlikely that Cyprus will be isolated. On a day to day basis member states have to forge coalitions, negotiate issues of common concern and, of course, count votes for and against a proposal. To achieve this member states need a close and continuous relationship with all other member states. In other words it is unlikely that Cyprus will encounter 'isolation' as a matter of routine. Early indications from Brussels confirm that, with the exception of proposals concerning trade or aid to the Turkish Cypriots, Cyprus is not isolated as a member state.[7] The problem is that these very issues on which Cyprus is isolated are often seen by the media as issues directly related to Cyprus's national interests and obviously receive the lion share of attention.

What should be noted, though, is that the pessimistic scenarios about Cyprus's EU accession without a resolution to the division of the island appear to be wrong. For example, the idea that '...Accession without settlement would trigger a situation of unpredictability and the prospect of guerrilla activity on the island'[8] appears to have been rather far fetched; similarly the possibility that '...the "TRNC" will be formally incorporated within Turkey'[9] no longer appears to be a valid supposition.

Of course, in reality the political problem persists. Cyprus continues to be a divided island and in practical terms the government of the Republic of Cyprus has no control of the northern part, which is why the EU has formally suspended implementation and enforcement of the acquis in the North. Yet, the Republic has formally joined the EU on behalf of the island as a whole, which implies that the Republic is responsible for the fate of the Turkish-Cypriot citizens of the Republic who should also benefit from accession. How the Republic deals with this problem will define Cyprus's 'reputation' within the EU in years to come.

Commenting on the EU's policy towards Cyprus in the 1990s Stavridis noted that it '...involved a lot of rhetoric and very little action',[10] which in turn widened the expectations-capabilities gap between Cyprus and the EU. It is interesting to note that following the referendum on the Annan Plan and EU accession – and irrespective of whether or not it is fair – expectations now seem to rest squarely on the Republic of Cyprus to find a solution to a thirty-years problem which was not even of its own making.

In the short-term Cyprus will continue to have a 'political problem' only this time it will have three aspects: (i) ending the division of the island; (ii) convincing the EU and the rest of the world that it is serious about its wish to end the division of the island; and (iii) convincing the people of Cyprus that there is a viable solution to the division of the island.

The test of effective membership

A small fish in a large pond

Can Cyprus really influence the rules so that it maximises its national interests? As Roderick Pace notes (Chapter 12), being a small country in the east Mediterranean when it came to the European or the international scene Cyprus had been the consumer of policies rather than their producer. In this sense the ability to influence policy making at the EU level – with the EU being a major world player in policy production – will be quite new and exciting for Cyprus. With 4 votes in the Council, 6 MEPs, 6 ESC members, 6 members in the Committee of the Regions, a Commissioner, a Judge in the ECJ and another in the CFI, and a member in the Court of Auditors Cyprus is omnipresent in the EU – and compared to other member states, such as Germany enjoys an above average representation. But does this mean that Cyprus can now influence policy making and safeguard its interests?

The debate over the power of 'micro-states' in the EU is still going. Strictly speaking, current arrangements allow them to 'punch above their weight'. However, since Luxembourg was the only real example of a micro-state in the EU appearances can be deceptive. Enjoying almost a special position as one of the original six member states, and being in close geographic proximity to France and Germany, Luxembourg has often played the role of the honest broker. In contrast, Cyprus is a latecomer located in the periphery of the EU with problems to solve rather than services to offer. Nor does the ability of Cyprus to influence EU policy rest on its 4 votes in the Council – because if a proposal needs just 4 votes to pass under QMV then there is probably a serious split within the member states and in these circumstances the practice, so far, has been to shelve the proposal until a wider consensus has been reached.

The ability of Cyprus to influence EU policy goes hand in hand with its ability to persuade other member states and with the ability of the Cypriot EU contingent to learn to negotiate using formal and informal channels. Unlike forms of 'one-off' international negotiations, within the EU there is continuous contact between the parties and repeated negotiations. Under these circumstances 'tricking' or 'misinforming' your fellow member states does not pay-off in the long term. In fact, the close and repeated interaction of the negotiators means that knowledge of each other's domestic constraints is extensive.

Then, of course, we have the issue of protecting national interests, which is usually the stumbling block for new member states. Before accession most member states defined national interest in fairly straight forward zero-sum *realist* terms counting gains and losses and having sovereignty as the basic benchmark. EU membership brings a re-evaluation of national interest as a standard, realist, sovereignty-linked concept. Thus, sometimes member states have to opt for an *interdependence* perspective of accepting present 'restraints' in the hope that there will be future 'opportunities'.[11] On other occasions member states will have to sever the traditional link between national interest and sovereignty in favour of a communitarian solution. In other words, member states often have to go through the traumatic experience of redefining national interest. The quicker a member state reacts to these new conditions the better it will adapt. It took member states, such as Greece, almost a decade of being the EU's *bête noir* before it was able to redefine its approach towards the EU and get rid of the 'syndrome of the underdog culture' and the 'syndrome of foreign protection'[12] which dominated its understanding of national interest in the context of the EU.

For all new member states the learning curve is quite steep during the first few years. In Cyprus the additional burden of the 'political problem' counsels for caution rather than optimism. Being a small fish in a larger EU pond Cyprus will have to adapt to a whole new way of viewing the world and itself.

Can Cyprus enforce the acquis?

As we have already seen, Cyprus has transposed the acquis. However, as always, EU policy *implementation* is the real test of harmonisation. Within the EU, putting Union policy into practice is not regarded merely as a technical matter for the member states' civil services. It is the job of the Commission as the 'guardian of the Treaties' to ensure that EU law is correctly enforced in all member states and, of course, member states who do not comply are referred to the ECJ. Not surprisingly, prospects for and progress towards full implementation of the acquis has been one of the points emphasised by the European Commission in its Regular Reports on individual accession countries.

Traditionally we distinguish between two general approaches to policy implementation:

- the *top-down* approach where the task of the implementers is to ensure that the outcomes and outputs of policy are delivered according to the wishes of the policy makers;[13] and
- the *bottom-up* approach where the implementers of policy are allowed to make changes to the outcomes and outputs of policy according to local needs.[14]

In both approaches the key element is the 'implementers', in other words the civil services. Unlike the CEECs Cyprus did not emerge from forty years of communism and had always operated a market economy. When compared to the large and somewhat inefficient civil services of the CEECs, which in many cases are still in the process of restructuring, the civil service in Cyprus has always been seen as small, efficient and competent, that is capable of delivering acquis enforcement. Of course, there have been a few voices of dissent, e.g.:

> Cyprus was a star player in the negotiating process and was far and away the most efficient state in getting legislation passed, but there are questions being asked about the extent to which implementation is being carried out in the same way.[15]

However, on the whole there has been satisfaction with the way Cyprus has handled acquis enforcement, so far. That does not mean that Cyprus's public administration is on the verge of Europeanisation. The Ministry of Agriculture (MANRE), for example, will undoubtedly have a difficult job in trying to implement the relevant 11,000 pages of the acquis. Many of the EU provisions transposed are new and so are the institutions entrusted with their enforcement. In this sense, inevitably there will be a need for assessment and adjustment.

The question of implementation is also connected to the performance of national Courts in enforcing the acquis. Cypriot Courts will be called upon to enforce general principles, such as direct effect or state liability as well as the rather technical issues covered by environmental or health and safety Directives. In the first few years, the performance of judges, their knowledge and understanding of EU law can make all the difference in labelling Cyprus an acquiescent or a recalcitrant member state. Like judges from other applicant countries Cypriot judges have had training in EU law. However, past experience indicates that this type training, usually in the form of seminars, is not enough. More systematic and in depth training is usually needed and as Nicolaides noted: 'training should also be provided to those that have to comply with EU rules, not only those that have to enforce them'.[16]

With an efficient civil service and given that it is after all a small jurisdiction there is no reason why Cyprus should not be able to enforce the acquis. Yet, at the same time, its small size and relatively small civil service can jeopardize effective implementation of the acquis. Lacunae in the law or lack of experts or lack of know-how or lack of training – i.e. the usual excuses for lack of proper implementation of the acquis – will not win Cyprus many favours with the Commission or the ECJ. For the time being we will have to accept the Commission's and the government's assurances that Cyprus is in a position to implement the acquis fully.

Maximising the opportunities that the EU membership offers

Strictly speaking Cyprus had a thriving trade with the EU and the Customs Union of 1987 gave some Cypriot companies the opportunity to do business in the EU. Although the opportunities offered to entrepreneurs by Europe's single market are unlimited in practice new member states, such as Cyprus, will first have to absorb the shock of EU companies' expansion into their domestic market.

The state of affairs in the economy of Cyprus prior to harmonisation did not differ from that existing in the EU before 1992. There were state monopolies, 'national champion firms', protective regimes for certain products as well as state subsidies to selected firms that specialised in exports. After harmonisation and over the next few years the economy of Cyprus will undergo the same changes as the economies of the member states in the early 1990s. From a practical point of view this means that the relatively small Cypriot firms (because of the small size of the market) will have to compete with some of Europe's strongest and fittest firms. Normally this could spell disaster for a micro-state. However, in the case of Cyprus because of the very specialised industries which form the backbone of its economy (tourism, services to off-shore companies) the effects may not necessarily be as devastating as they were in some member states. Certainly the small size of the Cypriot economy – about the size of a large city in continental Europe – is unlikely to cause a rush for its market by European firms. Cyprus certainly hopes to attract foreign investment, but then again so do Malta and the Baltic states and practically every new member state. Whether Cyprus is successful or not will depend on the government's ability to attract foreign investment. The celebrated Irish model of development through foreign investment has been the example most often used, forgetting that it took Ireland over 20 years to prepare its economy. The positive aspect in the case of Cyprus is that because of the small size of the economy a small investment can go a long way.

Ability to maximise the opportunities of the single European market is, of course, very important because in the long term prosperity or lack of it after accession to the EU might determine the Cypriot people's perception of the EU and might even define pro- or anti-European stances by political parties. Not that this is problematic in Cyprus at the moment where political parties from across the political spectrum have been in favour of accession. However, it is quite important for the government to ensure that Cypriot businesses are aware of the opportunities opened to them. To this end the Cyprus Chamber of Commerce and Industry (CCCI) and its branches throughout Cyprus have been active in promoting the EU and the new business opportunities it offers to local businesses.[17]

What Cyprus must do at all costs is avoid the example of Greece which by 2002, after 21 years of EU membership, had managed to remain comparatively as poor as it was when it joined in 1981 (see Table 13.1 below). Greece's bad performance has become so legendary within the EU that it is now used as a basic example for applicant countries of what *not* to do after EU accession. In contrast, Ireland's exceptional performance has become the shining model to emulate.

Table 13.1 GDP per capita as a percentage of the EU's average[18]

	Joined	*-10 years*	*Accession*	*+15 years*	*2002*
Ireland	1973	63	61	67	126
Greece	1981	66	69	65	66
Spain	1986	78	71	84	84
Portugal	1986	53	54	69	69

Greece's bad performance is attributed to:[19]

- Bad or no implementation of single market rules
- Inability to absorb EU aid well
- Mismanagement of aid received from the EU
- Maintenance of a very complicated business environment
- Lack of macro stability for many years

The lesson here is that EU membership does not automatically guarantee better economic performance or increased income per head. Although Cyprus is well ahead of Greece in most economic indicators and has an inviting business environment the bad example set by Greece may well be repeated by the new member states.

Of course, anyone who has followed the debate over EU accession in Cyprus understands that the single market was not at the top of the political and popular agenda when Cyprus applied for EU membership. Micro-states are 'consumers' of security and, for obvious reasons, no country in Europe craves security more than Cyprus. A brief look at the indicators proves this point. *Eurobarometer* indicates that support for EU membership has fallen from 73% down to 59% in autumn 2003 and down to 42% in spring 2004. Opposition to EU membership has increased from 4% to 7% in Autumn 2003 up to 16% in spring 2004.[20] In just eight months, support for EU membership appears to have dropped by 29%. Coming on the heels of the Cypriots' rejection of the Annan plan and the criticism they received from the EU such results are expected. Yet, the true picture is revealed by the Cypriots' unwavering support for the EU's common foreign policy, unchanged at 81%, and the common defence and security policy, up from 87% to 91%.[21]

Clearly the perceived need for security is so overwhelming that even when Cypriots feel that the EU has abandoned them (e.g. the heavy criticism for the rejection of the Annan Plan) support for its security policies increases. This is perhaps the greatest testament to Cyprus's pro-EU orientation. It is also an indication of what most Cypriots regard as the greatest 'benefit' of EU membership. Even though the EU is not a military pact it is hoped that membership will create vested interests in the EU and the member states to minimise future security threats. Interestingly, these are the very reasons the EU had for insisting that the 'political problem' was solved before accession.

Absorbing EU funds

Irrespective of whether one agrees with the EU's possible future federal polity, fiscal federalism, in other words the redistribution of wealth within the EU, is a feature of the current EU system. The new member states will be net recipients of EU funds, at least for the first three years of EU membership. In this sense Cyprus can expect to have some immediate benefits from accession.

Ability to absorb EU funds does not come without conditions. For example, the Commission no longer releases funds to a member state directly. Instead, appropriate institutions have to be set up and appropriate procedures must be put in place that will allow Cyprus to benefit from the EU's pool of money destined for the less developed regions of the EU. Moreover, in order to maximise funding from the Structural Funds programmes a member state must be able to co-finance projects. In other words a member state needs to have money in order to receive aid. This is not as paradoxical as it sounds. Over the years the EU has realised that giving the member states 100% funding is usually a recipe for mis-management, wastage and even fraud. In contrast, co-financing encourages member states to invest in their own infrastructure and usually avoids bad management and wastage. Finding the money for co-financing is always a problem as most member states, and certainly the new member states, have budget deficits. As tax-increases are usually avoided by governments borrowing is one solution which, though, governments also tend to avoid as infrastructure projects have a very long-term pay-off. The only alternative solution is to reduce public sector inefficiency by restructuring or by introducing very stringent financial regulations which will weed-out wastage.

Cyprus is all too aware of these conditions and constraints which is why the government was keen to create appropriate structures and institutions, that can absorb EU aid, at a very early stage. With a GDP per head just 17 points below the EU's average[22] (ahead of Portugal and Greece) Cyprus is ahead of the new member states – which also means that it will not be a pressing priority for the EU. It is impossible to say whether a new member state is well prepared to absorb and benefit from EU aid. Receiving money from the EU was certainly a major incentive for the CEECs, many of which are well below Cyprus in their level of development and general economic indicators. I certainly have yet to hear from a new member state that does not believe and expect that it will benefit from EU funding after accession.

Redefining 'effectiveness'

Being an effective member state has two dimensions: Firstly, it is connected to a member state's relationship with other member states and the central EU institutions, what loosely is referred to as EU loyalty. Secondly, it is related to the ability to make the best of the opportunities the EU has to offer. A sort of ethical invitation to 'do the right thing for others and for yourself'.

However, in practice member states tend to have almost unique 'reputations' inside the EU, each with its own niche for certain activities or approaches to the EU. Thus, Italy the member state that the Commission has referred to the ECJ most often for breaches of EU law is also a member state which has consistently aimed to advance the process of European integration; the UK, the member state most often cited as a Eurosceptic is also a member state that enforces rigorously EU law. Does this mean than one can be classified as more loyal or more effective than the other? In an EU of 25 member states there is little doubt that despite all the precautions taken by the Commission member states will continue to breach EU law, will have problems in utilising the opportunities offered by the EU, including aid, and will generally adopt pro- or anti-European stances depending on the issues at stake. Unless the practice of trying to seek a consensus in the Council is abandoned in favour of a straight forward vote-count on every proposal brought forward, in which case recriminations will follow every single Council decision, it is unlikely that loyalty will be a real issue. If 'loyalty' was a measure of a member state's effectiveness then all member states would have failed this criterion since they have all at some stage breached EU law and have been referred to the ECJ. Similarly, inability to make use of the opportunities offered by the single market or absorbing structural funds reflects more on the governments of the member states which, though, are judged by their electorates every four years or so. The example of Ireland is often cited as an indication of a member state's 'effectiveness' in the context of the EU. Yet, by doing so effectiveness is tied to prosperity, which depends on many variables from geography to the attitudes of individual citizens.

Perhaps the true measure of 'effectiveness' is a member state's ability to achieve what it set out to achieve through EU membership. Prosperity is always an underlying goal for every government but experience shows that different member states had different priorities for accession. For example, even during the negotiations for Greece's accession political criteria concerning stability of democratic institutions were advanced by both

Greece and the Commission as major contributing factors in Greece's application. Similar political criteria were used during the negotiations for the EU's Iberian enlargement.[23] The very fact that democratic institutions in all three member states stabilised and thrived, could be seen as achievement of their primary goal for accession. In fact, it might even partly explain why Greece and Portugal, and to a lesser extend Spain, did not achieve levels of development similar to those of Ireland. Of course, by interpreting 'effectiveness' in this subjective manner we almost completely remove any objective way of measuring it. However, this interpretation seems to be consistent with the way EU citizens seem to disregard 'effectiveness' – in terms of use of opportunities offered by the EU – when assessing their country's membership of the EU. For example, Greece and Portugal (and Spain) have well above average levels of support for EU membership[24] even though their countries cannot really be seen as 'effective' member states in terms of making use of the opportunities offered by the single market or absorbing EU funds.

As we have already seen, for micro-states EU accession satisfies a mixture of security needs and economic needs. It also elevates their presence in the international scene offering them the ability to involve themselves directly with policy making at the highest level. For Cyprus, EU accession represents all of the above with particular emphasis on security. Especially after the rejection of the Annan Plan, and despite the EU's critical response, Cyprus is still looking to the EU for assistance with its 'political problem'. The obvious question here is: if in ten years' time a solution to the island's division was the only tangible outcome of accession could Cyprus be regarded as an effective member? Unless Cyprus was a persistent recalcitrant state constantly causing problems within the EU, good or bad economic performance would not really be a factor in the perception of Cyprus by other member states. Cyprus would certainly regard a solution to its political problem as a victory in itself and for most of its citizens EU accession would be measured as 'effective'.

The point here is that 'effective' membership should not be seen as a precise notion or as a list of tasks to be completed for its achievement. It is more of a wider assessment of a member state's accomplishments since accession, which should take into consideration that member states' performance in conjunction with its primary goals for acceding. A reasonable performance matched by successful achievement of its goals for accession should be seen as 'effective membership'.

Concluding remarks: maintaining the momentum

In the last five years, such has been Cyprus's eagerness to complete successfully the accession process that practically every other political issue, except for the 'political problem', has been by-passed. Thus, harmonisation bills went through the House of Representatives with only minimum discussion, if at all, and emphasis has been placed on the positive aspects of EU membership, as is usually the case with new member states. If it were not for the failure of the Annan Plan, EU membership would be heralded as Cyprus's indisputable greatest achievement since independence in 1960.

Of course, as full implementation of the acquis begins to take effect and as the various protective regimes in the Cypriot economy are gradually dismantled this euphoria might not last for very long. Given the current state of the 'political problem' and the EU's sharp reaction it is essential for Cyprus to maintain the momentum and be the EU's *Musterknabe* when it comes to enforcement of the acquis or it will be all too easy at this stage to acquire a reputation for being a 'difficult' member state. The best way to maintain the momentum is not through political action but by ensuring top performance of public administration.

It is usually the aftermath of formal accession that reveals chinks in the armour of civil services. The worst assumption for both government and the civil service will be that the hard work is behind them, when in fact it is just starting. In some member states some of the good work achieved by the rigorous efforts for accession will be undone as key civil servants, who played a major role in harmonisation, are rewarded by being moved to Brussels or to 'easier' but well paid posts. Training might cease as it is taken for granted that it has been successfully completed and the role of trainers is no longer necessary. Away from the close scrutiny of the Commission government departments might revert to their old habits while even government might flout the rules by delaying acquis enforcement in order to help an ailing national industry or a 'national champion firm'.

To some degree all member states try to use the EU rules to their advantage. In this sense, attempts by Cyprus to do the same would hardly constitute a major act of rebellion. Maintaining the momentum after accession is obviously the difficult part for all new member states. But it should not necessarily be seen as such by Cyprus which has an efficient public administration. In any case, for Cyprus the first few years of accession will probably also determine what kind of a solution will be found to its political problem and it is obvious that this is the focus of both government and the citizens. Having completed transposition of the acquis so promptly and efficiently it would be a shame to see the momentum lost just when Cyprus is ready to reap the fruits of its hard work.

Notes

1. Republic of Cyprus, House of Representatives Parliamentary Proceedings, January 2003–February 2004.
2. K. Hanf and B. Soetendorp, 'Small States and the Europeanisation of Public Policy' in K. Hanf and B. Soetendorp (eds), *Adapting to European Integration Small States and the European Union*, Longman, London and New York, 1998, pp.8-11.
3. P. Nicolaides, 'Preparing for EU Membership: The Paradox of Doing What the EU Does Not Require You to Do', *Eipascope*, No.2, 2003, p.11.
4. Ibid, p.12.
5. See for example: C. Hitchens, *Hostage to History Cyprus from the Ottomans to Kissinger*, Verso, London, 3rd edition, 1997; F. Marbagheri, *Cyprus and International Peacemaking*, Hurst, London, 1998; K. Kyle, *Cyprus: In search of Peace*, Minority Rights Group International Report, London 1997.
6. See for example, 'EU to Reward Turkish Cypriots', *The Guardian*, 26 April, 2004.
7. Interview with members of Cyprus's permanent representation in June 2004.
8. N. Neuwahl, 'Cyprus, Which Way? – In Pursuit of a Confederal Solution in Europe', *Harvard Jean Monnet Working Paper*, No.4, 2000, p.6.
9. N. Nugent, 'EU Enlargement and the Cyprus Problem' in *Journal of Common Market Studies*, Vol.38, No.1, March 2000, p.145.
10. S. Stavridis, 'Double standards, ethics and democratic principles in foreign policy: the EU and the Cyprus problem' in A. Theophanous, N. Peristianis and A. Ioannou (eds), *Cyprus and the European Union*, Intercollege Press, Nicosia, 1999, p.169.
11. See: R. Keohane and J. Nye, *Transnational Relations and World Politics*, Harvard University Press, Cambridge Massachusetts, second printing, 1973. Also see R. Keohane and J. Nye (1989), *Power and Interdependence*, Scott Foresman, Boston, 2nd edition, 1989.
12. See P. Ioakimidis, 'Contradictions in the Europeanisation Process' in K. Featherstone and K. Ifantis (eds), *Greece in a Changing Europe*, Manchester University Press, Manchester, 1996, pp.46-47.
13. See the classic study of B. Hogwood and L. Gunn, *Policy Analysis for the Real World*, Oxford University Press, Oxford, 1984.
14 See the representative study of S. Barret and C. Fudge, *Policy and Action*, Methuen, London, 1981.
15. Comments by the Executive Director of Civilitas Research, James Ker-

Lindsay in 'After Athens: what next?', *Cyprus Mail*, 18 April 2003.

16. Nicolaides 2003, *op.cit.*, p.14.
17. See http://www.ccci.org.cy/info_2.shtm.
18. Source Nenad Pacek, Director, Central Eastern Europe, Middle East and Africa, The Economist Group, Vienna, 'Benchmarking key lessons from previous enlargement rounds', Powerpoint Presentation, 29 October 2003. Also see: www.oracle.com/pl/industryforum/6th/p2.pps.
19. Ibid.
20. Comparison between the two most recent figures. See *Eurobarometer 2003.4, Public Opinion in the Acceding and Candidate Countries*, Autumn 2003, p.18 and *Eurobarometer 2004.1, Public Opinion in the Acceding and Candidate Countries*, Spring 2004, p.7.
21. Ibid, p.25 and p.14 respectively.
22. *Eurostat* News Release, STAT/04/73, 3 June 2004
23. If you can still find a copy, see L. Tsoukalis, *The European Community and its Mediterranean Enlargement,* George Allen & Unwin, London, 1981.
24. See *Eurobarometer 2003.4, Public Opinion in the Acceding and Candidate Countries*, Autumn 2003, p.3.

Index